Introduction

The number of people who garden organically has increased dramatically over the past decade. The reasons for this include a growing concern for our environment and health. It is also now accepted that organic methods do work and are a viable way of achieving a healthy, productive and attractive garden.

"Going organic" is not just a question of changing your brand of fertilizer or, indeed, giving them up altogether. It means a change of attitude: getting away from the idea that every small creature is a pest, every plant out of place is a weed, and that the solution to every problem is in a spray. An organic garden is designed to encourage nature. This not only helps keep the garden healthy, but also provides safe habitats for wildlife.

Every garden can be run organically, from the smallest to the largest, whatever the location. Even in the middle of a city you can create your own miniature ecosystem. With a little effort, sources of manures and other materials can be found, and there are also many proprietary organic products available for those unable to bring in the raw materials.

Practising organic methods on edible plants while continuing to use sprays and artificial fertilizers on the rest of the garden is not to be recommended. This book shows how to maintain the whole garden organically: vegetables, herbs, fruit, shrubberies, herbaceous borders, roses, lawns, paths and ponds are all included.

The first section of the book describes how a garden can be made attractive to wildlife *and* the gardener. The many useful creatures that help pest control are introduced, for it is particularly important to recognize these garden friends rather than mistake them for pests. If areas of a garden require regular inputs of pesticides and artificial fertilizers, this implies that the plants are growing in a situation that does not suit them. In this case, a redesign may be in order. It is easier to manage a garden organically if it is designed from scratch or redesigned with organic methods in mind. There are plans showing a number of designs ranging in size from a back yard to an acre.

Having looked at the environment above ground, the book looks at that below ground, in the soil. A healthy, fertile soil with a good structure and a thriving population of living creatures is the basis of all effective organic growing. Detailed and practical information on this is given, including compost making and the use of animal manures.

Inevitably, nature cannot keep every pest and disease under control the whole time, but there are many organic techniques for protecting plants. When a problem does arise, correct identification is essential. Hints and tips to help with this are given, followed by a plant-led directory of problems and solutions.

Chemical fertilizers and pesticides are relative newcomers and for those who have never got involved with the chemical era, much of this book will be familiar. But there will also be much that is new. As well as using methods that have been tried and tested for centuries, organic gardening takes on board the discoveries of modern research, as long as they fit the basic principles of organic growing.

Henry Doubleday Research Association

The primary aim of the Henry Doubleday Research Association (HDRA) is to promote organic methods of growing with particular reference to gardening. The HDRA runs demonstration gardens which are open to the public. Apart from its advisory and education work, it has a thriving research department, a department of genetic resources working to preserve the genetic heritage of our vegetables, and a Local Authority/Consultancy Department, encouraging recycling and composting initiatives in towns and cities.

Organic standards

If produce is sold as organic it must, in most countries including Britain and the EU, be grown to a recognized set of "organic standards". By law, the grower must be registered with a recognized organic body and the farm or holding inspected to ensure that the standards are maintained. There is obviously no need for legally binding standards for gardeners, but organic gardeners do need to know the rights and wrongs of organic gardening. For this reason, the HDRA has compiled a set of Organic Gardening Guidelines based on the standards set for commercial growers but adapted to suit the different circumstances and requirements of the garden. The growing methods described in this book conform to the HDRA Organic Gardening Guidelines.

What is organic gardening?

The word "organic" itself means, simply, "of living origin", but when applied to gardening it describes a whole system of growing. The organic approach recognizes that the garden environment is much more than just the sum of its individual parts, and that all the living things in it are interrelated and interdependent.

The organic approach aims to minimize our impact on the wider environment by avoiding the use of materials from non-renewable resources, recycling where possible, and keeping the use of pesticides to a minimum. It also, of course, allows the gardener to achieve an attractive, healthy and productive garden.

Nature's example
Woods, forests and other natural plant communities survive for centuries without any outside intervention. A plant growing in the wild, for example, grows using only carbon dioxide (and nitrogen if it is a legume) from the air and the food available in the soil. They do not use up valuable resources or cause pollution. And, while no one can claim that an organic garden is entirely natural, organic methods do try to follow nature's example as far as possible.

In nature, everything is recycled; nothing is wasted. Leaves and fruit may fall from the plant to the soil, where they will decompose and the goodness they contain become available to the same plant or to others growing in the area. Their fibre will help to maintain soil structure. Plant-eating creatures (herbivores), such as caterpillars or rabbits, may eat parts of the plant, and the manure they produce will again return to the soil, as will the creatures themselves when they die. Alternatively, the caterpillars may be eaten by birds and the rabbits by a fox. These creatures will in turn also produce manure and return to the soil when they die.

In nature there is no need to bring in resources from outside as everything is recycled within the system. This whole cycle is kept in motion by the myriad micro-organisms that carry out the decomposition of plant material, manures and dead bodies. These essential creatures tend to be bypassed, ignored or even inhibited by artificial chemical methods of gardening.

In a garden situation as much as possible is recycled, although outside inputs are usually necessary to keep the garden fertile. However, the manures and fertilizers used in an organic garden are of natural origin and must also be processed by soil organisms before the goodness they contain is available to plants. Artificial fertilizers that dissolve quickly in the soil's water and are then taken up directly by plants, by-passing the soil life, are not used, for they can lead to over-lush growth, which is more attractive to pests and diseases. Natural materials contain a wider, more balanced range of plant foods than man-made chemical fertilizers. As well as the major nutrients, nitrogen, potassium and phosphate, they also supply minor and trace elements, essential for balanced growth. Many also help to improve soil structure.

To minimize the energy costs of production and transport, materials brought in to keep the soil fertile should be, as far as possible, recycled waste products, preferably of local origin.

Natural balance
Caterpillars, rabbits and other herbivores can, of course, be pests. In a natural system, the damage they cause will be kept to a reasonable level. Their numbers will be kept in check by their natural enemies, who in turn will be controlled by theirs. Every pest and disease, of whatever size, has its own pest and disease, and so on down the line.

Problems arise in a garden situation because unnatural collections of plants are grown in inappropriate situations and expected to thrive. This does not mean that we should abandon nature's complex web of control, destroying it with the use of harmful chemicals. We should encourage nature to do its best, only intervening when absolutely necessary. As a last resort, there are a few insecticides and fungicides that may be used. Although less harmful than many products, these sprays may still kill beneficial creatures, so their use is kept to a minimum.

How organic can we be?
In an ideal world, everything used in an organic garden should itself have been been organically grown. Unfortunately, this is not always possible, so compromises have to be made, such as choosing manures from less intensive farming systems, and using seeds that have not been chemically treated after harvest, even though they may have been grown using chemicals. Wherever possible, raise plants in the garden rather than buying them.

80003488114

The RHS Encyclopedia of Practical Gardening

ORGANIC GARDENING

PAULINE PEARS AND SUE STICKLAND

Pauline Pears runs the Information and Education Department of the Henry Doubleday Research Association – Britain's largest organization for organic gardening. She also writes regularly for the gardening press. Sue Stickland was formerly Head Gardener at HDRA's Ryton Organic Gardens. She is now a freelance gardener and writer, specializing in organic and wildlife gardening, and old vegetable varieties

MITCHELL BEAZLEY

The Royal Horticultural Society's Encyclopedia of Practical Gardening © Octopus Publishing Group Ltd 1995, 1999

The Royal Horticultural Society's Encyclopedia of Practical Gardening: Organic Gardening © Octopus Publishing Group Ltd 1995, 1999

First published in 1995
Reprinted 1997
New edition 1999 Reprinted 2000, 2001, 2003, 2004, 2006

ISBN 978 1 840001 587
ISBN 1 84000 158 5

Edited and designed by Mitchell Beazley, an imprint of Octopus Publishing Group Ltd
2-4 Heron Quays, London E14 4JP
Produced by Toppan Printing Co (HK) Ltd.
Printed and bound in Hong Kong

Contents

A NOTE ON PLANT HARDINESS	
Where appropriate, hardiness zone information is given for plants, denoted by the letter "z" followed by a number. This number relates to a range of average annual minimum temperatures and should be used as a guide to the best plants for a particular area. Most plants will succeed in warmer zones than the given one. The temperatures for these eleven zones are as follows:	**zone 1:** below -45.5°C (below -50°F) **zone 2:** -45.5 to -40.1°C (-50 to -40°F) **zone 3:** -40.0 to -34.5°C (-40 to -30°F) **zone 4:** -34.4 to -28.9°C (-30 to -20°F) **zone 5:** -28.8 to -23.4°C (-20 to -10°F) **zone 6:** -23.3 to -17.8°C (-10 to 0°F) **zone 7:** -17.7 to -12.3°C (0 to +10°F) **zone 8:** -12.2 to -6.7°C (+10 to +20°F) **zone 9:** -6.6 to -1.2°C (+20 to +30°F) **zone 10:** -1.1 to +4.4°C (+30 to +40°F) **zone 11:** above +4.4°C (above +40°F)

DO'S AND DON'TS

Do's

DO manage the whole garden organically. Organic methods can be used for every area in the garden, edible and ornamental

DO keep a regular watch on your garden and get to know what goes on so problems can be caught early.

DO get to know the useful pest-controlling creatures. They do a valuable job that is often unrecognized

DO create habitats for wildlife. A bird box, a pond or a heap of wood will shelter wildlife, helping pest control

DO use crop rotation for vegetables. This makes better use of the soil's fertility and helps prevent the build up of pests and diseases

DO grow flowers that will attract and feed garden friends. Many of these useful creatures need to eat pollen and nectar to supply energy for egg laying

DO grow a mixture of plants whenever possible. Pests and diseases are then much less likely to get out of hand

DO recycle kitchen and garden waste through a compost heap. The compost will give healthy, fertile soil

DO collect autumn leaves and make them into leaf-mould, which is easy to make and very useful

DO apply bulky organic materials like compost, leaf-mould and manure to the soil to improve its structure

DO feed the soil's living creatures with organic manures and fertilizers so that they in turn can provide plants with a balanced food supply

DO keep soil covered with plants or mulched with organic material. This will improve soil structure and keep weeds under control

DO use hand weeding, hoeing and mulching to keep weeds under control. Leave those that are not causing a nuisance; they can provide useful habitats

DO cut grass only when necessary and leave mowings to feed the lawn whenever possible. This encourages healthy growth and reduces the need to feed

Don'ts

DON'T grow fruit and vegetables organically and then resort to chemical methods on non-edible plants. The whole garden environment is important

DON'T ignore what is going on because problems are then much more likely to get out of hand

DON'T assume creatures are pests. They may be harmless or even beneficial

DON'T tidy up every area of the garden; excessive neatness can drive away garden friends

DON'T grow the same vegetables in exactly the same place every year. This can lead to a build up of persistent soil pests and diseases that are difficult to control

DON'T use sprays that might harm natural predators and parasites. Most sprays kill beneficial creatures as well as pests and diseases

DON'T grow large areas of one type of plant only for this may encourage the quick spread of pests and diseases

DON'T throw away kitchen and garden waste. Its disposal causes pollution of our environment

DON'T burn autumn leaves if at all possible; bonfire smoke pollutes the atmosphere

DON'T harm the soil structure by digging or working it too often, or by walking on it in unsuitable conditions

DON'T use artificial fertilizers. They can encourage growth that is attractive to pests and inhibit the activity of the soil's inhabitants

DON'T leave soil bare for months on end, especially over winter. This allows the goodness to be washed out and the soil structure to be damaged by rain

DON'T use weedkiller sprays because they can be harmful to other creatures and plants, not just to weeds. There are also many beneficial weeds

DON'T cut lawns too short or too often; this prevents the grass growing strongly and allows weeds to take over

Products for the organic garden

Unfortunately, it is not always easy to know which products on the market are suitable for an organic garden. A few products carry a recognised organic symbol, but there is no legal definition of the word "organic" as applied to gardening products. This may simply mean that some or all of the ingredients are of living origin and not all of these are suitable for organic gardening use. The relevant sections of this book will help you through this maze.

Glossary

Acid Applied to a soil with a pH of below 7.

Alkaline Applied to a soil with a pH of over 7.

Anaerobic (process) One carried out in the absence of air.

Annual A plant that completes its life cycle within one growing season.

Bare-rooted (plant) A plant lifted from the open ground (as opposed to a containerized plant).

Bedding plant A plant used for temporary garden display, usually in spring and summer.

Beneficial insect Any insect that preys on plant pests or diseases or assists pollination.

Biennial A plant that completes its lifecycle over two growing seasons.

Biodegradable (material) A naturally derived material that can be broken down into its constituent parts by micro-organisms.

Biological control Control of a pest or disease by another living organism, usually one that has been introduced for this reason.

Biological control agent A living organism introduced to kill a pest or disease.

Bolting The premature production of flowers and seeds.

Brassica A member of a group of plants which includes the cabbage, cauliflower, Brussels sprout and turnip.

Broadcast Sowing seed by sprinkling it evenly over an area rather than in rows.

Canker A sharply defined diseased area, often with deformed bark, on a woody stem.

Caterpillar See *Larva.*

Chlorophyll The name given to the green pigment present in most plants.

Compost (seed or potting) A mixture of materials used as a medium for sowing seeds or potting plants.

Compost activator Material that promotes the initiation of the composting process.

Compost (garden) Rotted organic matter.

Containerized (plant) A plant grown in a pot or some sort of container (as opposed to a bare rooted plant).

Cordon A tree or bush pruned to form a main stem bearing fruiting spurs.

Deciduous (plant) A plant that loses all its leaves annually at the end of the growing season.

Deficiency Adverse condition in plants caused by a shortage of one or more nutrients.

Die-back The death of branches and shoots which starts at the tip and spreads back towards the main stem.

Disorder Adverse condition of plant that are commonly caused by environmental factors.

Drill Narrow furrow in which seeds are sown.

Earthing up Mounding up of soil around the base of a plant such as a potato.

Erosion The process of soil being washed away or blown off the surface of the ground.

Evergreen A plant that retains its leaves throughout the year.

Fan A tree or shrub with branches trained in the shape of a fan against a wall or other support.

Flame weeder A piece of equipment in which paraffin or gas is used to produce a high-temperature flame for killing weeds.

Foliar feeding Application of liquid fertilizer to plant foliage.

Frass Excreta or droppings of caterpillars and other larvae.

Gall An abnormal outgrowth of plant tissue.

Germination The development of a seed into a seedling.

Green manure A plant grown with the specific aim of improving the soil.

Growing medium A mixture in which plants are grown.

Growing season The period during which a plant is actively producing leaves and flowers.

Habitat The natural home of a plant or animal.

Half hardy A plant that is unable to survive the winter without protection but does not require protection all year round.

Hard pan A hard, compacted layer in the soil.

Harden off To acclimatize plants raised in warm conditions to cooler conditions.

Hardy A plant capable of surviving the winter in the open without protection.

Herbicide A weedkiller.

Hibernate To spend the winter months in a dormant state.

Honeydew Sticky substance exuded by aphids and some other insects.

Horticultural fleece A lightweight, man-made material used to keep pests and frost off plants.

Larva An active, immature stage of some insects. The larva of a butterfly, moth or sawfly is known as a caterpillar; of a weevil or beetle as a grub; of a fly as a maggot.

Leaching The removal of soluble substances from soil or potting mixtures by water passing through them.

Leafmould Decomposed autumn leaves, used as a soil conditioner.

Legume Vegetable of the Leguminosae family that produces pods, like peas and beans. It has the ability to take up nitrogen from the air.

Lump hammer Heavy hammer with a block-shaped head.

Maggot See *Larva*.

Micro-organism A microscopic living organism.

Mixed border A border containing different types of plants: a mixture of shrubs, herbaceous plants, bulbs and annuals.

Modules Moulded plastic or polystyrene trays divided up into cells which are filled with compost for sowing seeds.

Mulch A layer of organic or other material applied to the soil surface.

Multi-sow To sow more than one seed in a pot or module cell and leaving them all to grow on.

Native (plant) Originating in the country where they are grown.

Natural enemy One creature or organism that preys upon another.

Nematode A microscopic eelworm.

Nitrogen An important plant food, especially used in the growth of leaves and shoots.

Nitrogen robbery An effect that occurs when undecomposed woody material, low in nitrogen, is dug into the soil. Micro-organisms that decompose this material take nitrogen from the soil in order to enable them to work and this results in a shortage of nitrogen for growing plants. Although the effect is only temporary, it can last for a year or more.

Non-degradable (material) One that is not biodegradable.

Nutrient A plant food.

Organic matter Material consisting of, or derived from, living organisms, such as compost, leaf-mould and farmyard manure.

Perennial A plant that lives for at least three growing seasons.

Pesticide A product that will kill a pest, disease or weed.

pH The degree of acidity or alkalinity.

Pheromone A chemical substance secreted by certain animals affecting the behaviour of other animals.

Phosphate A phosphorus compound (P_2O_5).

Phosphorus One of the major plant foods, important in the germination and development of seedlings and in root growth.

Pollination The transfer of pollen to the stigma of a flower to fertilize it.

Potash A potassium compound (K_2O). Potash is often used as a general term to mean potassium.

Potassium One of the major plant foods affecting the size and quality of fruit and flowers. It can increase pest, disease and frost resistance.

Predator A creature that feeds by preying on other creatures, including garden pests.

Pricking out The transplanting and spacing out of seedlings.

Pupa The resting stage between adult and larva in some insects.

Resistant variety A plant variety which shows particular resistance to a pest and/or disease.

Resting body A structure produced by a fungus which remains dormant for a period of time before germinating.

Rootstock The root system of a grafted or budded plant used in grafting.

Rotation The practice of growing plants, usually vegetables, in a different site each year to avoid the build up of pests and diseases.

Rotovate To use a machine with rotating blades to break up the soil.

Soil conditioner Material that improves the soil structure without necessarily adding plant foods.

Spore A reproductive body of a fungus.

Spur A slow-growing, short branch system that usually bears a cluster of flower buds.

Strimmer A machine with a rotating blade or nylon cord used for cutting long grass or other soft vegetation.

Subsoil The layer of soil below the topsoil which is lighter in colour and lacking in organic matter, soil life and nutrients.

Tap root A strong-growing, vertical root.

Tilth A fine, crumbly surface layer of soil.

Top-dress To apply a material such as organic matter or fertilizer to the surface.

Top soil The upper layer of dark, fertile soil in which plants grow.

Trace elements Food materials required by plants in very small quantities.

Water table The level in the soil below which the soil is saturated by ground water.

Watering in To water around the stem of a newly transplanted plant in order to settle the soil around its roots.

Whip Small, bare-rooted, deciduous tree, shrub or hedging plant.

Worm compost Plant material that has been converted to compost by worms.

Habitats 1: Ponds

Introduction

When planning an organic garden you should introduce features that will encourage a good variety of wildlife, from birds and butterflies down to tiny insects. This may seem of dubious value, but relatively few creatures actually damage plants, and they all have their own natural enemies. By building up a wildlife community in the garden you will establish a balanced environment in which pests are less likely to get out of hand.

This does not mean that the whole garden has to look like a nature reserve. Features such as a pond, a hedge, a mixed border, a dry stone wall or a wild-flower meadow will significantly boost the garden's value to wildlife without making it untidy and will make it more attractive for you, too.

A watery habitat

Consider putting a pond in your garden if it is at all feasible. It guarantees an influx of new creatures – those that live permanently in the water and those such as toads, frogs and newts that need ponds to breed. In addition it will attract passing animals, birds and insects needing to drink or bathe. A pond designed for wildlife can be ornamental too, but it must have certain characteristics.

Pool design

While the pond does not have to be large, the bigger it is the more different plants and water creatures it will accommodate and the better conditions for them will be. The temperature of the water in a small pond can fluctuate considerably and can freeze solid in a hard winter. Ideally, you need a pond that is at least 60cm (2ft) deep at some point in the centre to ensure an ice-free area for pond life. The pond should have at least one shallow edge so creatures have easy access. You can create this "beach" with rocks and gravel even in an existing pond with steep sides.

Build in several shelves at different levels around the sides of the pond for a range of water plants; a shallow bog area adjacent to the pond will accommodate plants that like damp soil but not standing water.

Construction

The best way to construct a wildlife pond is to use a flexible sheet liner, as this enables you to create the exact shape you want. A butyl rubber liner is more expensive than polythene or PVC but lasts much longer.

After excavating, remove any sharp sticks or stones and rake the surface smooth. This will prevent the liner from being punctured. Lay a

Making a pond and bog

1 Lay a soft underlining over the excavated surface then cover this with a waterproof liner, smoothing it over the pool contours.

2 Spread a 10cm (4in) layer of subsoil on the pool floor and marginal shelves, and a little way up the sloping sides.

soft underlining of sand, old carpet or poly-ester matting to protect the liner from sharp stones. Put the liner over the centre of the excavation and mould it into the contours of the pool, smoothing it down as you go.

Filling the pond

Put a thin layer of subsoil on the bottom of the pond and then fill it with tap water or from rainwater butts. Adding a bucket of water from an established pond will help to build up the pond community more quickly. Frogs and toads normally return to their home pond to breed, so the best way to introduce them is to beg some spawn from a neighbour in the spring, or obtain some from a wild pond through your local wildlife trust. Do not put in goldfish, as these eat frogspawn, tadpoles and insect larvae.

Planting the pond

Once the pond is full of water you can intro-duce a variety of plants. Mid-spring is the best time for planting, although any time in spring or summer is acceptable.

Water plants

You will need several types of plants for a healthy, balanced pond.

In small ponds, it is best to grow plants in lattice-work planting baskets. This stops them spreading too far and enables you to lift and divide them more easily. The exception is floating plants, which are simply put on the water surface. Plant bog plants directly into the moist soil.

Submerged plants grow under the water. They provide hiding places for pond life and use up excess nutrients in the water, thus preventing the growth of algae such as blanketweed.

Floating plants drift on the surface. They reduce the amount of sunlight entering the water, providing shade for aquatic creatures and starving unwanted algae of light.

Deep-water plants have their roots on the pond bottom and their leaves float on the sur-face. They play a similar role to that of floating plants. Ideally, about one-third of the surface of a pond should be covered with foliage.

Marginal or emergent plants grow in the shallows of a pond and give good shelter for amphibians. Choose these plants to flower in succession throughout the summer to attract a variety of insects. Always grow each plant in the correct depth of water.

Bog plants grow in permanently waterlogged ground. They can be among the best plants for attracting bees and butterflies.

3 Make a gently sloping beach on one of the sides using large stones as an edging, infilled with pebbles.

4 Line the bog area and build a barrier of stones to separate it from the pool; fill the bog with soil.

Habitats 2 : Ponds

Cross-section of a pond

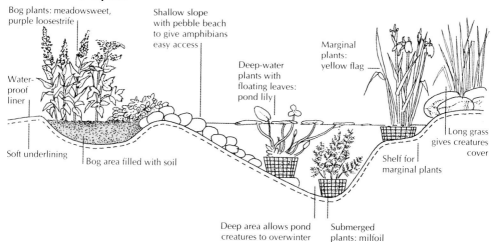

Bog plants: meadowsweet, purple loosestrife

Shallow slope with pebble beach to give amphibians easy access

Deep-water plants with floating leaves: pond lily

Marginal plants: yellow flag

Water-proof liner

Long grass gives creatures cover

Soft underlining

Bog area filled with soil

Shelf for marginal plants

Deep area allows pond creatures to overwinter

Submerged plants: milfoil

A pond does not have to be particularly large, although the larger the design the greater the variety of water plants that can be grown and the more wildlife it will attract.

Native water plants will help to make it a richer habitat for wildlife. Many of these plants are as beautiful as exotic species, and they are easy to buy. A large proportion of the water plants sold by garden centres and specialist suppliers are in fact natives.

Ideally, the pool should have a deep area where wildlife can go if the pool freezes, a shallow beach for easy access and some shelves for plants to grow on.

Most of the following plants are suitable for a small garden pond with a surface area of about 3sq m (33sq ft) and a depth of about 60cm (2ft), with marginal shelves. However, the water lily ideally needs a depth of at least 1.8m (6ft).

WATER PLANTS

Submerged plants
Callitriche spp. (water starwort) z 6–9
Ceratophyllum demersum (hornwort) z 6–9
Fontinalis antipyretica (willow moss) z 6–9
Myriophyllum verticillatum (milfoil) z 6–9

Floating plants
Hydrocharis morsus-ranae (frogbit) z 5–9
Lemna minor (duckweed) z 5–9
Stratiotes aloides (water soldier) z 4–9

Deep-water plants
Hottonia palustris (water violet) z 6–9
Nuphar lutea (yellow pond lily) z 5–9
Nymphaea alba (white waterlily) z 5–9
Nymphoides peltata (fringed waterlily) z 5–9

Marginal plants
Caltha palustris (marsh marigold) z 5–9
Iris pseudacorus (yellow flag) z 4–9
Menyanthes trifoliata (bog bean) z 3
Myosotis scorpioides (water forget-me-not) z 5–9
Ranunculus flammula (lesser spearwort) z 5
Veronica beccabunga (brooklime) z 5–9

Bog plants
Ajuga reptans (bugle) z 4–9
Cardamine pratensis (lady's smock) z 4–9
Filipendula ulmaria (meadowsweet) z 4–9
Lychnis flos-cuculi (ragged robin) z 6
Lysimachia nummularia (creeping Jenny) z 5–9
Lythrum salicaria (purple loosestrife) z 4–9

NOOKS AND CRANNIES

You only have to move an old pile of logs or a heap of stones to realize just how many creatures make their homes in the damp, cool crevices. Spiders, centipedes, beetles and newts, for example, can all be found, and perhaps a mouse or two as well. To encourage them, build one or two piles of logs in the shrubbery, for instance, (you can hide them behind taller-growing subjects if you wish), or put a few large stones in an inconspicuous place, such as behind the shed, to provide useful habitats.

Dry-stone walls constructed without mortar also provide plenty of nooks and crannies for insects and other small creatures. Furthermore, the reflected warmth from the stones encourages butterflies and slow-worms to bask.

You do not have to be an expert to build a low retaining wall for a border. Not only will this harbour wildlife, but it can also add to the look of the garden, especially if you use local stone. Suitable stone can be obtained from stone merchants and from some garden centres.

Building a dry-stone retaining wall

You will need about 0.5t/cu m (7½cwt/cu yd) of stone per wall.

To make a firm foundation, dig out the topsoil over the area needed for the base of the wall. Fill in this trench with hardcore (broken stones or bricks), compacting it with a sledge hammer, and put sand on the top to make the surface level.

Choose some large, flat foundation stones for the base and lay them down in a single layer, firming them in place. Build up the wall, overlapping the courses of stone in a staggered manner.

To make the wall stable, slope it back and downwards towards the border so that it will be retaining at an angle of about 8° from the vertical. Finish the top with a layer of flat stones. Push small stones behind the main blocks which make up the courses of the wall to reinforce it, before levelling off the border soil behind.

Building a dry-stone retaining wall

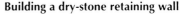

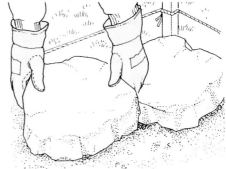

1 Make a firm foundation with hardcore, then lay down large flat stones for the base.

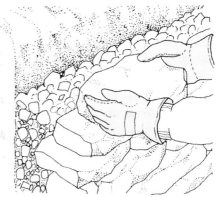

2 Build up the wall, sloping it backwards slightly and overlapping the courses of stone.

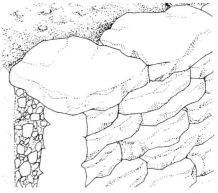

3 Infill behind with small stones to reinforce it and finish with a layer of flat stones.

11

Habitats 3: Hedges

Planting a hedge

1 Dig out the topsoil from a trench 1m (3¼ft) wide and fork over the subsoil; mix leafmould or compost with the topsoil.

2 Refill the trench with the soil mixture and put in the hedging plants at the required spacing, firming them in well.

Regularly clipped hedges that are dense and twiggy make excellent nesting sites for birds. Some also provide berries for food, and the plant debris that builds up underneath provides a place for hibernating hedgehogs. A hedge also acts as a corridor, allowing creatures to move between gardens and into the wilds beyond.

Planting a hedge is cheaper than putting up a fence and hedges make good windbreaks, filtering instead of blocking the wind. However, a hedge does take up more space. You should allow a strip about 1m (3¼ft) wide for the hedge, and leave 1m (3¼ft) before planting vegetables, fruit or moisture-loving flowers.

Plan a hedge at least on one side of the garden if you can, using walls or fences clothed in climbers for the rest if space is limited.

Types of hedges (see pages 180–1)
Formal hedges The best plants for closely clipped hedges are neat slow-growing species such as yew (*Taxus baccata* z 6), holly (*Ilex aquifolium* z 6), beech (*Fagus sylvatica* z 5) and hornbeam (*Carpinus betulus* z 5). They can be used for medium-height hedges (around 1.2m (4ft) or for much taller ones. The close cutting will remove most seeds or berries, but they still provide cover and nesting sites for birds.
Conifer hedges Two of the best species of conifer for garden hedges are Western red cedar (*Thuja plicata* z 6) and Lawson's cypress

(*Chamaecyparis lawsoniana* z 6). These are most suitable for tall hedges (2m (6½ft) or more). Some conifer species are not suitable for hedges, particularly in a small garden, as they grow very tall and become bare at the base and do not like clipping or topping. Conifer hedges make dense cover for birds, particularly in winter.
Informal flowering or berrying hedges Some hedging species can be left to grow more naturally so that they give an attractive show of flowers or berries, and these can also benefit wildlife. Good species include *Cotoneaster simonsii* z 5, *Pyracantha rogersiana* z 8, *Berberis* x *stenophylla* z 5 and some *Rosa rugosa* hybrids such as 'Scabrosa' z 2. They are mostly suitable for medium-height hedges of 1–2m (3¼–6½ft).
Barrier hedges For a hedge that is child- or animal-proof, choose a prickly species such as hawthorn (*Crataegus monogyna* z 5), holly (*Ilex aquifolium* z 6) or berberis (*Berberis* spp. z 3–8).

A mixed native hedge
There is a wide range of shrubs and trees traditionally used for countryside hedgerows which together will clip to form a tidy garden hedge. As well as providing dense cover and nesting sites, they form a rich habitat for a variety of smaller creatures that rely on them for food.

Before planning a native hedge, look at field hedgerows to see what species they contain. They will give you an idea of which species you

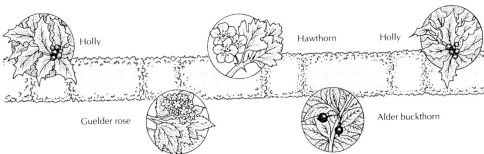

Holly   Hawthorn   Holly

Guelder rose   Alder buckthorn

In this hedge of native species, hawthorn is the main species, planted in blocks of 15 plants; the hawthorn is interspersed with blocks of five plants of other native species.

can expect to grow well, and you may want to follow this planting scheme in your garden.

Choose one main species to make up the majority (70–80 per cent) of the hedge. Use prickly hawthorn or blackthorn to keep animals out or in. Field maple also makes a good basis for a hedge. Choose several other native species to make up the remaining plants: it is usually best to plant a block of at least five of each species. Try to include at least one evergreen for winter cover.

Native hedging plants are available as bare-rooted whips 45–60cm (18–24in) high from tree and shrub nurseries. It is best to buy plants this small as they establish well and you can clip them to make them bushy right from the start. Allow five plants per 1m (3¼ft) of hedge, planted in a staggered row.

Planting a hedge
Deciduous hedges should be planted from late autumn to early spring; autumn is the best time. Ideally, plant evergreen hedges such as holly and conifers in mid- to late spring.

Prepare a strip for the hedge about 1m (3¼ft) wide. On cultivated ground, fork or hoe to remove any weeds and add well-rotted compost or a proprietary organic planting mixture. Leafmould is a good alternative on heavy soils. On uncultivated ground, remove any rough turf and dig out the topsoil from the strip, keeping it separate from the turf. Loosen the subsoil at the bottom of the trench and put the turf on top, chopping it up with a spade. Refill the trench with a mixture of soil and compost, planting mixture or leafmould. Plant the hedging plants at the recommended spacing. Lightly firm the soil and water them well. In spring, mulch them

with hay, straw, shreddings or bark to retain moisture and keep down weeds (see pages 52–5). Use newspaper under the mulch if necessary. Native hedging whips are generally bare-rooted and have small enough roots to be planted through black polythene on very weedy ground (see page 146).

Trimming a hedge
Never trim a hedge in the nesting season (spring and early summer). An annual trim in late summer or early autumn is sufficient for most hedges mentioned. Informal hedges need even less attention – prune these only to prevent them becoming straggly. Wait until winter when the berries are gone.

PLANTS FOR NATIVE HEDGES

Acer campestre (field maple) z 4
Carpinus betulus (hornbeam) z 5
Cornus sanguinea (dogwood) z 5
Corylus avellana (hazel) z 4
Crataegus monogyna (hawthorn) z 5
Euonymus europaeus (spindle) z 3
Fagus sylvatica (beech) z 5
Frangula alnus (alder buckthorn) z 3
Ilex aquifolium (holly) z 6
Ligustrum vulgare (wild privet) z 4
Malus sylvestris (crab apple) z 3
Prunus spinosa (blackthorn) z 4
Quercus petraea (oak) z 4
Quercus robur (pedunculate oak) z 6
Rhamnus cathartica (buckthorn) z 3
Sorbus torminalis (wild service) z 6
Viburnum opulus (guelder rose) z 3

Habitats 4: Woodland edges

The edge of a wood, where partial sunlight allows a range of shrubs and wild flowers to grow beneath the tree canopy, is always teeming with life. Each tier of vegetation provides homes for a different creatures; for example, in the case of birds, the song thrush lives in the tree tops, the finches among the shrub branches and the wrens and blackbirds in the low vegetation and ground cover.

Even in a small garden, it is easy to re-create this woodland edge in a mixed border.

Tree layer

Grow at least one tree if you have the space; if space is limited grow a dwarf ornamental tree such as a crab apple or one large shrub. There is plenty of choice for large gardens.

Many tree species can be kept small by coppicing, cutting back trees to within 15–30cm (6–12in) of the ground every few years and allowing vigorous new growth. This gives a thicket of attractive stems and foliage. Ideally, you need several trees that can be coppiced in rotation so that there is always one tall specimen. Height can also be provided by a wall, fence or pole covered in climbing plants. Native honeysuckle and ivy are good for wildlife, but many exotic species also provide nectar, pollen, seeds or berries (see page 25).

> **NATIVE TREES AND SHRUBS**
> (Figure gives approx. height at maturity)
>
> *Acer campestre* (field maple) z 5 15m (50ft)
> *Betula pendula* (birch) z 1 18m (60ft)
> *Corylus avellana* (hazel) z 4 6m (20ft)
> *Crataegus monogyna* (hawthorn) z 5 6m (20ft)
> *Frangula alnus* (alder buckthorn) z 3 2.4m (8ft)
> *Ilex aquifolium* (holly) z 6 15m (50ft)
> *Malus sylvestris* (crab apple) z 3 9m (30ft)
> *Prunus avium* (wild cherry) z 3 15m (50ft)
> *Prunus padus* (bird cherry) z 3 10m (33ft)
> *Sambucus nigra* (elderberry) z 5 10m (33ft)
> *Sorbus aria* (whitebeam) z 5 10m (33ft)
> *Sorbus aucuparia* (rowan) z 2 9m (30ft)
> *Tilia cordata* (lime, small-leaved) z 3 15m (50ft)
> *Viburnum lantana* (wayfaring tree) z 3 3m (10ft)
> *Viburnum opulus* (guelder rose) z 3 4m (13ft)

Making a climber curtain

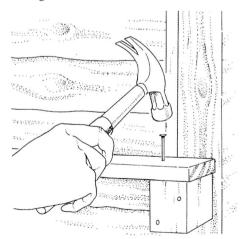

1 Nail blocks of wood onto the fence posts and fix across strips of wood to form simple nesting ledges for birds.

2 To screen the ledges, train a climbing plant on a latticework of wires between the outer faces of the blocks.

A CLIMBER CURTAIN

Nail blocks of wood a few centimetres thick onto your fence posts. The total distance between the surface of the fence and the outer faces of the blocks should be about 10cm (4in). Fit a few simple ledges across the blocks on which birds can nest. Stretch a latticework of wires between the outer faces of the blocks or put up a light trellis on which climbing plants can be trained. These form a green curtain to screen the wildlife.

Shrub layer
Shrubs provide a framework beneath tree height and are a good source of berries, flowers and attractive foliage (see page 27). Include some evergreens for winter cover and deciduous shrubs to give dappled shade.

Flower layer
Choose flowers that are shade tolerant or those that flower in early spring before the trees have put out their leaves. Many woodland wild flowers are ideal. Not only can they look attractive, but they provide nectar and pollen for insects at an important time of year.

WILD FLOWERS FOR WOODLAND

Ajuga reptans (bugle) z 6
Anemone nemorosa (wood anemone) z 5
Arum maculatum (lords and ladies) z 6
Campanula trachelium (nettle-leaved bellflower) z 3
Digitalis purpurea (foxglove) z 4
Hyacinthoides non-scriptus (bluebell) z 5
Fragaria vesca (wild strawberry) z 5
Galanthus nivalis (snowdrop) z 4
Galium odoratum (woodruff) z 5
Glechoma hederacea (ground ivy) z 3
Helleborus foetidus (stinking hellebore) z 6
Lamium purpureum (red dead nettle) z 4
Oxalis acetosella (wood sorrel) z 3
Polygonatum multiflorum (Solomon's seal) z 4
Primula vulgaris (primrose) z 6
Silene dioica (red campion) z 6
Viola riviniana (common violet) z 5

Ground cover
The decaying material on a woodland floor harbours many insects. Use a mulch of leaf-mould, shredded prunings, woodchips or bark (see pages 52–5) to re-create this condition.

Woodland edge border

The different layers of this border make it ideal for wildlife. The silver birch tree gives height, the evergreen shrubs (holly and mahonia) provide berries and permanent shelter and woodland wild flowers such as primroses grow in the areas of dappled shade.

Habitats 5: Lawns/Grass

Lawns are a good habitat for a variety of creatures in the garden. A lot of activity goes on below ground, with worms and insects, some of them quite large, feeding on the dead grass and roots. These are a source of fast food for many birds: easy to get at because the grass is short, and safe because on an open lawn they can see approaching danger.

You can create another habitat in the garden simply by letting some grass grow long on a bank, in an odd corner or on a patch in the middle of your existing lawn. This will give lawn "weeds" and grasses a chance to flower, attracting different insects, which in turn make food for different birds. It will also provide shelter for amphibians and small mammals. You may also get a show of flowers, particularly from a lawn where no weedkillers have been used.

An even better plan would be to make a patch into a wild-flower "meadow" by creating the conditions in which the wild flowers of traditional hayfields and pastures grew. Meadow wild flowers do best in poor soil because this reduces the competition from coarse weeds and grasses. You can create a patch of low fertility in a small area by digging out the turf and topsoil and replacing it with subsoil. Make sure you remove all weed roots. For large areas, it is more practical to grow a hungry crop such as potatoes for several years without any compost or fertilizers, or to grow and remove a green manure crop such as grazing rye (see page 85).

MEADOW WILD FLOWERS

Latin name	English name	Hardiness zone	Flowering period	Soil preference
Bellis perennis	Daisy	4	Early spring–mid-autumn	Most types
Primula veris	Cowslip	5	Mid-spring–late spring	Alkaline
Cardamine pratensis	Lady's smock	4	Mid-spring–early summer	Damp
Hypochaeris radicata	Cat's ear	3	Late spring–early summer	Most types
Ranunculus acris	Meadow buttercup	5	Late spring–early autumn	Most types
Rhinanthus minor	Yellow rattle	6	Late summer–early autumn	Most types
Stellaria graminea	Lesser stitchwort	5	Late spring–mid-autumn	Most types
Chrysanthemum leucanthemum	Ox-eye daisy	3	Early summer–mid-summer	Most types
Anthyllis vulneraria	Kidney vetch	7	Early summer–late summer	Most types
Lotus corniculatus	Bird's foot trefoil	5	Early summer–late summer	Most types
Prunella vulgaris	Selfheal	3	Early summer–early autumn	Most types
Leontodon taraxacoides	Hawkbit	6	Early summer–early autumn	Most types
Hypericum perforatum	Perforate St John's wort	3	Early summer–early autumn	Most types
Achillea millefolium	Yarrow	2	Early summer–late summer	Most types
Centurea scabiosa	Greater knapweed	4	Mid-summer–early autumn	Most types
Knautia arvensis	Field scabious	6	Mid-summer–early autumn	Well-drained
Campanula rotundifolia	Harebell	3	Mid-summer–early autumn	Very poor, dry

Creating a wild-flower meadow

1 Dig out the topsoil from the area and fill with subsoil.

2 Mix the seed with an equal amount of silver sand.

3 Rake and firm the bed and broadcast the seed evenly.

Choosing wild flowers and grasses Choose flower species that bloom over a similar period so they will all set seed before the hay is cut. Check they are suitable for your soil type – most will grow in any ordinary garden soil, but if you have extreme conditions (very acid or chalky soil or heavy clay, for example) you may be restricted in what you can grow.

You also need several fine grass species. Either buy seeds of meadow grasses from a specialist seedsman, or use an ordinary lawn mixture without rye grass sown at a lower rate than recommended, say 3g/sq m (0.1oz/sq yd). Some companies sell mixes of wild flowers and grasses suited to particular soils and situations.

Sowing The best time to sow wild-flower seed is in early autumn, because the seeds of some species need to experience winter cold before they will germinate. Alternatively, sow in mid-spring when conditions are warm and moist, but be prepared for some seed remaining dormant until the following spring.

Prepare a fine crumbly seedbed by raking and firming, just as you would for an ordinary lawn. Mix the wild-flower and grass seed with an equal amount of silver sand: this makes it easier to distribute the small amount of seed more evenly. The sowing rate for wild-flower seed is only approximately 1g/sq m (0.03oz/sq yd). Broadcast the seed, rake it in and lightly firm the soil.

Cutting Meadow wild-flowers developed as a result of the traditional farming practices of haymaking and grazing. To re-create this on a patch of your lawn, you have to adopt a particular schedule of mowing and not mowing and stick to it each year.

For a spring meadow, select plants that flower between early spring and early summer. Leave the patch to grow until mid-summer. Cut it (remove the hay) and then mow the patch and lawn until the end of the season.

For a summer meadow, choose plants that flower between early summer and early autumn. Mow up until early summer, but not too closely – set the mower blades at a height of 7.5cm (3in). Leave the patch to flower until mid-autumn, then cut it and remove the hay.

A small patch can be cut with a sickle or shears. Meadows were traditionally cut with scythes, but a strimmer is a good substitute. It is important to rake up the hay and remove it to keep the fertility of the meadow low.

Adding to a lawn or meadow Sowing seeds into an established lawn or meadow is unlikely to work. Instead, plant out wild flowers from pots, preferably in mid-autumn after mowing. Wild flowers are found in nurseries, but you can get a greater variety if you grow your own from seed (see page 157). You can also plant bulbs of wild flowers such as wild daffodils.

Know your friends 1

Although you should encourage a whole range of wildlife into your organic garden, creatures that are predators of garden pests are particularly welcome. It is important to be able to recognize these creatures and know something of their habits and lifecycle, because this can help you tip the balance between friend and foe in your favour, and is an important part of organic pest control (see pages 90–141).

Some predators have a limited diet and target specific pests: hoverfly larvae, for example, feed mainly on aphids. Others are less discerning: centipedes and hedgehogs, for example, are among those which feed on a wide range of grubs, insects and eggs, some of which are pests, some of which are not. However, because their diet will consist of what is most available, they will eat more pests during a pest outbreak, and thus they still help to restore the natural balance in the organic garden.

The first step in encouraging any of these creatures is to stop using pesticides – some predators are sensitive even to organic sprays. The second step to take is to increase the wildlife value of your garden in the ways that are described on pages 8–17. In addition, knowing the habits of some of the most useful garden friends means you can artificially boost their populations. As well as putting up nest boxes for birds, for example, you can put up boxes in which bats can roost and even "refuges" in which lacewings can overwinter (see page 21).

Sometimes the dividing line between friend and foe is not clear-cut. Earwigs, for example, can be pests if you have prize dahlias, but they can help by preying on aphids and codling moth eggs. Blackbirds stop at nothing to get at ripe strawberries, but they also eat caterpillars, and even wasps feed their young on small insect pests. The best strategy is to tolerate such creatures and protect vulnerable crops when necessary.

Below is a description of the most beneficial insects commonly found in the organic garden. As a general rule, check when you come across something you do not recognize – certainly before you squash it! The larvae of ladybirds and hoverflies, for example, can easily be mistaken for harmful grubs.

INVERTEBRATES
Ladybirds
Appearance Adult beetles have red and black or yellow and black markings – but most commonly red with black spots. Larvae have tapering bodies which are segmented, greyish-black with orange markings; these insects are active from late spring to late summer.

Usefulness Both adults and larvae feed mainly on greenfly, but also eat other pests including mites, scale insects, mealybugs and small caterpillars.

To encourage them Cultivate a nettle patch for early aphids (see pages 26–7) and tolerate some aphids around the garden for ladybirds to feed on. Do not do too much tidying up in the garden during autumn: leave some dry plant debris, loose bark and hollow stems to provide hibernation sites for these insects. Avoid using pesticides.

Beneficial insects (not to scale)

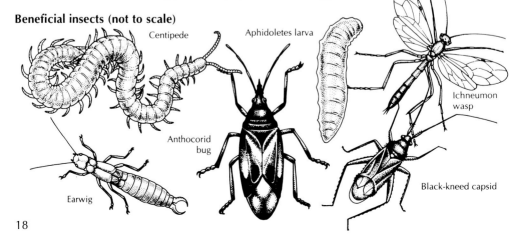

Centipede

Aphidoletes larva

Ichneumon wasp

Anthocorid bug

Earwig

Black-kneed capsid

Hoverflies

Appearance Adults resemble small wasps or bees but they have only one set of wings. Their flight is characteristic: darting then hovering motionless as they visit flowers in summer and autumn. The legless larvae are generally translucent brown or green, appearing from late spring onwards.

Usefulness The larvae of many species (about 100) feed on aphids, eating them at a significant rate – sometimes up to as much as 50 a day. They also eat fruit tree spider mites and small caterpillars.

To encourage them Grow flowers that attract adult hoverflies by providing nectar and pollen for them to feed on (see page 25). Tolerate some aphid colonies as sites for adults to lay eggs. Avoid using pesticides.

Lacewings

Appearance The most commonly seen species of lacewing are green, with two pairs of flimsy wings and large eyes. The larvae are small, bristly and active, variable in colour but often a creamy-brown, appearing from late spring to mid-autumn. Sometimes these insects fix the skins of sucked-out aphids on to the bristles on their backs to act as camouflage.

Usefulness Both adults and larvae feed on aphids. The larvae also eat mites, leafhoppers, scale insects and small caterpillars.

To encourage them Grow flowers to attract adults, which also feed on nectar (see page 25). Make lacewing "refuges" to encourage them to overwinter in the garden. Avoid all pesticides, even organic ones.

Ground beetles and rove beetles

Appearance These are dark scuttling beetles with long legs and antennae; few of them fly. Rove beetles tend to be longer and thinner than ground beetles, more like oversized earwigs. They are seen all year round.

Usefulness Both types of beetle are important predators of slugs. They also eat the eggs and larvae of cabbage and carrot root flies and lettuce root aphids.

To encourage them These beetles live in the soil or under debris, logs and stones – anywhere that it is moist and shady (see page 11). Leave the soil undisturbed where possible, and use mulches and ground-cover plants. Put down shelters such as old tiles or pieces of wood. Avoid using pesticides.

Centipedes

Appearance Centipedes are long, segmented, fast-moving creatures with many legs, distinguished from millipedes by the fact that they have only one pair of legs per segment (whereas millipedes have two). Most garden species are yellow or brown.

Usefulness They often prey on slugs and snails, although a range of insects is also included in their diet.

To encourage them Some species live in the soil, others under logs and stones. Encourage them as for ground beetles.

Earwigs

Appearance Dark brown in colour, flattish, slender insects with a prominent pair of pincers at the rear.

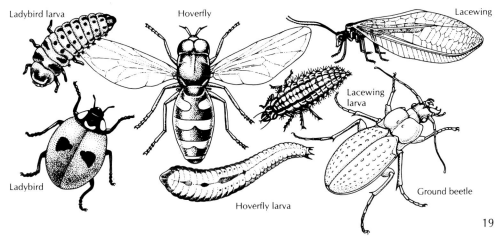

Ladybird larva · Hoverfly · Lacewing · Lacewing larva · Ladybird · Ground beetle · Hoverfly larva

Know your friends 2

Usefulness These insects cause some damage, often to flower buds and petals, but they make up for this by eating caterpillars, large numbers of aphids and insect eggs, particularly those of the codling moth.

To encourage them Earwigs like to rest during the day in narrow crevices – in loose bark or old seedheads, for example. If you find them in flowerheads or curled round an apple stalk, the chances are that they are taking refuge rather than doing damage.

If you want to keep these insects away from your dahlia or chrysanthemum plants, provide alternative night-time accommodation in flowerpots stuffed with straw fixed upside down among the flowers, then release the ear-wigs well away from the flowers anytime in the morning.

Anthocorid bugs
Appearance These are small, reddish to dark brown, beetle-like creatures with a sharp snout. They are active from late spring to early autumn.

Usefulness They feed mainly on aphids, but also eat scale insects, capsid bugs, caterpillars, mites and blossom weevil larvae.

To encourage them They overwinter under bark and in leaf litter, so will be more likely to be found in gardens with trees and hedges. Avoid using pesticides.

Aphidoletes
Appearance Aphidoletes are tiny delicate midges with long antennae. The larvae are orange with

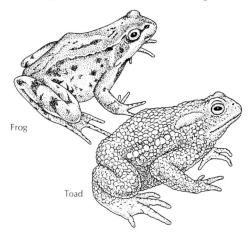

Frog

Toad

no legs, and are just visible to the naked eye. They are active from late spring to early autumn.

Usefulness The larvae eat aphids.

To encourage them Grow nursery plants for aphids (see page 26).

Black-kneed capsid
Appearance These greenish beetle-like bugs have overlapping wings and long antennae. The knee-joints are black, distinguishing them from other species, some of which are pests.

Usefulness They are a major predator of fruit tree red spider mites; they also eat greenfly, thrips, leafhoppers and small caterpillars.

To encourage them Never use winter washes on fruit trees, and avoid all pesticides (even organic ones) as capsids are extremely sensitive to them.

Ichneumons
Appearance Ichneumons are leggy brown insects with a wasp-like waist. They are one of the several groups of parasitic wasps found in the garden.

Usefulness They parasitize the caterpillars of butterflies and moths.

To encourage them Grow attractant flowers (see pages 25–6).

Making a lacewing refuge
Cut the bottom off a large (1- or 2-litre) plastic drink bottle. (Do not wash it out – the remains of any sugary solution is an added attraction.) Cut a piece of corrugated cardboard 82–100cm (32–40in) long to fit the height of the bottle, roll it up and push it inside. Make two tiny holes in the base of the bottle and push a piece of thin wire through to secure the cardboard. Tie a piece of string round the neck of the bottle so that you can suspend it from a fence or tree branch. Leave the top on to keep out rain.

VERTEBRATES
This section covers a selection of the larger, more easily identified garden friends and the ways in which you can make your garden more hospitable to them.

Frogs and toads
Both these amphibians rely on water for breeding, but the rest of the year can be found in

damp, warm, shady places at a considerable distance from ponds. Frogs can change their colour to match their background, so you might find a vivid green and yellow one in the lush vegetation at the edge of a pond and a dark brown one in the compost heap.Toads have a grey-brown warty skin.

Most male frogs hibernate at the bottom of a pond, while toads and other frogs overwinter in damp, hidden places such as under stones or old logs. They return to their home pond in early spring, where they mate and the female lays the spawn. Frogspawn is the familiar blobs of spotted jelly; toads lay long strings of eggs. Both spawn and tadpoles have many predators including newts, ducks, goldfish and many insects.

Usefulness Frogs are major predators of slugs. Toads also include some snails and numerous ants and woodlice in their diet.

To encourage them Build a suitable pond in the garden if possible (see pages 8–11). Make sure you have secure, damp places where adults can shelter and hibernate.

Hedgehogs

Hedgehogs do not like wet places, but otherwise live well in all rural and suburban areas. They hunt mainly at night from mid-spring to mid-autumn, sometimes travelling a mile or two in search of food. They hide during the day, perhaps under shrubs or a hedge or in long grass. By mid-winter they will have constructed a winter nest to begin hibernation.

Usefulness A hedgehog's diet includes a large proportion of pests such as slugs, millipedes, cockchafers and caterpillars, although it will eat almost any insect and sometimes birds' eggs and small mammals.

To encourage them Make sure that your garden has plenty of daytime shelter and hibernation sites such as low, thick shrubs, leaves in hedge bottoms, behind a shed or under log piles (see page 11) or a heap of prunings. Avoid using slug pellets and other pesticides. Check hazards such as fruit nets regularly, and put ramps in cattle grids and steep-sided pools. If you must have a bonfire, first make sure there are no hedgehogs under the bonfire pile. If you have a hedgehog in the garden, supplement its diet with cat food in the autumn to help it build up strength for hibernation.

Making a lacewing refuge

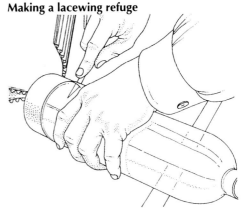

1 Use a sharp knife to cut the bottom off a large plastic drink bottle.

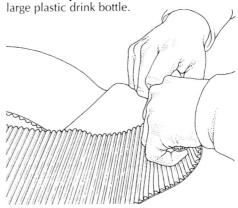

2 Roll up a piece of corrugated cardboard 90cm (3ft) long and the height of the bottle.

3 Push the roll inside the bottle and secure it with a piece of thin wire.

Know your friends 3

Slow-worms

Slow-worms look like snakes (although they are legless lizards), varying in colour from grey to coppery or dark brown. They bask in partial sunlight, in long grass at the base of a wall, for example, but spend much of their time underground, so they are rarely seen.

Slow-worms need a warm place to have their young, and sometimes choose a garden compost heap, where you may find them during late summer. They hibernate underground.
Usefulness Slugs form a major part of the slow-worm's diet.
To encourage them Long grass and stones in a warm, sunny spot provide ideal conditions for these creatures.

Newts

Newts look something like lizards, but have no scales and move very slowly. The adults spend the summer and autumn on land, hiding under stones or logs or in thick grass and emerging at night to feed. Most newts also hibernate on land during winter, returning to pools to breed in the spring. They wrap their eggs individually in water plant leaves.
Usefulness Newts eat slugs and snails, worms and a variety of insects.

To encourage them Build a suitable pond in the garden (see pages 8–10) and make sure there is long grass and other shelter nearby.

Bats

All bats have mouse-like furry bodies and large wings. The bats that you are most likely to see around the garden are the small pipistrelles, but there are several other common species. Pipistrelles roost mainly in warm, dry hollows in trees and in crevices in buildings, often behind tiles or weatherboarding and sometimes as low as 2.1m (7ft) from the ground. Some other species use cellars and tunnels. Bats hibernate in winter.
Usefulness Bats eat many insects including cockchafers, midges, craneflies (daddy long-legs), moths and aphids. Some species eat insects as they fly around, while others eat them from foliage or the ground.
To encourage them To provide food, encourage insects into the garden with, for example, a meadow and attractant plants (see pages 16 and 25). Put up a bat box if there are no natural roosts. Bat boxes simulate tree holes or crevices in buildings and can be used by many bat species. They are simple to make or, alternatively, you can usually buy them from your local Wildlife Trust. Fix your box in a sheltered

Making a bat box

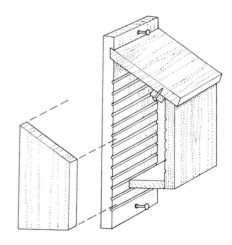

1 Use rough-sawn timber to make a bat box as this will help the bats to cling. Do not use wood preservatives on the timber as these can be toxic to bats.

2 The box need be only about 20cm (8in) high and 10cm (4in) inside from front to back – bats like narrow spaces. Leave an access gap of about 1.9cm (¾in) wide underneath.

position, which preferably has some morning sun and shade in the afternoon, and where the entrance is clear of overcrowding branches.

Birds

Some gardens may attract up to a dozen bird species to nest, but many more may visit in search of food.

Usefulness Birds can be a mixed blessing: some, such as blackbirds, peck ripe fruit and sparrows savage seedlings and crocus flowers (see page 112). However, there are many birds that are beneficial to the organic garden.

The song thrush is well known for its snail bashing, and both blackbirds and thrushes eat caterpillars. Small birds such as bluetits, long-tailed tits and even house sparrows will pick aphids off plants, and bluetits have been known to account for 95 per cent of codling moth cocoons. Robins are particularly welcome when you are digging a plot where soil pests may be overwintering as they will feed on them. Starlings on a lawn are probably probing for leatherjackets, and even seed-eaters such as finches will collect insects to feed their young.

To encourage them Provide different levels of vegetation: a tall tree as a song post if possible, as well as shrubbery and undergrowth (see pages 14–15). A hedge, thick shrubs and climbers (especially evergreens) will make good nesting sites for many birds, and you can provide artificial sites with nesting ledges on walls and fences (see page 14) and nest boxes.

Nest boxes attract birds that naturally nest in hollow branches and tree cavities, which are not often found in a suburban garden. The design of the nest box will influence which birds take up residence. A closed box with a small entrance hole suits bluetits and great tits. Bluetits need an entrance of only about 2.8cm (1 1/10 in) diameter, and increasing this to approximately 3cm (1⅛in) will allow great tits in. Any larger, and sparrows will take over. Site these nest boxes on a wall or tree, making sure they are in a fairly open position so that the hole is directed away from prevailing winds and shaded from hot sun.

The other main type of nest box is simply an open box with sides and a roof. Robins and spotted flycatchers will nest in this type of box. Site the nest box where it is surrounded by

plenty of vegetation to act as camouflage. Alternatively, you can fix one inside the garden shed if the window is left permanently open so the birds can get in and out.

A pond or bird bath is another useful garden feature, valuable for providing drinking water and a place to bathe (see pages 8–10). Thaw out or break any ice that forms on the bird bath in winter. Some birds may be particularly attracted by running water – a small bubbler fountain, for example, will provide this.

Provide a natural "larder" by growing flowers which attract insects, which in turn provide food for birds. Choose shrubs which have a good berry crop, and leave seedheads on flowers until the seed-eating birds have visited (see pages 26–7). In winter, put out food on a bird table every day. Site the table at least 1.5m (5ft) above the ground, and at least 2.1m (7ft) away from bushy cover in which a cat could hide. Put out a range of hard and soft food: seeds (especially sunflower seeds for the tits and finches), peanuts, fat and scraps such as cheese rind, bread and cooked potato. Clear away any stale food regularly, and put any damaged apples on the lawn for the blackbirds to eat.

Bird box

A wooden nest box with one small entrance hole suits birds such as tits. Lift the lid to clean the box at the end of the season.

Choosing plants 1

Plants for an organic garden need not differ widely from those in any other garden, but there are a number of points to consider.

Diversity

An organic garden should contain as many different types of plant as possible. Where similar plants are growing in a large area, whether it be a vegetable plot full of cabbages or a border full of roses, a pest or pathogen can build up numbers and soon get out of control.

This plant diversity goes hand-in-hand with creating different habitats: a pond, meadow, dry stone wall and woodland edge (see pages 8–17) all give you the chance to introduce different types of plants. You can also make more variety in areas such as the vegetable patch by, for example, including some annual flowers and herbs.

Plants for places

Make sure that any plant you choose for a particular spot in your garden is going to like it there. This may seem obvious, but it is surprisingly easy to get carried away by attractive blooms in the garden centres and pictures in nursery catalogues.

Find out what type of soil the plant likes – light or heavy, acid or alkaline, moist or dry. Does it do best in sun or shade? Is it prone to damage by wind or frost? Plants that are put in the wrong place will never thrive and are more susceptible to pest and disease attack. It helps to take note of which plants are doing well in neighbouring gardens. Also check which wild plants grow in woods, commons, and open spaces nearby – closely related garden varieties are likely to flourish.

Resistant varieties

Some plant varieties have more resistance to specific diseases than others, and these are worth looking for if you have a particular problem in your garden. Disease resistance is increasingly a concern of modern plant breeders; for instance, many new roses have been bred to have some resistance to blackspot and mildew. It may also sometimes be worth growing different, but similar, species in order to avoid problems. For example, you could grow the aster *Aster* x *frikartii* instead of the traditional Michaelmas daisy, *Aster novae-angliae* and *Aster novi-belgii*: it flowers slightly later but is not troubled by mildew. For more detail on resistant varieties see page 92.

Food for wildlife

Many garden plants are a good source of food for wildlife: they can provide nectar and pollen for insects and seeds and berries for birds and animals (see pages 18–23). Try to include at least some of these plants with the aim of providing a "natural larder" over as long a period of the year as possible.

Nectar and pollen

Thymus vulgaris

Achillea millefolium

Nectar and pollen Open and small flowers where the pollen and nectar are easily available will attract the widest range of insects. Most of the old cottage-garden flowers come into this category, but many modern flowers have been bred for size and "frilliness" and are completely inaccessible to insects. Some are sterile so that no pollen, nectar or seeds are produced at all.

Plants in the Umbelliferae family, with their characteristic flat umbels of flowers, are particularly popular with hoverflies, parasitic wasps, and other beneficial insects that have short mouthparts and cannot reach into deep flowers. Many herbs such as fennel, angelica and dill are umbellifers, as are many vegetables – carrots and parsnips, for example. However, the latter are biennials – they only flower if you store the roots overwinter and replant them the following spring. Beneficial insects are also attracted to plants in the Compositae or daisy family that have flowerheads composed of many tiny flowers. Good examples of these are sunflowers, yarrow, and shasta daisies.

Although you will see bees on these plants, these insects have their own additional favourites. Their longer tongues enable them to feed from, for example, flowers in the Labiatae family, which includes other herbs such as marjoram, mint, lavender and thyme. These also attract butterflies, although the best butterfly plants tend to be those such as buddlejas, hebes and heliotropes which have tubular flowers and, often, a sweet scent.

FLOWERS PROVIDING NECTAR AND POLLEN FOR BENEFICIAL INSECTS
Achillea millefolium (yarrow) z 2
Anaphalis spp. (pearl everlasting) z 3–7
Anethum graveolens (dill) z 8
Angelica archangelica (angelica) z 4
Anthriscus cerefolium (chervil) z 7
Aster spp. (Michaelmas daisies and other asters) z 2–9
Calendula officinalis (pot marigold) z 6
Chrysanthemum maximum (shasta daisy) z 6
Convolvulus tricolor (annual convolvulus) z 8
Corylus avellana (hazel) z 4
Echium vulgare (viper's bugloss) z 3
Erigeron spp. (fleabane) z 2–9
Eschscholzia spp. (Californian poppy) z 7
Polygonum fagopyrum (buckwheat) z 3
Foeniculum vulgare (fennel) z 5
Fragaria vesca (alpine strawberry) z 5
Helianthus annuus (sunflower) z 4
Levisticum officinale (lovage) z 4
Limnanthes douglasii (poached egg plant) z 8
Myrrhis odorata (sweet cicely) z 5
Nemophila menziesii (baby blue eyes) z 8
Phacelia tanacetifolia (phacelia) z 6
Salix spp. (willow) z 1–8
Solidago spp. (golden rod) z 2–8
Thymus spp. (thyme) z 5–9

Choose your plants so that there are blooms throughout the season. Those that flower very early and very late are particularly important as they provide much-needed nourishment for insects that are emerging from or going into hibernation. Catkin-bearing willows, flowering currants, forget-me-nots, honesty and wallflowers are rich spring sources of nectar, and herbaceous plants like Michaelmas daisies and golden rod often last until mid-autumn.

Seeds Many of the same cottage-garden flowers that supply nectar and pollen also produce good seedheads. Do not be too eager to chop off all the dead flowerheads in the border as soon as the flowers have faded. Leave them until seed-eating birds such as goldfinches and greenfinches have had a chance to feed.

Anethum graveolens

25

Choosing plants 2

FLOWERS PROVIDING SEEDS FOR BIRDS

Achillea millefolium (yarrow) z 2
Antirrhinum spp. (snapdragon) z 7
Aster spp. (Michaelmas daisies and other asters) z 2–9
Centaurea cyanus (cornflower) z 4
Cosmos atrosanguineus (cosmos) z 8
Cynara cardunculus Scolymus group (globe artichoke) z 6
Dipsacus fullonum (teasel) z 3
Echinops ritro syn. *E. bannaticus* (globe thistle) z 3
Foeniculum vulgare (fennel) z 5
Geranium spp. (cranesbill) z 3–9
Helianthus annuus (sunflower) z 4
Lavandula spp. (lavender) z 5–9
Lunaria biennis (honesty) z 8
Lychnis coronaria (rose campion) z 4
Myosotis spp. (forget-me-not) z 4–9
Oenothera spp. (evening primrose) z 3–9
Scabiosa caucasia (scabious) z 3
Solidago spp. (golden rod) z 2–8

CHECKLIST

These are questions to ask yourself when deciding what plants to grow in your organic garden.

Conditions
What growing conditions do the plants grow best in?
    Sun/shade
    Moist soil/well-drained soil
    Light soil/heavy soil
    Acid soil/alkaline soil
    Open/sheltered site

Pests and diseases
What pests and diseases are the plants prone to?

Flowering period
When do they flower?

Beneficial qualities
Do the flowers attract insects?
Do the plants have seeds or berries for birds to feed on?

Fruits and berries

Berrying shrubs and trees in the garden supply food for birds and small mammals in autumn and winter.

Again, try to extend the harvest over as long a period as possible. Some berries are inevitably stripped early in the season – mountain ash and the hips of species roses, for example. However, most last long enough to brighten your garden for several months. Even the unpopular berries on skimmias and snowberries will be eaten by birds as a last resort during late winter. The fruits of the Japanese quince (*Chaenomeles*) are useful once they have fallen to the ground and begun to soften and ivy, of which the berries only ripen to black in spring, forms one of the most valuable food sources at a time when all other supplies are exhausted.

Native plants

Although pollen- and nectar-seeking insects are happy to feed from a selection of garden plants, the same is not true of many leaf-eaters; for them only the native plants on which they evolved will do.

You might not at first want to encourage this sort of insect. However, remember that they are the first step in the food chain which supplies creatures that are both beneficial and a source of pleasure in the garden. Hedges, ponds, wild-flower meadows and woodland-edge shrubberies (see pages 10–17) are an ideal way of introducing native plants.

Nursery plants

It is important to tolerate some pests in your garden, otherwise there will be no food for the beneficial creatures. A nursery plant is one that supports a significant population of pests without any ill effects and therefore acts as a food source to give predators a good start. These creatures can then move out into the garden to prevent damage to other plants.

The common nettle is a good example of a nursery plant. Nettle aphids are among the first aphids to appear in spring and provide food for ladybirds emerging from hibernation (see page 18). Nettle aphids do not attack other plants.

TREES AND SHRUBS FOR FRUIT AND BERRIES

Berberis (berberis, all berrying species) z 3–8
Chaenomeles spp. (Japanese quince) z 5
Cotoneaster spp. (cotoneaster) z 4–7
Crataegus monogyna (hawthorn) z 5
Ilex aquifolium (native species*, holly) z 6
Mahonia aquifolium (Oregon grape) z 5
Malus (crab apple varieties, M. 'John Downie'*) z 2–8
Pyracantha spp.* (firethorn) z 6–8
Rosa rugosa (species rose) z 2
Sambucus nigra (elder) z 5
Skimmia japonica (skimmia) z 7
Sorbus spp. (sorbus; *S. aucuparia**, mountain ash) z 2–9
Symphoricarpos spp. (snowberry) z 2–9
Viburnum davidii (viburnum) z 7
*Viburnum opulus** (guelder rose) z 3

* Shrubs that are usually most liked by birds, although this does depend on what birds you have in your area and what other food supplies are available to them.

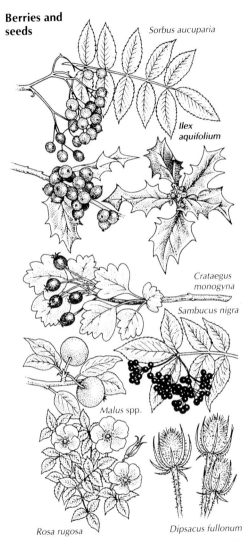

Berries and seeds

Sorbus aucuparia

Ilex aquifolium

Crataegus monogyna

Sambucus nigra

Malus spp.

Rosa rugosa

Dipsacus fullonum

Many other aphids are specific to their own group of plants, so you can often tolerate them on vigorous ornamentals without fear that they will spread to your crops.

Companion planting

Some ornamental plants are said to make "good companions" to particular fruit and vegetable crops because they enhance plant growth or help combat pests and diseases. Similarly, bad companions have a deleterious effect on each other.

While plants can have various effects on one another – thriving tomatoes cannot be grown near a walnut tree, for example – there are few cases of companion planting that have been researched well enough to give thorough, consistent and practical results (see page 95). The practice of companion planting is also difficult to fit in with a crop rotation and all the benefits this brings (see pages 46–9).

However, any mixed planting, such as those that include annual flowers or herbs in the vegetable plot, is likely to be beneficial in some way simply because it adds further diversity to the garden and may attract beneficial insects. The main problem is judging sowing times and spacing so that the yields of crops and the appearance of ornamentals are not adversely affected.

Garden plans 1

SMALL GARDEN 2cm = 1m (¾in = 3¼ft)

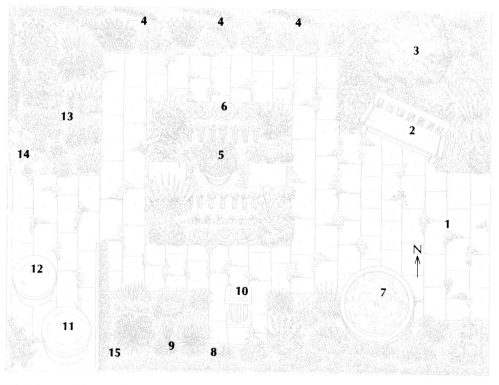

This is a small, semi-formal organic town garden approximately 7 x 5m (23 x 16½ft). Despite its size, it is possible to grow salads, herbs and fruit as well as ornamentals in the space available. It is also a place to relax in and enjoy gardening, as well as being a wildlife refuge.

The central bed is given to fresh salads and culinary herbs (see pages 172–3), and other plants in the border are chosen to attract bees and other beneficial insects (see page 25).

Paving with creeping herbs in the crevices takes the place of a lawn. A low fountain bubbles over stones; as well as being a pleasant garden feature it attracts birds and insects to drink (see pages 20–3). The damp vegetation around the water will also harbour frogs and the fences are covered with climbing plants, thereby giving leafy height and nesting sites for birds (see pages 14–15).

Although space is at a premium, there is a worm bin for recycling kitchen waste and a small compost bin. These are screened off at the wider end of the garden. The compost bin takes the garden debris and any bags of brought-in manure (see pages 50–79).

KEY
1 Patio with creeping herbs
2 Garden seat
3 Small tree/large shrub and ground cover
4 Cordon fruit trees, perennial herbs/attractant plants
5 Tub of frost-tender herbs
6 Annual herbs/salad bed
7 Bubbler fountain over stones
8 Climbing plants/nesting hedges
9 Ornamental/attractant plants
10 Bird table
11 Compost bin
12 Worm bin
13 Wild area: small shrubs and wild flowers
14 Stone pile
15 Trellis with climber

LARGE GARDEN 1cm = 5m (½in=16½ft)

This garden is large enough to grow a wide selection of fruit, vegetables and ornamentals. There is also a terrace, lawn (see pages 182–3) and herb garden (see pages 172–3) near the house and a large pond (see pages 8–10) borders the lawn. For wildlife, there is a dry stone wall (see page 11), as well as a marshy area, semi-natural woodland (see page 14) and a pile of woody material which has been left to rot (see page 15). The wild-flower meadow (see page 16) is a reservoir of beneficial insects for the mini-orchard of apples, pears and plums on semi-dwarfing rootstocks (see page 174).

The vegetable garden has a four-year rotation for annual crops and flowers (see pages 46–9), and separate beds for permanent plants. The greenhouse (see pages 184–5) is used for raising plants and growing tender crops, and soft fruit (see pages 176–7) is grown in a cage. Nearby, compost and leafmould are made and organic matter stored (see pages 50–79).

The garden is bounded by hedges (see pages 12–13) and there is also a wall to provide warmth and shelter for trained fruit trees.

KEY
1 Herb bed
2 Lawn
3 Garden seat
4 Pond
5 Dry-stone wall
6 Marshy area
7 Semi-natural woodland
8 Log pile
9 Long-term compost heap
10 Wild-flower meadow
11 Fruit trees
12 Wall-trained fruit
13 Perennial vegetables
14 Greenhouse
15 Vegetables
16 Soft fruit
17 Ornamental border
18 Composting area
19 Comfrey bed

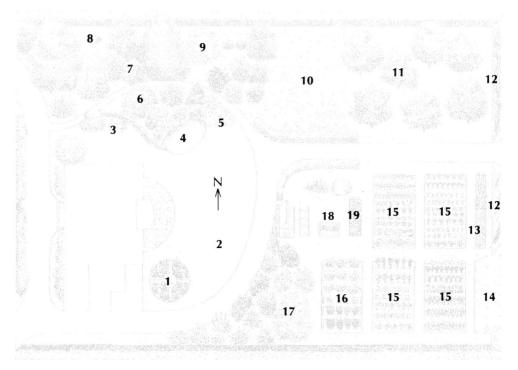

Garden plans 2

AVERAGE GARDEN 1cm = 2m (½in = 6½ft)

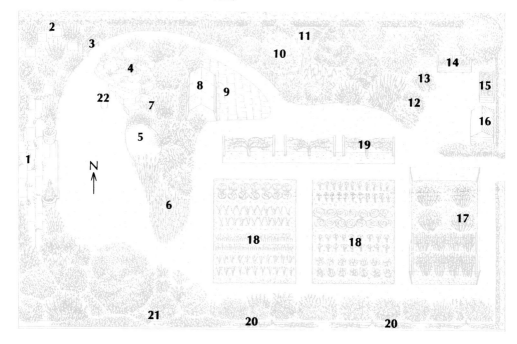

This is a medium-sized garden about 30 x 17m (100 x 56ft). It is an attractive garden with space for relaxation but at the same time is as productive as possible, given the space.

A lawn (see pages 182–3), tree and herb bed (see pages172–3) are near to the house. The small pond (see pages 8–10) and wild-flower meadow (see pages 16–17) on the edge of the lawn give extra interest and are good habitats for wildlife. They are flanked by a bed of shrubs and ornamentals (see pages 178–9), and a hedge (see page 12–13) joins them to the wild area at the end of the garden.

The vegetables are intensively grown on a bed system (see pages 42–3) and there is a small greenhouse in which to raise plants (see pages 184–5). Some soft fruit is grown in a fruit cage (see pages 176–7). Espalier fruit trees border the vegetable beds and there is space beneath them for low-growing attractant plants (see pages 24–7). There is room for more to be trained on the west-facing fence. Althrough space is limited, there is an area for composting, leafmould, shredding and storing organic materials (see pages 50–79).

KEY
1 Patio with planted tubs
2 Herbs with stepping stones
3 Garden seat
4 Rock garden
5 Pond and marsh
6 Wild-flower meadow
7 Shrubs/herbaceous plants
8 Greenhouse
9 Water butt
10 Shrubs/groundcover – wilder area
11 Log pile
12 Manure heap
13 Material for shredding
14 Compost bins
15 Leafmould bins
16 Shed
17 Soft-fruit cage
18 Bed system for vegetables
19 Espalier fruit trees
20 Wall-trained fruit/low-growing plants
21 Ornamental border
22 Bird table

ALLOTMENT 1cm = 5m (½in = 16½ft)

This allotment is a typical size of 30 x 11m (100 x 36ft). An organic allotment must have diversity of planting, and there must also be shelter for wildlife as well as space for composting and storing organic matter.

The vegetables have a four-year rotation (see pages 46–9). There are annual flowers for cutting on each plot according to crop families. Many of these annual flowers are good attractant plants for bees and other beneficial insects (see page 25). A separate seedbed provides the opportunity for raising bare-rooted plants for transplanting.

Some sites do not allow fruit trees or bushes. However, there are beds for long-term vegetables which also contain perennial attractant plants. The screen at the end of the plot could be formed from sunflowers or Jerusalem artichokes, for example, if hedges or trellis are not allowed.

The composting area has large compost bins to recycle vegetable waste, a space for storing manure and leaf bins for leaves collected off site (see pages 50–79). Leafmould is used for the seedbed and root crops. There is a patch of nettles and rough long grass for wildlife (see pages 16–17). A comfrey bed provides material for mulching the crops or making liquid feed (see pages 88–9).

KEY

 1 Screen
 2 Comfrey bed
 3 Manure heap – covered
 4 Nettle patch
 5 Compost bins
 6 Leafmould bins
 7 Perennial vegetables/attractant plants
 8 Seedbed
 9 Brassicas
10 Roots
11 Onions and related crops
12 Annual flowers for cutting
13 Cut flowers
14 Flowers for cutting and drying
15 Legumes
16 Potatoes and related crops

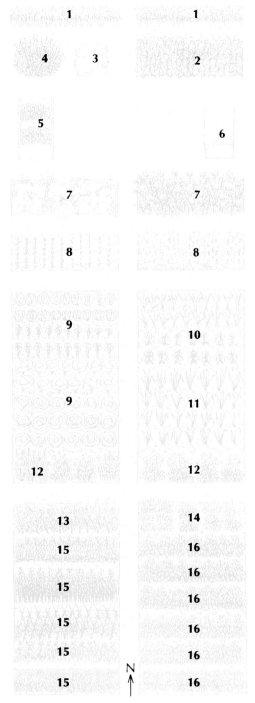

Know your soil 1

Below the surface of the garden there is as complex a living world as there is above it. The soil has been formed over thousands of years from the breakdown of rocks into mineral particles of sand, silt and clay. However, this is only its "skeleton", usually making up about half the volume of a soil. The rest is made up of air, water, organic matter, plant roots and the all-important creatures that live in the soil.

The soil skeleton
A soil is determined by the different amounts of sand, silt and clay particles it contains. Those with a fairly equal mixture of particles are called loams; a clay loam contains a higher percentage of clay, a sandy loam more sand.

You can easily work out what type of soil you have in your garden by picking up half a handful of moist topsoil and feeling it. Knead the soil with your fingers – a sandy soil feels gritty, clay feels sticky and silt feels smooth and silky. Now roll the soil between your hands. Very sandy soils will not form a ball without crumbling. If the soil forms a cohesive ball, rub your finger over the surface: a clay-rich soil will take a shine.

Air and water
The mineral particles in the soil are held together in aggregates, or "crumbs", with spaces, or "pores", between them. This is the soil structure. The pores are very important: large pores allow drainage so that air can get into the soil and small pores hold water. The pores also form the living spaces for all the soil-dwelling creatures and a passage for plant roots. In a well-structured soil, plant roots can spread easily and exploit a large volume of soil for nutrients and water.

To assess the structure of your soil, crush a clod in your hand. A well-structured soil is friable whether it is wet or dry; it is not sticky or dusty. Take a look at the soil profile as well (see page 34).

The structure can be destroyed when the soil is compacted by walking on it or using machinery, by heavy rain or irrigation and by cultivating in the wrong conditions, such as when the soil is very wet or frozen.

Organic matter (see pages 50–7)
Organic matter is material of living origin. In the garden this is usually plant debris, animal manures and the remains of its living inhabitants, including microscopic organisms as well as insects and small mammals. Organic matter therefore contains a complex range of ingredients: proteins, sugars, carbohydrates and all the other materials that make up plants and animals. It is continually decaying as it is worked on by micro-organisms and various small creatures, and simpler substances such as minerals and salts that plants can use as food are released into the soil.

Organic matter has many benefits, including helping soil particles adhere together into crumbs, thus improving the soil structure. This

TYPES	ADVANTAGES	DISADVANTAGES
Clay	Usually contains a rich supply of plant foods because clay particles have the ability to retain nutrient elements until they are released to plant roots.	Sticky when wet and hard when dry, so difficult and heavy to cultivate. Slow to drain, so prone to waterlogging and slow to warm up in spring.
Silt	Typically alluvial in origin, deep, fertile and with good water-holding capacity	Silt soil packs down easily, so becomes airless. Sticky and cold when wet and dusty when dry.
Sand	Easy to work. Free draining, so quick to warm up in spring.	Does not retain moisture. Can be naturally deficient in nutrients as many are easily washed out.

helps drainage on heavy soils, making them more workable and easily penetrated by plant roots. Because it holds water, organic matter makes light soils more moisture-retentive. In addition to this, it provides a food supply for soil inhabitants, helping them to thrive and multiply and, in turn, release plant nutrients. Organic matter also holds onto nutrient elements in the same way as do clay particles, preventing them from being washed out.

MANAGING YOUR SOIL

Knowing all about your soil enables you to manage it properly, to provide ideal conditions for soil life and plant roots. This may mean improving drainage or adjusting the acidity of the soil. You will also need to add organic matter, but what type and how? When do you cultivate and how much? Techniques like mulching and crop rotation are also part of good soil management.

Clay soil

pH Check; add lime if necessary. The calcium in limestone can also help aggregate clay particles, hence improving the soil structure. (On alkaline soils, it is possible to add gypsum for the same effect.)

Drainage The drainage of the topsoil is likely to be poor: improve soil structure by adding organic matter. Avoid walking on the soil, particularly when it is wet. Use a bed system. If the subsoil is clay, you may need a drainage system.

Watering Clay soil retains moisture well; mulch to help prevent drying and cracking in summer.

Cultivation It is particularly important only to cultivate when the soil is just moist, not too wet or too dry. Fork seedbeds in autumn and leave the frost to break up the clods until the structure improves.

Organic matter This is needed to make the soil more workable and improve drainage. Use as a mulch or fork into the top 15cm (6in) of soil. You do not need nutrient-rich organic matter: leafmould is valuable. Do not bury organic matter unless it is very well rotted as there is little air to help decomposition.

Green manures These are useful to break up the soil.

Nutrients Clay soils are usually rich in nutrients, but a good structure is necessary to allow roots to exploit them.

Silty soils

pH Check; add lime if needed.

Drainage As for clay.

Watering As for clay.

Cultivation This is necessary to remove initial compaction, but avoid over-cultivating as it will destroy the weak structure. Use mulches to protect the surface and to prevent a hard "cap" from forming.

Organic matter This is needed to build up structure and help drainage as for clays, as well as to provide nutrients.

Green manures Use to protect the surface of the soil and build up structure.

Nutrients Silty soils are not as fertile as clays. Check for deficiencies and correct if necessary.

Sandy soils

pH Check every year as lime is easily washed out of a sandy soil. Correct if necessary.

Drainage Sandy soils are free-draining and the presence of water may mean that a hard pan needs breaking or a drainage system is necessary.

Watering Add plenty of organic matter to retain moisture and apply a mulch.

Cultivation Avoid turning over the soil if possible as this speeds up the loss of water and organic matter. Mulch the soil to prevent the surface from drying out because it will not rewet easily.

Organic matter This is needed to hold water and provide plant foods and prevent them being washed out. Use some nutrient-rich manures and compost.

Green manures Use bulky green manures to add organic matter, stop nutrients washing out and prevent erosion.

Nutrients Sandy soils may lack nutrients, which are easily washed out. Check new soils and add fertilizers if necessary.

Know your soil 2

Finally, the addition of organic matter helps to prevent soil erosion and strengthens the soil against the effects of heavy rain and cultivation. The organic matter also makes the soil darker and therefore warmer.

The organic matter in the soil needs replenishing regularly, particularly when the soil is disturbed. This introduces more air and speeds up the decaying process.

Soil life
Even just a spadeful of garden soil contains thousands of living creatures. Although a few are pests or disease organisms, the vast majority are harmless, while some of them are positively beneficial.

One of the most useful is the familiar earthworm. These tunnel through the soil, partly by pushing between the soil particles and partly by eating through the soil and organic matter.

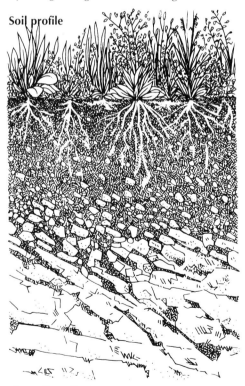

Soil profile

The **soil profile** shows the different layers in the soil: the dark topsoil, the lighter subsoil, and the bedrock beneath.

They leave channels, which help drainage and aeration, and make it easier for plant roots to penetrate. They also produce casts which contain more nutrients than the surrounding soil and are cemented together with gums, making them more stable.

Other soil inhabitants are much less noticeable and microscopic organisms are not visible to the naked eye. Many play an invaluable role in breaking down organic matter, controlling diseases and making the minerals in the soil more available to plants. One group of fungi, the mycorrhizas, form a close relationship with plant roots, helping them to absorb nutrients – particularly phosphorus – and protecting them from disease organisms.

You can see the extent of soil life in the top layer of the soil profile and encourage a healthy population by making sure that the soil is not too acid and by adding organic matter. Disturb the soil as little as possible and always make sure that the surface is covered, either by plants or a mulch.

Soil profile
For a cross-section or "profile" of the soil in your garden, dig a hole with vertical sides. It must be at least 1m (3¼ft) deep.

The dark topsoil is where plant roots feed and most of the soil life is found. Ideally, this should be approximately 60cm (2ft) deep, but it is often much shallower, which has a bearing on the range of plants that will grow well. The lighter subsoil contains few plant roots and less soil life, and its nature, along with the bedrock beneath, affects the drainage of the topsoil.

Soil pH
The pH of the soil is a measure of its acidity or alkalinity, both of which affect the soil life, the availability of nutrients to plants and the range of plants that flourish. Either buy a soil pH testing kit or get a professional soil analysis.

Depending on the garden's history, the pH of the soil may differ from area to area and you may need to test several samples. Even if the pH is at a satisfactory level, recheck it at least every two or three years (more often on sandy soils). Vegetables, fruit and most other plants will grow within a pH range of 5.5 to 7.5, although fruit tends to do better in acid soils around pH 6.0. Above and below this range nutrients become less available and more plants will begin to struggle. However, there are specific plants which need very acid soil in which to grow, and some which tolerate very alkaline soils.

If your soil is too acid for the use intended, you can raise the pH by adding ground limestone or dolomite limestone. Follow the instructions in the pH kit, or add approximately 200g/sq m (7oz/sq yd) annually until the soil reaches the required pH. Calcified seaweed (see page 55) will also raise the pH – add approximately 40g/sq m (1⅖oz/sq yd) annually. Slaked lime, hydrated lime and caustic lime are very soluble and quick-acting and therefore should not be used in the organic garden.

If your soil is pH 6.5 or above, you should not add any of these materials. Some vegetable plots that have been limed every year as part of the rotation (see pages 46–9) end up being far too alkaline. Be wary of using comfrey (see pages 88–9) or mushroom compost (see page 53), as these materials raise the pH of the soil.

Do not add any type of lime to the soil together with manure as the two can react and release ammonia gas, wasting valuable nitrogen. Apply lime in the autumn and manure in the spring, or dig in the manure and apply lime to the surface.

If your soil is too alkaline, add compost and manure every year and eventually the pH should become lower. Creating raised beds can help as these are not affected by seepage of lime-rich water from the surrounding land.

Nutrient analysis

A chemical analysis will indicate the amounts of important plant nutrients that are present in the soil. It will give the phosphorus and potassium levels and usually those of magnesium and calcium. Other minor or trace elements may sometimes be analysed. If all your plants are growing well a soil analysis is not essential. However, it is advisable if you are starting a new garden, particularly if you are growing fruit or other long-term plants. An analysis is also advisable if you have soil problems that do not appear to be caused by poor drainage, poor structure or the wrong pH.

Advertisements for soil analysis services often appear in gardening magazines. Most of these do not take into account the contribution made by the organic matter in the soil and the reserves of nutrients that can be released by the action of micro-organisms. If possible, get an analysis that is intended specifically for organic growers. This will measure the organic matter and activity of soil organisms, so giving a better indication of the true potential of the soil in your garden. It will also make recommendations for correcting any deficiencies with organic fertilizers.

SOIL pH						
	acid		**neutral**		**alkaline**	
pH 3	**4**	**5**	**6**	**7**	**8**	**9**
Most plants fail	Acid-loving plants such as camellias and rhododendrons thrive	Most fruit thrives	Most plants thrive	Tolerable to most plants	Some plants thrive such as spinach and clematis	Most plants fail
Substances toxic to plants released into the soil	Some plant nutrients washed out of the soil	Phosphorus becomes less available to plants	Iron and manganese become less available to plants	Phosphorus becomes less available to plants		
Earthworms generally absent	Potato scab disease cannot survive	Most soil life thrives	Clubroot disease less rampant			

Mulching

Mulching means covering the ground with a layer of material. Mulches can either be biodegradable (generally loose organic materials such as compost, manure, leafmould and bark, which will eventually rot down) or nondegradable (sheet materials such as plastic, which do not add organic matter to the soil). Both types of mulch help to control weeds, and this is the most important use of nondegradable mulches and other sheet mulches such as newspaper (see pages 146–9).

Mulches help retain moisture in the soil, in particular the top several centimetres, which is beneficial to shallow-rooted plants. They also protect the soil surface from pounding rain and can keep crops clean and free from disease. They can also alter the temperature of the soil and the air just above them. Dark mulches absorb heat in the day and radiate it at night, while light-coloured mulches reflect heat rather than store it. The temperature above light mulches can thus be significantly lower at night.

Biodegradable mulches

It is biodegradable mulches that play the most important part in soil management. Organic matter is added to the soil as the mulch is taken under by worms and other soil-living creatures and gradually broken down. This improves the soil structure and supplies plant nutrients. The quantity and rate at which the nutrients become available depends on the particular mulch. Even stemmy materials such as straw, which would normally induce nitrogen robbery (see page 55),

SLUGS AND MULCHES

Rapidly decaying mulches, such as compost, grass mowings and hay, provide the moist, nutrient-rich environment that slugs love. However, some argue that the mulch provides an alternative food source for slugs and encourages slug predators such as ground beetles, so less damage is done to plants. A dry mulch such as bark or shredded prunings is less likely to encourage slugs, and cocoa shell is said to deter them.

can be used as a mulch if dug into the soil; the small amounts taken under gradually by soil organisms do not usually cause problems. However, only use such mulches around permanent plantings or where they can be removed easily at the end of the season so you do not accidentally incorporate them into the soil.

Applying a loose mulch

It is essential that the soil is wet before you apply a mulch, since rainwater will only percolate slowly through the mulching material and some will be absorbed before it reaches the soil. It is also vital that the soil is warm, since the mulch can act as an insulating barrier and prevent the soil from warming up quickly. This is particularly the case with light-coloured mulches. Never apply such a mulch in winter or early spring.

Applying a loose mulch

1 If the soil is dry, water it well before mulching.

2 Spread the mulch out by hand around small plants.

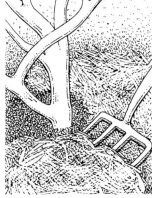

3 Keep the mulch clear of plant stems and tree trunks.

USE OF LOOSE MULCHES
(For more details of the properties and source of these materials see pages 52–5)

Mulch	Example of use	When	Main reason for use
Leafmould	On seedbeds	In autumn before sowing	To improve soil structure
	Around bedding plants, herbs, herbaceous plants	Any time when soil conditions are suitable	To improve soil structure and moisture and look attractive
Compost	On vegetable crops with a long growing period	When well-established and still actively growing	To provide nutrients and keep in moisture
	Around herbaceous plants	In spring	To provide nutrients, keep in moisture and improve soil structure
Worm compost	On plants in pots or individual garden plants that need feeding	Any time when growing strongly	To provide nutrients
Well-rotted manure	Around plants that need a lot of feeding	When making quick growth, usually in spring	To provide nutrients, particularly nitrogen
Lawn mowings	Around widely spaced vegetable crops	Any time when soil conditions are suitable	To control weeds and keep in moisture
Shredded prunings	Around trees and shrubs	Any time when soil conditions are suitable	To protect soil surface and control weeds
	On paths	Any time	To keep the surface clean
Bark/woodchips	Around trees and shrubs	Any time when soil conditions are suitable	To protect soil surface, look nice and control weeds
Straw	Around fruit on the ground	Before fruit forms	To keep fruit clean and keep in moisture
	Between widely spaced shrubs, fruit trees and bushes	Any time when soil conditions are suitable	To control weeds and keep in moisture
	On paths	Any time	To keep surface clean
Hay	Around fruit trees, canes and bushes	In late spring	To control weeds, provide nutrients and keep in moisture
Cocoa shell	Around bedding and herbaceous plants	When in active growth	To control weeds, look attractive and provide nutrients
Sawdust/ woodshavings	On paths	Any time	To keep surface clean

However, once in place on a warm moist soil, the mulch helps to keep it warm and moist but prevents it getting too hot or wet. This moderating effect is very beneficial to soil life and plant roots.

Spread the mulch evenly over the soil surface. How thick you apply it will depend on the size of the plants and how much material you have available. Even a 1cm (⅜in) layer will help to improve the soil structure, but it takes 7.5–10cm (3–4in) of a loose mulch to control weeds effectively.

In most cases you should keep the mulch a few centimetres away from the plant stems as it can encourage rotting and cause a grafted tree or shrub to shoot from the rootstock. However, occasionally mulching right round the stem can be beneficial. Tomatoes and brassicas, for example, will make new roots into a mulch and this helps them to grow.

No-dig gardening 1

In no-dig gardening, the soil is never turned over; all manure, compost and other organic materials are applied to the surface.

Digging is such a common practice that it is rarely questioned, despite the fact that it is such hard work. In fact, it is possible to grow a full range of vegetables without even lifting a spade, and you certainly do not need to dig the ground between fruit and ornamental plants.

For information on mulching see pages 36–7 and 146–9.

When to dig

Traditional reasons for digging include improving the aeration and drainage of the soil, and burying weeds and organic matter.

However, most soils do not become airless and waterlogged if they are not dug, provided they are mulched with organic matter. The material spread on the surface will gradually be taken into the soil by worms and other creatures, creating drainage channels and a good soil structure in which there is plenty of air.

Digging can in fact have a detrimental effect on the soil structure by disrupting the aggregates of soil particles and disturbing the soil life. It can also lead to the loss of organic matter from the soil by continually exposing it to the atmosphere where it breaks down more quickly. Loss of moisture from the soil is another disadvantage.

Digging is certainly a quick way of clearing ground that is covered in annual weeds. The benefit is short-lived, however, since below the surface of the ground there are hundreds of dormant weed seeds, all just waiting for the right conditions in which to germinate. When you bring them to the soil surface by digging over the ground, they will do just that. Instead, it is far more efficient to get rid of troublesome surface weeds by shallow hoeing or mulching with a non-degradable or biodegradable mulch. You do not even have to dig a new patch of ground – you can clear weeds or grass using a long-term mulch.

However, there are times when digging is beneficial. Soils that have been compacted or have a hard pan benefit from an initial digging to break up the solid layer. Digging can also expose pests to predators and cold weather, so dig over any ground that you know is infested (for example, an old strawberry bed where vine weevil has been a problem) before you grow another crop.

Obviously, you need to dig holes in order to plant trees and shrubs, and you may want to grow some crops such as potatoes in the conventional way, or to dig in a bulky green manure such as grazing rye. There is no need to be fanatical about not digging, but be aware that over-cultivating the soil is not necessary and can be harmful.

Sowing on a no-dig plot

1 Before sowing, hoe to remove any weeds and rake aside any coarse remains of the mulch from the previous crop.

2 Use a hoe to draw a drill: the mulch should have left the surface of the soil fine and crumbly in texture.

TO DIG OR NOT TO DIG?

No dig	Digging
Encourages the activities of soil-living creatures which do the digging for you	Hard work is required
Protects soil structure and produces friable soil surface	Can destroy soil structure
Reduces loss of moisture and organic matter from soil	Increases loss of moisture and organic matter from soil
Does not bring weed seeds to the surface	Kills annual weeds and surface-rooting perennials, but turns up weed seeds
Does not expose soil pests to predators and cold	Exposes soil pests to predators and cold
Can take longer to improve poor soils	Breaks up compaction and hard pans

Growing on a no-dig vegetable plot

If starting a new plot from pasture or weedy ground, clear it by putting down a light-excluding mulch for at least a growing season. This does not necessarily mean you cannot grow crops during this time: vigorous, widely spaced plants such as Brussels sprouts, broccoli and squashes can be planted through some mulches.

Once the ground is thoroughly cleared, growing on a no-dig system is easy. You will need the same amounts of compost, manure or fertilizers for individual crops as you would on a conventional plot, but instead of digging them into the soil, simply put them directly on the surface.

Remember to make sure that the soil is moist before you apply any mulch.

3 Water along the drill if the soil is dry, then sow the seeds, taking care to space them out thinly in the row.

4 Cover the seeds with soil, or if this is cloddy, use leafmould or old potting compost; firm the surface lightly.

No-dig gardening 2

Transplanting on a no-dig bed

1 Part the mulch and make a small hole with a trowel, keeping the soil removed separate from the mulch.

2 Put in the plant, and firm it in with the spare soil and water it; then even out the surrounding mulch.

Sowing seeds on a no-dig bed

Crops such as carrots, beetroot, peas and parsnips can be sown directly in a seedbed on a no-dig bed, in the same way as on a conventional plot. If any compost or other nutrient-rich organic matter is required, it is usually easiest to apply it once the plants have become established and start to grow.

Before sowing, remove any weeds by hoeing the soil and rake aside any coarse remains of the mulch from the previous crop. Draw a shallow drill in the soil using a hoe. Water along the drill if the soil is dry and sow the seeds thinly.

On an established no-dig bed, the surface soil will be fine and crumbly and can be raked back over the drill. If the soil is cloddy, however, use leafmould or old potting compost for covering the drill. Firm the surface lightly with a rake.

Growing transplanted crops

Before planting out vegetable crops such as courgettes and brassicas, hoe the ground to remove weeds and spread compost, manure or other organic matter required by the crop on the surface.

Part the mulch where you want to plant and make a small hole with a trowel. Keep the soil removed separate from the mulch. Put in the plant and firm it in with the spare soil. Even out the mulch, but in general keep it 5–10cm (2–4in) away from the stem of the plant to prevent rotting.

Growing potatoes

This is the only crop that needs more mulching if grown on a no-dig system. The tubers are placed on the soil surface at the same spacing as on a conventional plot: typically 30–38cm (12–15in) apart in rows 38–50cm (15–20in) apart for early potatoes, and 38cm (15in) apart in rows 76cm (2½ft) apart for maincrop. Layers of organic matter are used to exclude light: initially, cover the tubers with 7.5–10cm (3–4in) of moist hay or straw. When the plants are 20–30cm (8–12in) tall, add another layer of hay or straw the same depth as the first and top with grass mowings. Add grass clippings every so often throughout the season.

Planting potatoes

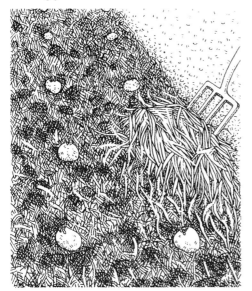

1 Place the seed tubers on a thin layer of manure on the soil surface and cover them with 7.5–10cm (3–4in) of hay.

2 When the plants are 20–30cm (8–12in) high, add another layer of hay and top with grass mowings to help exclude light.

The main advantage of growing potatoes in this way is that they are so easy to harvest – you simply pull back the mulch and pick up the tubers from the soil surface without having to loosen and lift the soil around the roots of the plants. With new potatoes you can harvest the biggest without disturbing the plant and then replace the mulch to allow the rest to grow on. There is also some evidence to show that the mulch can help reduce tuber damage from potato blight (see page 127).

However, in practice there are problems with this method and results can be poor. In cold areas, a light-coloured mulch can prevent the ground from warming up and may make the air above it even colder, so that frost is more likely to damage the foliage of the potatoes. Furthermore, because rain cannot easily get through the mulch extra watering may be necessary, and penetration of light through the mulch can give a high proportion of green tubers at harvest.

You can avoid some of these problems by planting the potatoes in holes. Use a trowel or dibber and dig individual holes approximately

15cm (6in) deep. You can either mulch the plants as before once they have come up, or make the planting holes through a black plastic mulch. If you use a type of good-quality, thick plastic, it should be reusable for several years afterwards.

Growing green manures (see pages 80–5)
On an established no-dig bed the surface of the soil will be friable enough for you to be able to broadcast fine green manure seeds as normal. Larger green manure seeds should be sown in drills.

As an alternative to digging in, annual green manures can instead be hoed off or chopped down to ground level and left on the soil surface in the form of a mulch. One treatment will be sufficient to stop most of these regrowing, although grazing rye is likely to be a little bit more persistent. If this is indeed the case, an easy way of clearing the crop is to chop it down and cover it with a light-excluding mulch for a couple of weeks. This treatment is also necessary in order to incorporate long-term green manures.

41

The bed system 1

In a bed system, the ground is divided up into a number of permanent beds by paths. The beds are narrow enough for all work to be done from the paths, so that there is no need to tread on the soil. While beds like this can be used for fruit, flowers and herbs, they are usually set up to grow vegetables. They look noticeably different to a conventional plot.

Since there is no need to have space to walk between them, crops can be planted more closely and be distributed evenly over the bed in blocks rather than rows. This gives a higher yield, which should more than compensate for the space lost to the paths.

The bed system has a number of advantages: it helps improve the soil structure because compaction caused by walking on the soil is avoided; you can plant, weed and harvest beds during rainy weather, when a conventional plot would be too wet to walk on; and valuable supplies of compost and other organic materials are concentrated on a smaller growing area and are not wasted on ground that will become path.

Close spacing of crops means that weeds are quickly smothered and less weeding is necessary, especially for leafy crops such as carrots and beetroot. Furthermore, because the plants are spaced evenly over the bed you have more control over their size at harvest: closely spaced onions, for example, give smaller bulbs which are a more convenient size for many people.

Shape and size of beds

The beds do not have to be rectangular – they can be parts of a square, segments of a circle or any other shape, provided you can reach to the centre from the paths. Most people find that a comfortable width is about 1.2m (4ft). Paths can be as narrow as 30cm (12in), although you should make them at least 60cm (2ft) where you want to take a wheelbarrow.

A bed can be any length, although it is sensible to set a limit or it can be a long walk to the other side: 2.5–4m (8½–13ft) is a good length for vegetable beds. If possible, orientate rectangular vegetable beds so that their length runs approximately north–south, as this will minimize the shading effect of tall plants.

Raised beds

Where drainage is poor or the topsoil thin, beds can be raised above the level of the paths. They must have a high edging to retain the extra topsoil, compost and other organic materials that are added.

However, even beds that are not deliberately built up tend to become slightly raised: as they are cultivated, organic materials and air are mixed into the soil, increasing its volume, whereas the paths are compacted by feet and wheelbarrows.

Edging

Unless they are artificially raised, beds do not have to be edged. However, a permanent

Creating the beds

1 Mark out the beds and paths with pegs and string.

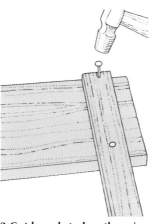

2 Cut boards to length and nail on wooden pegs.

3 Use a lump hammer to knock the boards into place.

Typical bed system for vegetable crops

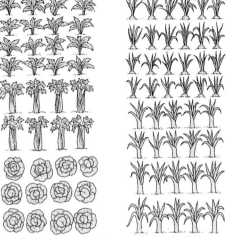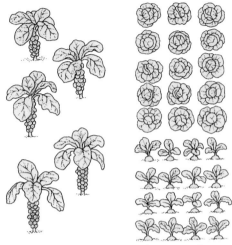

A convenient width for vegetable beds is about 1.2m (4ft), with paths 30–40cm (1–1⅓ft) wide. To minimize shading from tall plants, orientate them so their length runs north to south. Plant the crops in blocks rather than rows to give a higher yield.

edging can help keep them defined, preventing soil getting onto the paths and loose path material from getting onto the soil. It will also protect newly sown or planted crops on the bed edges.

For most beds an edging 10–15cm (4–6in) high should be sufficient. Raised beds need a higher edging – about 30cm (12in) is usually the maximum practical height. There is a wide choice of materials to use: new wooden planks, scrap wood, bricks, tiles, slates and kerbstones. The choice depends on what is available locally, the size, shape and function of the beds, and how much you want to pay.

Wooden edging is convenient for rectangular vegetable beds. Mark out beds and paths with pegs and strings and cut wooden boards to fit their length and width. Wood 10–15cm (4–6in) high and 1.8–2.5cm (¾–1in) thick is ideal. Cut pegs 23–37cm (9–15in) long from wood approximately 2.5 x 3.6cm (1 x 1⅖in) in cross-section to hold the boards in place. Cut one end of each peg to a point. Nail a peg to each end of all the boards and, for a long board, at intervals along its length – approximately every 1.5m (5ft) is about right for 2.5cm (1in) thick board. Thinner wood will need more pegs. Use a lump hammer to knock the boards into place.

For beds which are curved or irregular in shape, wooden boards are not so suitable. Here, you could use shaped concrete kerbstones, frost-resistant bricks, tiles or half logs set into the ground.

Paths

The paths between the beds can be left as bare earth and hoed or they can be covered with a light-excluding mulch, which will not only keep weeds down but keep your feet clean. Suitable mulches include newspaper under straw in an informal situation and polypropylene sheet under woodchips for a more ornamental finish. Sawdust is another simple and cheap alternative suitable for paths between vegetable beds. Top up the mulch regularly.

In a formal garden you could have brick, paving or gravel paths. These are more expensive and more difficult to lay, but they are easy to maintain and have a long lifespan.

Spacing of vegetable crops

Spreading plants out over an area rather than growing them in rows reduces competition between them for nutrients, light and water and is a more productive use of space. There are several ways of getting an roughly even distribution across a 1.2m (4ft) bed.

43

The bed system 2

Equidistant spacing

In this system of spacing, the plants are grown in staggered rows, with each plant an equal distance from all the others. This is the best layout for closely spaced crops. To get the spacing correct, check the distance of each plant from its neighbours by using a stick cut to the required length.

Square spacing

This involves the plants being grown in rows with the in-row spacing the same as the between-row spacing. Use this layout if the distance between plants is such that you can only get two or three across the bed – it allows more plants to be accommodated.

Staggered rows

This is the best way to lay out very widely spaced crops where there is only room for one in the width of the bed.

Planting

Simply plant out transplanted crops in the required pattern. For direct-sown crops there are two options: you can "station sow" them in the same pattern (that is, sow two or three fine seeds or one or two large seeds in every place where an individual plant is required) then thin them later to one seedling at each station; or you can sow in accurately spaced rows and thin the seedlings in the row to produce the final layout.

What spacing?

The spacing of plants on a bed system will be somewhere between the in-row spacing and the between-row spacing of the crop on a conventional plot. For example, Chinese cabbage normally spaced 30cm (12in) apart in rows 45cm (18in) apart on a conventional plot would be grown at an equidistant spacing of approximately 37cm (15in) on the bed system. The exact distance will depend on your soil and situation.

On poor, dry soils some crops may require a wider spacing in order to obtain sufficient water and plant foods. In a damp climate a wider spacing for some plants may help to prevent fungal disease.

With vegetables such as onions and cabbages, the spacing will affect their final size. Within limits, the more space you give them the larger they will grow. Reducing the spacing can produce vegetables of a more convenient size for many families and also increase the overall yield. For example, if you plant summer cabbages at an equidistant spacing of 60cm (2ft), you are likely to get the biggest heads that the variety is capable of producing. Reduce the spacing to 35cm (14in) and you should get a higher total yield of heads which are smaller but still of a useful size. However, there comes a point when reducing the spacing further is counterproductive because none of the plants have room to grow to a size worth harvesting.

Types of spacing

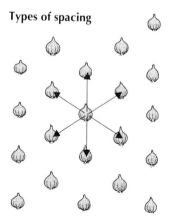

Equidistant: arrows show recommended crop spacing.

Square: in-row and between-row spacings are equal.

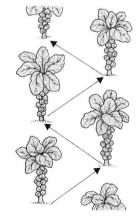

Staggered: the best layout for very widely spaced crops.

DRAINAGE

Where the water table is near the surface or the subsoil is of heavy clay or rock, rubble drains are effective in a small plot. Dig a trench 60–90cm (2–3ft) deep and 30cm (12in) wide, with a slope of 1 in 40. Half-fill with rubble, top with gravel and replace the topsoil. If there is no ditch or drain to which the drain can connect, lead it to a soakaway. Dig a hole 1.8m (6ft) across and at least 1.8m (6ft) deep. Line the sides with unmortared bricks, fill with rubble and top with turf.

On a large plot you may need ditches or land drains. Ditches should be 90–120cm (3–4ft) deep and slope outwards at a 20–30° angle. If the land slopes, dig a cut-off ditch to intercept water from higher ground. Dig another parallel ditch at the bottom of the slope. Connect the two by a ditch or a land drain. Discharge the water from the bottom ditch into a soakaway or stream. Land drains are sections of earthenware or perforated pipe. Dig a trench 60–100cm (2–3¼ft) deep and 30cm (12in) wide and lay the pipes on a 5cm (2in) bed of coarse gravel. Cover with a similar layer of gravel before replacing the soil.

On poorly drained land it also helps to grow crops using a bed system.

The effect of spacing on size

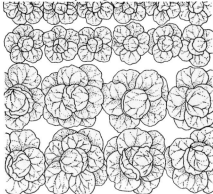

Reducing the spacing of crops such as cabbages gives smaller heads.

SUGGESTED SPACING

Artichokes (Jerusalem)   37cm (15in)
Beans (broad)   30cm (12in)
Beans (dwarf French)   15cm (6in)
Beans (runner)   15 x 60cm (6 x 24in)
Beetroot   13–15cm (5–6in)
Brussels sprouts   55–75cm (22–30in)
Cabbage, winter   45cm (18in)
Calabrese   15–30cm (6–12in)
Carrots   15cm (6in) or 5 x 20cm (2 x 8in)
Celery, self-blanching   15–25cm (6–10in)
Courgettes   60cm (24in)
Lettuce   15–30cm (6–12in)
Onions, maincrop   10–20cm (4–8in)
Parsnips   10–20cm (4–8in)
Peas   7.5cm (3in) or in rows*
Potatoes   30cm (12in) earlies, 38cm (15in) others
Spinach beet   23cm (9in)
Sweetcorn   30–45cm (12–18in)
Swiss chard   23cm (9in)

*Although an even distribution of plants over the bed works well for most crops, there are times when other spacings are more convenient:

Beans (runner) Tall varieties can be grown in a double row along the middle of the bed or up a wigwam of canes at the conventional spacing.

Carrots Maincrop can be station sown at 10cm (4in), but it is less time-consuming and makes weeding easier if you sow in wider rows 15cm (6in) apart and thin to about 5cm (2in).

Peas Short leafless peas can be grown at an equidistant spacing of 7.5cm (3in), but most varieties are best grown in close double rows or bands, either across the bed with 45cm (18in) between the bands or up the middle of the bed.

Potatoes Can be grown at close equidistant spacing of 30cm (12in) for earlies and 38cm (15cm) for others, but will have to be mulched instead of earthed up.

Crop rotation 1

VEGETABLE FAMILIES

The groups of vegetables given below are organized according to botanical families. When planning a crop rotation, keep vegetables in the same family together and "rotate" them so they grow in different ground in subsequent years.

Brassicas
(Cruciferae)
Brussels sprouts, cabbage, broccoli, calabrese, cauliflower, kale, radish, swede, turnip

Legumes
(Leguminosae)
Pea, bean (broad, French and runner)

Potato family
(Solanaceae)
Potato, tomato, aubergine, peppers

Umbellifers
(Umbelliferae)
Carrot, parsnip, parsley, celery, celeriac, Florence fennel

Daisy family
(Compositae)
Lettuce, chicory, endive, scorzonera, salsify

Onion family
(Alliacae)
Onion, garlic, shallots, leeks

Beetroot family
(Chenopodiaceae)
Beetroot, spinach, Swiss chard, spinach beet

Cucurbits
(Cucurbitaceae)
Cucumber, courgette, marrow, squash, pumpkin

Not related to any other vegetable
Jerusalem artichokes, sweetcorn, asparagus

What is crop rotation?

The basic principle of crop rotation is to keep closely related vegetables together and grow them on a different piece of land each year. The crops are moved around in a regular sequence so that they do not return to the same spot for three or four years, or longer.

Benefits

There are several reasons for crop rotation: it helps to control pests and diseases and weeds; it maintains soil fertility and also helps to improve soil structure.

Pest and disease control

The most commonly recognized benefit is that it helps to avoid problems of soil pests such as eelworm and diseases such as onion white rot, which attack only a closely related range of crops. By growing crops belonging to different botanical families in successive years, you can prevent such pests and diseases building up.

Weed control

Rotation helps weed control. Moving weed-suppressing crops such as potatoes and squashes from plot to plot can minimize problems for crops that follow, and help to prevent any one weed from getting out of hand.

Soil fertility

Rotation is equally important for maintaining the soil fertility. Different crops make different demands on the soil, and growing one crop continually may exhaust the ground of a certain nutrient. Changing crops from year to year (and hence also the soil management) allows the soil reserves to be replenished. Many leguminous crops like peas and broad and runner beans add nitrogen to the soil, which helps to feed the following crop.

Soil structure

Similarly, rotation helps to improve the soil structure. Alternating between crops with deep tap roots and those with a mass of shallow fibrous roots benefits the soil at all levels.

Problems

In practice it is not always easy to adhere to a strict crop rotation. This is particularly true if you have a small garden.

Weather
The weather may upset sowing and harvesting times by several weeks.

Garden conditions
There may also be parts of the garden that are ideally suited to – or indeed the opposite and completely unsuitable for – certain crops. Only one end of the plot may be sunny and sheltered enough to grow tender crops such as tomatoes, for example.

Club root
Where club root is a problem, it may even be advisable to keep aside one area for brassicas, and to improve it for them by liming until the pH is high.

Is it worth it?
It is sometimes argued that crop rotation is not worthwhile in a small garden, since some diseases such as clubroot and white rot persist in the soil for much longer than four years and crops can only be moved a few metres.

However, even if rotation cannot guarantee complete control of pests and diseases, in most cases it does help towards it. In any event, it is still valuable for improving the soil. This is particularly the case in an organic garden, where fertility building relies on different organic materials and green manures being used in conjunction with different crops.

PLANNING A CROP ROTATION
The first step in planning a rotation is to divide the garden up. Next, select your crops and then start cultivating the ground.

Dividing up the garden
Divide your vegetable garden into equal sections, one for each year of the rotation. This can mean anything from simply putting in wooden marker pegs at the side of the bed to physically dividing it with a network of paths. In most gardens, there is only space for a three- or four-year rotation. On a bed system, you will need to group beds together into three or four groups.

Selecting crops
Decide which crops you are going to grow together and which are going to follow which.

This will be determined in first by their botanical families (see table opposite), and second by their soil and nutrient requirements. Salsify and scorzonera (the Compositae family), for example, can be grown with the Umbellifers (carrots and parsnips) because they have similar soil and nutrient requirements. If these follow a crop to which manure or compost was applied the previous year, their needs will be satisfied.

Another factor which can affect the crop groupings is their sowing and harvesting times. It is more convenient if you can clear a good part of a plot (or a whole bed on the bed system) at more or less the same time so you can prepare it for replanting. For example, leaf beet fits well with overwintering brassicas such as purple sprouting broccoli because, as well as having similar nutrient requirements, they both need to stay in the ground until harvesting is finished in spring.

Green manures must also fit in with the crop rotation (see pages 80–5).

Putting crop rotation into practice
While it is no use sticking slavishly to a rotation if it is to the detriment of the crops, it is still worth having an overall plan. On the bed system, a plan for a crop rotation is easier to make and is more flexible in practice. Records are also valuable. Keep a note, not only of what is grown where, but of when the crops are sown and when they are cleared. This will help you to plan more accurately in future.

The vegetables you grow and the quantities in which you grow them are a matter of personal choice, so it is almost impossible to follow an off-the-peg rotation plan exactly. The traditional four-year rotation of potatoes–brassicas–legumes–roots assumes that potatoes and brassicas make up much of the bulk of the plot. This might still be the case on an allotment, but in a small garden you are more likely to concentrate on vegetables that are best picked fresh or are difficult or expensive to buy, for example, salads, spinach and unusual crops such as kohlrabi and celeriac. Thus a different plan may be required.

The example of crop rotation on page 49 is designed to show the way a rotation is planned, so that you can then formulate a scheme of your own.

Crop rotation 2

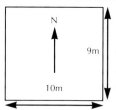

PLANNING A ROTATION

What area is available for vegetables?
A rectangular plot 10 x 9m (33 x 30ft).

Which crop families are to be grown?
Potato family Early and salad potatoes only (buy maincrop). Tomatoes are in the greenhouse.

Brassicas White cabbage for salads; Brussels sprouts; calabrese for eating and freezing; a few radish and kohlrabi; Chinese greens for winter salads.

Peas and beans Lots, for eating fresh and freezing surplus.

Onions Red salad onions, and a few maincrop (buy bulk); shallots and spring onions; leeks.

Umbellifers Carrots (a succession for pulling fresh); parsnips if room; Florence fennel; celeriac; parsley.

Other Sweetcorn, courgettes, lettuce, chicories, endives, spinach beet, annual herbs and flowers.

How should the bed be divided?

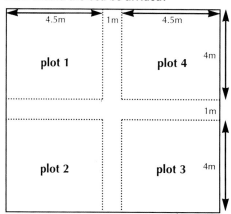

Peas and beans are the group required in greatest quantity, and would probably occupy up to a quarter of the whole bed. Therefore, divide the bed into four plots for a four year rotation. With rows running north–south, each will be 4m (13ft) long, a convenient length for the quantities required of most crops. On a bed system, each of the four plots could be divided into three beds.

How should the crops be grouped?
Peas, beans, catch crops like lettuce, annual flowers and herbs: Make use of organic matter left from previous crops. All cleared for winter green manures (tares or grazing rye) to be sown.

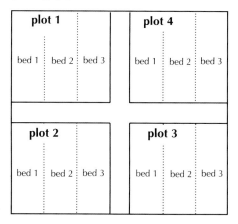

Potatoes, courgettes and sweetcorn: All need heavy feeding, all cleared for winter green manure (grazing rye) to be sown.

Umbellifers, onion family, catch crop spring onions, annual flowers and herbs: No feeding usually required for carrots and parsnips; compost the soil for celeriac, fennel and onion family. Use phacelia green manure for gaps.

Brassicas, leaf beet and catch crops of radish, kohlrabi and Chinese greens: All leafy crops benefit from nitrogen left by legumes. Use mustard as a green manure for gaps.

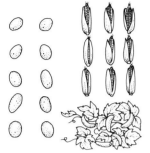

PLOT 1 TREATMENT

Compost trench for runner beans.

Grazing rye overwinter on rest of plot. If soil needs lime, add it here, after potatoes, which prefer acid conditions.

PLOT 2 TREATMENT

Well-rotted manure added in spring before planting.

Hay/straw or grass mowings to mulch growing crops for weed control.

PLOT 4 TREATMENT

Grow grazing rye over-winter after peas and beans, and tares after non-leguminous crops. Brassicas make use of added nitrogen from legumes. Mulch long-standing brassicas with compost/well-rotted manure.

PLOT 3 TREATMENT

Compost added before fennel, celeriac, leeks, onions and garlic.

Leafmould added for carrots and parsnips on heavy soil.

Introduction

Organic matter – bulky material of living origin – is an essential constituent of healthy, fertile soil (see pages 32–3), but one that is continuously being depleted. Soil-living creatures consume it, cultivation breaks· it down and gardeners remove replacement supplies which, in nature, would go back into the soil. Thus, to maintain soil fertility, organic matter must be applied regularly.

The value of organic matter in the garden
Soil structure Most organic matter improves the soil structure which, in turn, improves its fertility by making the plant foods it contains more available, as well as making it easier for roots to grow through the soil.
Plant foods Some materials supply plant foods. Being of living origin, they can contain the major elements (nitrogen, phosphate and potash) and the minor and trace elements essential for plant growth. Nutrient analyses can be variable and are not necessarily a good measure of the value of the product. The rate at which the nutrients are available can vary from weeks to years, depending on how long it takes the soil life to decompose the material.
Soil health Organic matter can help to keep soil pest and disease problems under control (see page 90).
Other uses Bulky organic materials can also be used to control weeds (see pages 148–9), as a mulch to keep the soil moist (see pages 36–7), and as an ingredient in growing media (see pages 160–5).

Processing before use
Bulky organic materials are usually composted or processed before use to make them easier to handle, stabilize the nutrients they contain, reduce toxins or make them more attractive.

Materials from non-organic sources should be stored for six months to allow a reduction in any chemical residues present. Those containing plant foods should be stored under cover to prevent the goodness being washed out.

Animal manures should never be used when fresh. In this state they contain freely available nitrogen compounds that can scorch plants, and both nitrogen and potassium may be in forms that are easily washed out by the rain, causing wastage and pollution. In well-rotted manures these compounds are stabilized.

Shredded conifer and other evergreen material should be stacked or composted before use to allow any toxic substances to decay or be driven off.

Sources
Bulky organic matter can be purchased or collected free from neighbours, farms, markets and other sources. Manures, composts, bark and other materials may also be purchased ready processed from garden shops. These may be easier to handle than unprocessed materials, but are likely to cost more.

Ideally, everything brought in should be organically grown. Buy products carrying a recognized organic symbol where possible, and avoid sources like intensive farms where contamination from pesticides, antibiotics and heavy metals is likely.

How to use bulky organic materials
Most materials can be dug into the ground or applied as a surface mulch. Certain materials which are high in carbon and low in nitrogen, including wood shavings, sawdust and wood chips, should only be used as a mulch because incorporating them into the soil could cause nitrogen robbery. Materials containing plant

Making animal manure

1 Straw animal manures should be heaped up and left to rot before use. This stabilizes the nutrients they contain.

PROCESSING ANIMAL MANURES

Straw manures Much of the goodness comes from the animal urine, so make sure the straw is well soaked and that the manure has not been standing out in the rain, which rapidly washes out nitrogen and potassium.

Straw manures can be added to a compost heap or stacked alone and left to decompose for several months. If the manure is dry, water it as the stack is built. Tread it down to expel excess air and cover with polythene.

Shavings-based manures Manure mixed with wood shavings rather than straw should be used with caution; the shavings can cause nitrogen robbery when mixed into the soil.

Only use this type of manure if the shavings are well-soaked in urine and/or you can add additional nitrogen, in the form of grass mowings, nettles or comfrey, for example.

Stack under cover until it is very well rotted – it should be a dark colour with individual shavings no longer distinct. This can take a year or two. When in doubt, use as a surface mulch only on permanent plantings. Do not apply to poor soil.

Poultry manures These are very high in nitrogen, contained in the white "dab" on the droppings. Mix with straw and rot as above or use as a compost heap activator.

foods are best mixed into the top 15–20cm (6–8in) of the soil as this is where the plants' feeding roots are at work.

How much to use
Nutrient-rich materials Increase for greedy feeders and poor soils; decrease for the opposite. Do not overfeed for fear of causing unhealthy, lush growth, and pollution.

Low/no-nutrient materials There is no real limit to the quantity of these that may be used.

When to apply it
Nutrient-rich materials Only apply to growing plants or to land where planting is imminent, never on bare ground in autumn and winter.
Low/no-nutrient materials These can be applied whenever soil conditions are suitable.

2 Stack up the manure, watering it very well if dry. Firm it down gently in order to get rid of excess air.

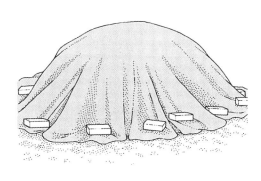

3 Cover the heap with polythene to keep moisture in and rain out. It should be ready to use within a month or two.

Types of organic matter 1

Autumn leaves

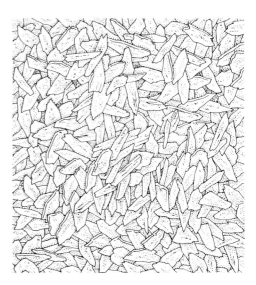

Shredded bark

Autumn leaves (low/no nutrients)
Use as a soil conditioner, an attractive mulch, for weed control and in growing media. Make into leafmould before use (see page 56–7). Use almost anywhere, especially to improve seedbeds. Apply at any time of year.
Sources: home garden; parks; cemeteries; streets in quiet neighbourhoods. Leaves collected from the side of busy roads may contain lead and other pollutants.

Bark, shredded (low/no nutrients)
Use bark as a soil conditioner, a decorative mulch, for controlling weeds and also in growing media.
Fine-grade bark can be dug in or applied as a mulch wherever soil improvement is required. Coarser grades should be used as a mulch only, around shrubs and other perennials.
Sources: proprietary garden products. Avoid products where nitrogen fertilizers have been used in processing.

Cocoa shells (nutrient-rich)
This provides plant foods as well as acting as a short-term weed control and soil conditioner. Use in most situations in the garden.
Sources: proprietary garden products. May contain residues of pesticides used in growing the cocoa beans.

Coir (coconut fibre) (low/no nutrients)
Use as an ingredient in growing media. Coir is suitable for use on acid-loving plants (pH 5.5–6.3).
Sources: proprietary garden products. Because it is imported from Sri Lanka, it should be used only where more local products are not available.

Compost, garden (nutrient-rich)
Use to feed and condition the soil, and also in growing media.
Use on all soils and plants where feeding is required. Mulch or dig in at one wheelbarrow load per 3–4sq m (3½–4¾sq yd).
Sources: home garden; proprietary garden products.

COMPOST ANALYSIS	
Average analysis of garden compost	
	% dry weight
Organic matter	80
Carbon	50
Nitrogen	3.5
P_2O_5	3.5
K_2O	1.8
CaO	1.5
Plus full range of trace elements	

Garden weeds

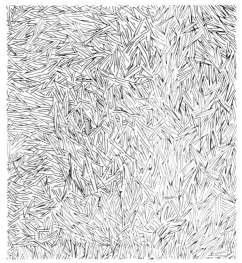

Grass mowings

Compost, spent mushroom (nutrient-rich)
Use to provide plant foods, to condition the soil and as a general mulch.

Stack mushroom compost under cover for several months before use, unless it is from organic sources. It can have a high pH and so is not advisable for use on acid-loving plants.
Sources: mushroom farms and proprietary garden products.

Compost, worm (nutrient-rich)
This is a rich source of plant foods and a useful potting compost ingredient; it also acts as a soil conditioner. It may be used wherever feeding is required, and is particularly useful for top-dressing pots, planters and hanging baskets. Sprinkle thinly and mix into the top few centimetres of soil.
Sources: home-made; proprietary products.

Green garden waste, excluding lawn mowings and prunings (nutrient-rich)
This material will vary in its value as a soil conditioner and a source of plant foods. It is best composted before use, but may be left as a surface mulch if not diseased.
Sources: home garden; other people's gardens.

Lawn mowings (nutrient-rich)
Lawn mowings are a rich source of quickly available nitrogen, a compost activator and a short-term mulch, and will control weeds if spread over newspaper.

Wherever possible, leave mowings on the lawn to feed the grass. Otherwise, process them through a compost heap or use them fresh, added to potato-planting trenches. They can also be used as a short-term feeding and moisture-retaining mulch. Do not apply a thick layer around young plants.
Sources: home garden; other people's gardens.

● CAUTION: Never use lawn mowings from the subsequent two cuts of a lawn that has been treated with weedkiller because the mowings may harm plants.

Manures, poultry (nutrient-rich)
These include chicken and pigeon manures. They are a rich source of plant foods. Use as a soil conditioner, to provide plant foods and, when fresh, as a compost activator.

Always compost these manures before use. If they are not already mixed with bedding material, mix them with straw or add to a general compost heap.
Sources: pigeon lofts; farms; proprietary garden products. Do not use chicken manure from intensive farms as it can be polluted with zinc and antibiotics.

Types of organic matter 2

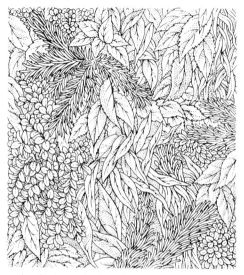

Hedge clippings and soft prunings

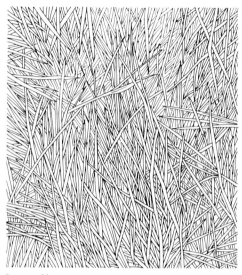

Straw and hay

Manures, straw (nutrient-rich)

These include horse, cattle, poultry, donkey and pig manures. Use as a soil conditioner, to provide plant foods and, when fresh, as a compost activator. They should be well rotted before use (see page 51).

Use wherever rich feeding and moisture retention is required – on potatoes, roses and blackcurrants, for example. Mulch or dig in at one wheelbarrow to 8–10 sq m (9½–11sq yd). Do not apply in autumn to empty ground.
Sources: farms; stables; proprietary garden products. Manure that has not been stacked out in the rain for months will be much richer. Do not use manures from intensive farms.

Manures, with wood shavings (variable)

Use as a soil conditioner and a feeding and moisture-retaining mulch. Shavings-based manure should be very well rotted before use. Use around shrubs and other permanent plantings; do not apply to poor soil.
Sources: stables.

Peat (low/no nutrients)

Peat has always been widely used as a soil conditioner and an ingredient of seed and potting composts, but concerns about the effect of extracting peat have encouraged organic gardeners to minimize their use of this material.

Prunings, conifers and other evergreens (low/no nutrients)

Use for general mulching and weed control around trees, shrubs and other perennial plants where they are not likely to be dug in.

Conifers and other evergreens may contain toxins that could inhibit plant growth. If they are being used as a mulch, they should be shredded or chopped first if possible, then heaped up and left to weather for several months before being used. This material can also be added to a mixed compost heap.

Do not use on young plants in case any toxins present should inhibit growth.
Sources: home garden; other people's gardens; proprietary products.

Prunings, soft and hedge clippings (low/no nutrients)

These materials will condition the soil and also provide plant foods in the long term. They make useful mulching materials.

Young prunings and hedge clippings can be applied fresh as a soil mulch, added to a compost heap, or heaped up on their own to compost. They are best shredded or chopped before being used.

Apply as a mulch to trees, shrubs and other perennial plants.
Sources: home garden; other gardens.

Vegetable waste

Seaweed

Prunings, woody (low/no nutrients)
Woody prunings are best shredded before they are used. They can then be used directly on soil or paths, or left in a heap to mature. This will darken the colour of the prunings and is likely to kill any diseases present.

Use for general mulching and weed control around trees, shrubs and other perennial plants, where they are not likely to be dug in.
Sources: home garden; other peoples gardens; proprietary products.

Sawdust/wood shavings (low/no nutrients)
Use as a mulch. Unless they are to be used on paths and other non-growing areas, sawdust and wood shavings must be left in the open to weather for a year or more before use.

Use sawdust and wood shavings only on perennial beds where soil is fertile and unlikely to be disturbed. They can cause severe nitrogen robbery if they are incorporated into the soil, unless they are very old.
Sources: wood yard; saw mill. All sawdust and wood shavings must be from wood that has not been treated with preservatives.

Seaweed (nutrient-rich)
Seaweed provides plant foods, especially potassium and trace elements. It also helps to activate a compost heap and improve soil conditions. It may be used fresh or composted, dug in or applied as a mulch.
Sources: pick up from unpolluted beaches below the tide line. Do not collect old, dry seaweed as this could be very salty. Never take growing seaweed from rocks.

Straw (low/no nutrients) and hay (nutrient-rich)
Both straw and hay will help to condition soil. They can be used as mulches and will give some weed control. Hay also contains useful levels of plant foods; straw is less rich. They can also be added to a compost heap.

Store for several months if newly harvested from non-organic sources. Use anywhere except round young plants that are susceptible to slugs. They are particularly useful around fruit bushes, where appearance is less critical. Hay can be used to supply all the foods needed by plants such as raspberries.
Sources: farms; stables; wildlife trusts. If the straw has been treated with a hormone weed-killer, do not use around tomatoes.

Vegetable waste (nutrient-rich)
Make into compost or worm compost before use, or add to a compost trench.
Sources: home garden; kitchen; local markets; greengrocers.

Making leafmould

Autumn leaves are one of the best sources of soil-improving organic matter. They take a year or two to decay into a dark, crumbly material known as leafmould. Newly fallen autumn leaves could be used directly on the garden, but converting them to leafmould makes them easier to handle and less likely to blow away if applied as a surface mulch. The advantage of leaves is that they are free, easy to obtain and clean to handle.

Which leaves?

Fallen leaves from any trees and shrubs, other than conifers and other evergreens, will make leafmould. Different species decay at different rates, but all will turn to leafmould eventually.

Diseased leaves which can pass on infection, such as those with rose blackspot or apple scab, are best avoided. Alternatively, use them to make a batch of leafmould which is used around unrelated plants.

Collecting the leaves

The best time to collect autumn leaves is when they are wet after rain. This saves watering them later. A quick method for collecting leaves on a lawn is to run the mower over them with the grass box on. This chops the leaves and adds some grass mowings, which will speed decay. Machines designed specifically to collect leaves are also available.

Sources of leaves

Leaves can be collected from parks and cemeteries (with permission) and from quiet streets. Leaves from busy roadsides are best avoided as they can be contaminated with lead and other pollutants. Some councils may deliver if you can cope with a lorry load. Ask for those from parks, not from the roads.

Making leafmould

The decay of autumn leaves is a slow, cool process carried out by fungi – very different from the composting process. To make leafmould, simply collect leaves together where they will not blow away, watering them well if they are dry.

The leaves may be piled up in a sheltered corner. Alternatively, use a simple container made by fixing wire mesh netting around four corner posts. Smaller quantities of leaves can be stuffed into black plastic sacks which are then tied loosely at the top.

Making leafmould

1 The best time to collect leaves is after rain, so they are moist. Rake them up or run the mower over them.

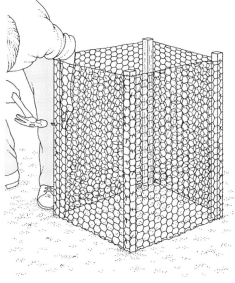

2 To make a container, hammer 4 posts into the ground. Staple wire netting to them. Use black plastic sacks for smaller quantities.

MAKING COMFREY LEAFMOULD

Fill a container such as a dustbin with alternate 7.5–10cm (3–4in) layers of 2–3 year-old leafmould and chopped comfrey leaves. Use when the comfrey leaves have virtually disintegrated.

darken in colour, they can be used as a mulch or dug into the soil. This may be as soon as the following spring, but the process can take much longer depending on the type of leaves used and on how moist they are. A finer grade of leafmould, suitable for potting mixes, will take 2–3 years to achieve.

Comfrey leafmould
Well-rotted leafmould mixed with chopped comfrey leaves (see pages 88–9) produces comfrey leafmould, a useful ingredient in seed and potting mixes.

The ingredients required are equal quantities by volume of fine 2–3 year old leafmould and chopped comfrey leaves.

Fill a dustbin or plastic sack with alternate 7.5–10cm (3–4in) layers of leafmould and chopped comfrey. Leave for 2–5 months (depending on the time of year), checking on the moisture levels occasionally. If the mixture turns soggy, or if it is so dry that little has changed, empty out the container. Leave the contents to dry, or add water as appropriate, before refilling the dustbin or sack.

The comfrey leafmould is ready to use when the comfrey leaves have virtually disappeared.

Using leafmould
Leafmould contains little in the way of plant foods but is an excellent soil conditioner. As soon as the leaves have started to break up and

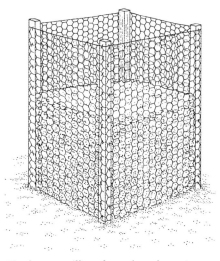

3 Fill the container with leaves, pressing them down and watering well if dry. The slow fungal decay process can then begin.

4 The leaves will settle as they decay into a dark friable material. They are usually left for 1–2 years before use.

Shredding

A shredder will transform a heap of prunings, hedge clippings and other garden waste that is too tough for composting into a neat pile of chips, and is ideal for the compost heap or for using as a surface mulch.

Shredding reduces the need for bonfires and trips to the rubbish dump and allows recycling of rich sources of organic matter and plant foods. These benefits, however, must be set against the use of energy to run the shredder, the noise, the time taken to shred material and the cost of purchase.

What can be shredded?
The most suitable materials for shredding are those that are fairly rigid, such as conifer and other prunings and Brussels sprout stems.

Softer materials are more likely to clog the system, especially in the smaller models. Domestic shredders can cope with branches approximately 2.5–4cm (1–2in) in diameter, although more powerful models can take material up to about 7.5cm (3in) thick.

Buying or hiring a shredder
There is a good selection of various types of shredders now available on the market and, increasingly, for hire.

Before purchasing a shredder, consider how much material your garden produces that can only be recycled if shredded. Buying a shredder is most appropriate for medium to large gardens with a number of hedges and shrubs that require regular pruning. Small gardens are

Shredding

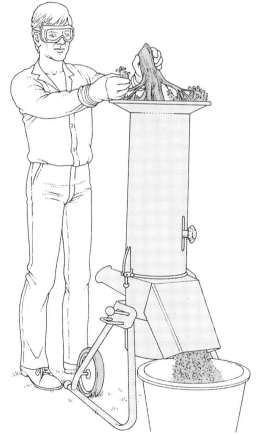

This machine shreds tough materials into small, easy-to-compost pieces. When using it, remember to wear the appropriate protective clothing to avoid accidents.

unlikely to produce enough material to justify the purchase.

Consider also the noise factor. Shredders can be extremely noisy, especially where there are walls and buildings to reflect the sound.

Hiring a shredder may be a more practical option than buying one. A great deal of material that could be shredded does not have to be, so the occasional hire of a machine may be all you need. This way you have the use of a larger model than you are likely to buy – which will shred larger items, and at a greater speed too.

Choosing a shredder
The following factors are important to consider when selecting a shredder:
Power Choose the biggest model you can afford. Small models can be frustratingly slow and may be of little value.
Petrol or electric? Electric models are quieter but petrol ones are more portable, faster and more powerful. There are no hand-powered models available.
Rate of throughput How quickly will it shred? Models of the same power may vary.
Maximum size of material Check that this meets your requirements.
Portability How easy is it to move?
Ease of unclogging Shredders, especially the smaller models, tend to clog up quite regularly. Check how long it takes to dismantle the machine, clear the blades and reconstruct it.
Working height It is important that this suits you, for shredding can be a time-consuming activity.
Outlet Check that a bag or basket can be set under the outlet to collect the shreddings.

Hints on using a shredder
• Always wear tough gloves and goggles; ear protectors are also advisable.
• Have a sturdy stick handy to push material down into the shredder.
• Avoid stones and soil as both will rapidly blunt the blades.
• Alternate softer and woodier material to reduce the risk of clogging.
• Take it slowly; do not try to force too much material through the shredder at once.
• Always use electric shredders with a socket that has a circuit-breaker fitted.

• Cover cable with carpet or similar to prevent anyone tripping over it.
• Make sure the machine is empty before switching it off or the blades will jam when it is restarted.

Using shredded material
Shredded green material and soft prunings are best processed through a compost heap, mixed with other ingredients (see pages 70–1). They will compost very rapidly.

Woodier shreddings, apart from those from conifers and other evergreens, can be used fresh as a mulch around perennial plants, where the soil is unlikely to be disturbed (see page 36–7). They may also be heaped up to mature before use. Such a heap may well heat up, and the colour of the shreddings will darken slightly.

Conifer and other evergreen shreddings may contain toxins that could inhibit plant growth. They may be used fresh to mulch paths and other non-growing areas, but should be composted for several months before use on growing plants. They may be added to a compost heap or heaped up on their own.

Other ways of dealing with wooden waste
Bonfires are, generally, a waste of valuable resources. The smoke produced is a pollutant which is bad for the health, and for neighbourly relationships! For these reasons, generally speaking, bonfires are not recommended in the organic garden.

There are times, though, when a bonfire may be necessary – to dispose of diseased woody material, for example. The bonfire should be quick and hot, producing the minimum of smoke. Have one on a windy day for quick burn and rapid dispersal; this can be achieved by burning only material that has had plenty of time to dry out. Never burn wet wood and green weeds.

Wood ash contains useful plant foods, but in a very soluble form. Add it to the compost heap before it is rained on.

If you have a spare corner in the garden, woody material can be simply heaped up and left to decay as woodpiles for wildlife. This can take many years, but the heap will be a source of food and a safe refuge for wild creatures in the meantime (see page 11).

Composting process 1

Compost-making is a keystone of organic growing. One of the basic rules of organic gardening is to recycle nutrients wherever possible, and to keep inputs to a minimum. Recycling kitchen and garden waste through a compost heap meets both these requirements.

Reusing waste in this way also helps to reduce the mountains of household rubbish that must be disposed of in landfill or in other ways. This fulfils another organic tenet – to keep pollution to a minimum.

What is garden compost?
Garden compost is a rich, dark, soil-like material made up of decomposed plant and animal material such as weeds, vegetable scraps and animal manure. It is an excellent (and free) soil improver which can be used throughout the garden.

When added to the soil, compost feeds the teeming microscopic soil life; as a result, plant foods are made available and the soil's health and structure are improved.

Garden compost should not be confused with sowing and potting composts, which should, perhaps, more properly be called growing media (see pages 160–5).

Why make compost?
There are several reasons why, in most cases, it is better to compost plant and animal remains rather than digging them straight back into the soil, or leaving them on the surface as a mulch.
- Uncomposted material left on the soil surface could act as a breeding ground for pests and diseases. It may also look unattractive.
- Digging in some uncomposted materials could induce nitrogen depletion.
- Composting converts soluble nutrients into a more stable form, so preventing wastage.
- Composting mixes different materials, giving a more balanced end product.
- Composting can kill weed seeds, pests and diseases.
- Composting reduces the volume of fresh material, making it easier to apply to the soil.
- In the form of compost, plant foods can be stored until they are required. This is not the case with fresh materials.

A natural process
The process of converting plant and animal waste into a useful product is not something that the gardener has invented – all plant and animal remains decay quite naturally without our interference. The key players in this decomposition process are microscopic creatures that inhabit our world. They tirelessly recycle the earth's resources, so keeping our planet green and fertile. In the garden we refine these natural processes, making them quicker, more productive and more practical for our own needs and circumstances.

Garden compost

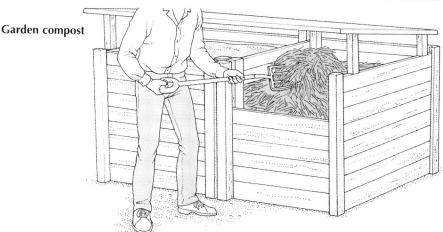

Compost-making micro-organisms start to feed on tender, juicy items. As they move on to tougher materials the process slows. Larger creatures such as worms and insects move in.

Making compost

There are many different ways of making compost, all of which should succeed as long as a few basic rules are followed (see page 62). The best method is the one that suits your particular requirements.

Valuable compost can be produced in as little as 2 months, or it may take a year or more; a compost heap may get so hot that it steams or it may remain cold; any weed seeds, pests and diseases that were added to the heap may or may not be killed. It all depends on the time of year, the type and quantity of material and how much time and trouble you take over it.

Ideally, compost should be fine, dark, crumbly and sweet-smelling and should contain no viable weed seeds. It may, however, be sticky, lumpy, stringy and odiferous.

The former is not difficult to produce, with a little extra effort, but the latter is still a perfectly useful compost.

The composting process

The process of converting kitchen and garden waste into compost is carried out entirely by naturally occurring organisms. When suitable materials are gathered together, these "compost workers" move in and start to feed on the more tender, juicy items. Their numbers build up rapidly, reaching 2 million per gram of moist compost in a few days, and so the rate of decomposition increases.

One result of all this activity is the production of heat, which can be quite noticeable if there is sufficient material to contain it. A large heap of mixed material can reach a temperature of 60°C (140°F) in just a few days. Weed seeds and many pests and diseases are killed, and the volume of the material decreases quite dramatically.

Compost workers need oxygen. As this becomes in short supply in the centre of an active heap, so the rate of work will slow down. Introducing more oxygen by remixing the heap will speed it up again.

If oxygen remains in short supply the process will proceed, but at a slower rate. If there is no oxygen – because the heap is too wet, for example – the material will start to putrefy rather than compost, which is not the desired result. Some moisture is essential, however; dry material will not compost.

Once the more tender ingredients have been consumed, the tougher material is worked on. The rate of decomposition slows. Heat is not produced so the larger creatures, such as worms and insects, are safe to move in to help with the work.

By the end of the process the original ingredients of the heap will be unrecognizable. They will have been broken down, mixed together and rebuilt into what we call compost. The original volume will have decreased by at least 50 per cent.

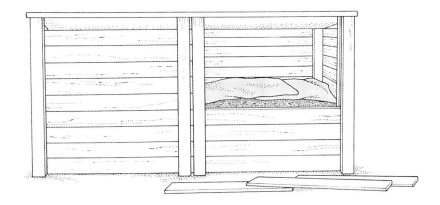

By the end of the process the original ingredients will be unrecognizable. They will have been broken down, mixed together and rebuilt into what we call compost.

Composting process 2

Essential rules of compost-making

When making compost, use a mixture of tough and sappy ingredients to ensure active composting and a good end product (see pages 70–1). Add as much as possible at once. It is important to provide sufficient moisture but do not let the heap become waterlogged. Build air into the heap, cover and enclose it to keep rain out and prevent moisture and heat loss. Never use pesticides on a compost heap. Experiment until you find a method that suits you, and do not worry if the end product is not perfect: it may still be usable.

Hot or cold composting?

The quick hot heap The quickest method of making compost is in a hot heap – that is, one where the ingredients heat up noticeably. This is done by filling a compost container in one batch using the right mixture of materials, preferably chopped or shredded if tough. A hot heap kills many weeds, pests and diseases.

The main disadvantage of a hot heap is that few people have sufficient material to achieve it. Another problem is that it may lose some of its value; nitrogen is given off as ammonia from a very hot heap, hence the smell.

PROS AND CONS

Hot heap
+ Quick-action, making compost in as little as 6–8 weeks
+ Most weed seeds and roots, as well as diseases, are killed
- Requires a lot of material at one time
- High temperatures can reduce fertility of end product by driving off ammonia
Cool heap
+ Can be built as materials become available
+ May be more fertile as nutrients are retained
- May take a year or more to compost
- Weeds and diseases may not be killed

The cool bit-by-bit heap Most gardeners add ingredients to the heap as they become available. It may or may not heat up and is called a cool heap. It can make excellent compost but can take a year or so. As the ingredients are unlikely to heat through, any diseases and weeds present may not be killed.

Making a cool heap

1 Use a sharp spade to chop compost material for quicker decomposition. Do this on a soft surface like a lawn to avoid jarring.

2 Air is an essential compost ingredient, so tease out "claggy bits" of material with a fork in order to allow air to penetrate.

Speeding up the composting process

One of the most common complaints that is made about making compost is that it takes such a long time to achieve a useful end product. However, whether you are making a cool heap or a hot one, there are ways of speeding up the process.

Filling the container

Although it may not be possible to gather sufficient material initially to fill a whole compost box, always make an effort to add as much material as you can at once. For example, mow the lawn, weed the border and collect a sack of manure or vegetable waste from the local market within the same few days. Never add individual items.

Chopping and shredding

Chopping or shredding tough compost material (see pages 58–9), such as old brassica stems, can increase the speed of decomposition dramatically. This is because chopping a stem into many pieces increases its total surface area, giving the composting micro-organisms a much greater area to work on, so the speed of breakdown is increased.

A compost shredder can be very useful here, but it is not worth buying one unless you have a lot of woody material to dispose of. Chopping with a sharp spade or shears and bashing tough stems with a hammer will do the job.

Turning the heap

A compost heap may sometimes heat up initially then slow down. This is because it has run out of air in the middle, or because it is too wet or dry. The answer here is to turn the heap. Remove the material from the container, then rebuild the heap. Tease out the contents to incorporate more air; add water or sappy ingredients if the mixture looks dry; add dry, tough material if it seems wet. The material that was at the outer edges of the heap should be moved into the centre. A hot heap can be turned every few weeks until it stops heating.

It is also worth turning a piecemeal heap that has not heated up, either after each new addition of material or with the last addition.

A simple way of turning a compost heap on a regular basis is to use a compost tumbler (see page 66). This can produce compost in as little as three weeks.

3 Always make an effort to collect together as much material as you can to add to the compost heap at one go.

4 Turning a compost heap will speed up the process. Empty the container then rebuild the heap, mixing everything together well.

Compost containers 1

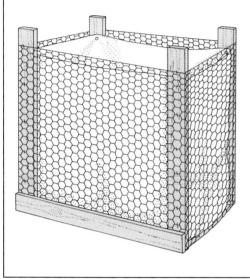

This is perhaps the simplest home-made compost container; it is easy to construct even if you have no carpentry skills.

Construction
Hammer four sturdy posts into the ground to give the size of container required and staple wire mesh netting around these posts. Line* the container with strips of old carpet or sheets of thick cardboard. This can be tied in with string threaded through both wire and lining. Carpet can also be held in place with nails hammered into the corner posts.

Remember to cover the compost with a sheet of polythene, a piece of carpet or a waterproof lid.

*You can easily adapt this container for making leafmould by simply leaving out the lining (see pages 56–7).

The simplest way to make compost is to heap up the ingredients on the ground and cover them with an old, hessian-backed carpet. Most people, however, use a container of some form. A compost box looks better (especially in small gardens), keeps the heap from spreading too far and can be easier to manage.

There are certain basic criteria to consider when making or buying a compost box.

Material
Wood is perhaps the most appropriate material for a compost box, providing insulation while also allowing some moisture loss. It is the most commonly used material for do-it-yourself containers, though these can also be constructed out of an imaginative array of other recycled materials (see pages 68–9).

Most commercial containers are plastic, an increasing number using recycled material. These have the advantage, generally, of being lighter, cheaper and easier to move than wooden models. They do not retain heat as well but warm up quickly in the sun. Plastic containers tend to produce a wetter compost.

Metal compost containers are available and can be useful where vermin are a problem.

Strength
A compost box should be sturdy enough to take the battering that it will incur during filling and emptying, and strong enough to contain the mature compost, which can be heavy.

Ventilation
The presence, or absence, of holes or gaps in the sides of a compost box is a subject that provokes a lot of argument. Some parties insist that they are essential for the supply of air into the heap. However, gaps also allow heat and moisture to escape, and the material next to them may dry out.

A compost box with solid sides is ideal; sufficient air can be included in the heap as it is built. Narrow gaps in the sides are fine, especially if your compost tends to be rather wet.

Weight
The weight of a container is an important consideration if the container itself must be removed for access to the finished compost.

Volume
When it comes to size, a volume of 0.7cu m (1cu yd) is often recommended as the most

Types of container

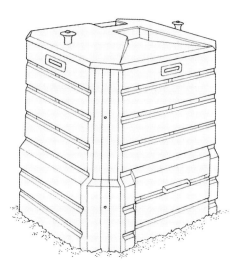

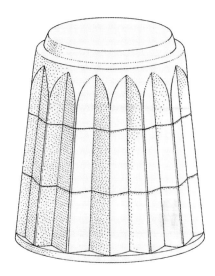

This commercially available compost container is made from recycled plastic.

This plastic compost container is known as a rotol container.

efficient for compost-making. Most compost boxes on the market are smaller than this, at around 200–300 litres. These can produce excellent compost and are more appropriate for most gardens. Anything smaller is not worth considering. Choose the largest you can fill. Proprietary compost bins are sold according to how many litres of material they hold.

Lid
A waterproof lid is important to keep the rain out. For ease of use, this should be simple to remove and replace and should not blow away in the wind.

Base
Most compost boxes are open at the bottom to allow drainage and easy access for worms and other composting creatures. If the container does have a base, it should be designed to allow good drainage.

Access
Access to the finished compost may be via a removable side on the box or, more commonly, by simply removing the container itself. Many commercial models have small

access doors through which compost is meant to be removed; these are of dubious value.

Siting the container
A compost box may have a permanent site or it may be moved around the garden so you can take advantage of the fertility that seeps out of the bottom. You may find it convenient to have a combination of, say, a home-made fixed model and a movable plastic container that you can reposition at will.

Compost boxes tend to be hidden away at the bottom of the garden. This is fine as long as the site is suitable. If it is difficult to get to and cramped to work around you will be much less likely to make compost.

A compost container should be set on bare soil to allow any liquid produced to drain away. It should be sited to allow easy access with a wheelbarrow or loads of compost material. There should also be space to store and mix compost ingredients and to turn the compost when necessary.

The ideal site is also warm and sheltered, but there is usually too much competition to allow the compost boxes to occupy such a prime spot!

Compost containers 2

How many containers?

It is possible to make a good supply of compost with only one container. When the time comes to start a new heap, the container is emptied or removed and the compost covered with a waterproof cover and left to mature.

However, having two or more compost boxes can make life easier. This is because the material from one box can be turned into the other, for example, or one box can be filled up while the compost in the other is maturing.

Compost tumblers

A compost tumbler can be rotated on an axle. This makes the regular turning of the composting materials much easier than with a conventional heap. However, even turning a compost tumbler can be quite strenuous.

There are other benefits too. Turning daily ensures a continuing supply of oxygen throughout the composting material. This, along with the fact that the ingredients are regularly mixed together, means that they heat up well and compost of sorts can be produced in as little as three weeks. This compost is not mature, but it can be used on the garden, stored under cover to mature or further processed through a worm compost bin.

The basics of composting are the same in a tumbler as in a conventional heap, but there are certain aspects that differ: for example, a tumbler should be sited on a firm, level surface such as concrete or paving and it should also be filled all at once, or over a period of a few days. Unlike a bin, it should not then be added to until you are ready to start up a new batch.

When using a tumbler, it is particularly important that the ingredients are chopped up and well mixed. Liquid may drip out of a tumbler; this can be collected and diluted for use as a liquid feed. If the right combination of ingredients is used this liquid should be minimal. When filling a tumbler it is best to mix the different ingredients together first, especially if there are large quantities of one type of material such as grass mowings. Alternatively, turn the tumbler occasionally when filling it.

If the ingredients are chopped first, the end product will be much more friable; otherwise it can turn out in the form of large balls. These can still be used on the garden or added to a worm bin for final processing.

COMPOST TUMBLERS

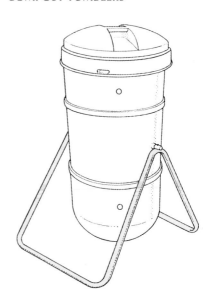

A compost tumbler is a container on an axle that can be rotated for easy mixing of the compost material.

Benefits

• Compost is available quickly when using a tumbler

• When using this type of container, good heating and mixing should help to kill off any weed seeds

• Where vermin are a problem in compost heaps, a tumbler is a useful alternative as it keeps them out

• A tumbler can be used where there is no bare soil to site a traditional heap

Disadvantages

• Can be hard work to turn

• Material should not be added to while composting

TRENCH COMPOSTING

A compost trench is a simple alternative to a compost heap and can be of use in dealing with kitchen waste over the winter months when the compost heap may not necessarily be active. A compost trench is a good way of disposing of old winter brassicas stems, especially those infested with whitefly and mealy aphid.

Siting
The most convenient place is in the vegetable plot, where runner beans or peas are to be grown next season.

Digging
In autumn, dig out a trench one spade wide and one spade deep (approximately 30 x 30cm/12 x 12in).

Filling
Gradually fill the trench with vegetable scraps and kitchen waste as it becomes available, covering each addition of material with some of the soil that was removed from the trench.

Once the trench is full, replace any remaining soil and leave it to settle for a month or two.

After filling
After the soil has settled you can either sow seeds or plant the area up, as the decomposed waste underneath provides an excellent source of plant foods and water for the following crop.

Planting
Make a series of individual compost holes in the filled compost trenches and then plant them with vegetables. Crops such as marrows, pumpkins and courgettes will all grow in such conditions.

1 In the autumn, dig out a trench one spade wide and one spade deep. Fill this with kitchen waste as available.

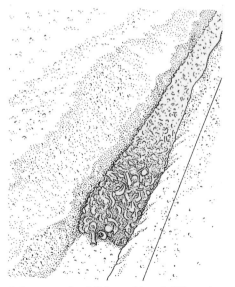

2 Cover each addition with soil. When the trench is full, replace remaining soil and leave to settle before planting.

Building a container

This movable wooden compost box consists of interlocking sections which are stacked up on top of each other to the required height. As the material in the box breaks down it decreases in volume, so the top sections of box can be removed and used to build a new container. Make a few extra sections and you will have a flexible composting system. To keep the material insulated and protected from the rain, cover it with a square of hessian-backed carpet, sacking or blanket, topped with waterproof material.

Materials and equipment

Recycled wood is the most economical material for a compost container. Wooden pallets or second-hand floorboards are perhaps the most easily obtained. Check in your local paper and contact recycled building material companies and demolition yards for sources.

Wider or slightly narrower boards may be used as long as the size of the blocks is adjusted (see instructions for details). There is no need to keep to the same width for each section if the timber available is variable.

SIZE

The following will make a box 75 x 75 x 75cm (30 x 30 x 30in). These dimensions can be easily adjusted as long as the sections remain square.

For one section of the box you will need:
• 2 x 75cm (30in) boards, 7.5cm (3in) wide, minimum 1.5cm (⅝in) thick
• 2 x 72cm (28in) boards, 7.5 cm (3in) wide, minimum 1.5cm (⅝in) thick
• 4 x 5 x 5cm (2 x 2in) blocks, 5.5cm (2¼in) long
• 20 x 3.6 cm (1½in) screws, size No. 8
• 1 screwdriver; 1 drill; 1 saw

For 10 sections for a box you will need:
• 30m (98½ft) of 7.5cm x 1.5cm (3 x ⅝in) board
• 2.2m (7¼ft) of 5 x 5cm (2 x 2in) timber
• 200 x 3.6cm (1.½in) No. 8 screws

Making a wooden container

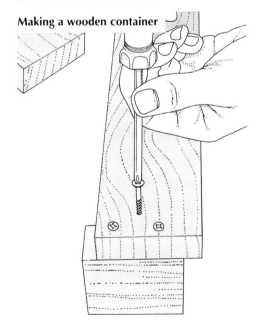

1 Cut all the required wood to size. Screw the corner blocks to either end of the two shorter boards.

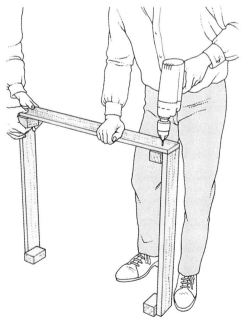

2 To complete the section screw one of the longer boards to the two shorter ones; repeat with the remaining long board.

Construction

1 First, cut two board, each 75cm (30in) long.
2 Cut two boards each 72cm (28in) long.
3 Cut four lengths of 5.5cm (2¼in) from the 5 x 5cm (2 x 2in) timber for the corner blocks. If using material with different dimensions from those above, cut two boards to the required length of one side of the box. Calculate the length of the remaining two sides by subtracting twice the thickness of the wood from the length of the first boards cut. calculate the length of the blocks by subtracting 2.1cm (¾in) from the width of the boards.
4 Once you have cut all the wood to the correct size, take one of the two shorter boards and place it in position on two of the corner blocks. The ends of the board should be flush with the blocks; the blocks should be offset so that they project 2.1cm (¾in) beyond the edge of the board, as shown in the diagram.
5 Hold the board in position on the blocks. Drill three holes 3cm (1¼in) deep at one end of the board, through the board and into the block below. Fasten with three screws.

6 Repeat this process for the other end of the board.
7 Fix the second shorter (72cm/28in) board in the same manner. You may need someone to help hold the pieces while you fix them together.
8 Stand the two shorter boards (with blocks attached) on their ends, approximately 75cm (30in) apart, with the protruding ends of the blocks away from you.
9 Place a 75cm (30in) board on top of these vertical boards to form the third side of the section. Ensure that the ends of the longer board are flush with the outer edges of the vertical boards. Drill and screw each end of the 75cm (30in) board using two screws only.
10 Finally, turn the section over so that the unfinished side is uppermost. Place the second 75cm (30in) board across between the shorter boards as before. Position squarely and drill and screw, again only using two screws.

You have now completed the first section of your compost box. Continue making sections until the desired number are completed.

3 Make more sections until you have the size of container required. The corner blocks act as locating pegs to keep sections together.

4 When you wish to take out the finished compost, simply remove individual sections of wood down to the level required.

Compost ingredients

Tough or tender?

On the table opposite, ingredients marked as tender (1) will start the composting process. They are nitrogen-rich and decompose quickly but provide little fibre to give the compost body. Too much will result in a soggy, smelly heap. Those marked as intermediate (2) will not decay as quickly as tender materials but will provide structure to the compost, and those marked as tough (3) will provide structure for the compost but will decompose very slowly unless mixed with more tender material. Living materials are variable, so these classifications should be taken as guidelines only. Plants get tougher as they age.

Sources

The average house and garden can produce a fair amount for the compost heap but if you are a keen gardener this will never be enough. Further supplies include straw, hay, vegetable scraps from the greengrocer, weeds and mowings from non-composting neighbours, pigeon manure from local lofts and stable manure. Materials to avoid are grass or straw recently treated with weedkiller, anything carrying a persistent weed, pest or disease, and manures from intensive farms.

Pests and diseases

The compost heap is often thought of as a breeding ground for pests and diseases, but this is not the case. A hot heap kills off all but the very persistent diseases like club root, and even in a cool heap the intense microbial activity can dispose of disease organisms.

As a general rule, diseases that only survive on living plant material can be composted. Those that survive in dead and decaying plant material are best omitted from a slow, cool heap. Diseases that produce resistant resting spores should be avoided altogether.

You may find a few pests, such as slugs and wireworm, in a maturing compost heap as they are part of nature's army of decomposers. Do not worry; the compost heap will not cause a population explosion in your garden. Never use a pesticide on a compost heap.

Compost activators

A compost activator initiates the whole process of composting. Natural activators include grass mowings, young nettles, comfrey leaves, urine and poultry manures. If one (or more) of these is used, there should be no need to add a purchased activator. If you purchase an activator, choose one based on herbs or bacteria; avoid nitrogen fertilizers.

Pet manures

Bedding and manure from pets such as rabbits, guinea pigs and gerbils can be added to a compost heap. Treat cat and dog manures with caution as they can contain organisms that are harmful to humans; if these manures are to be composted, they should be added to a good mixed heap that will heat up. The resulting compost should be handled with care, and used on ornamentals only.

The composting of cat and dog manures is not advised where children have access to the compost, either in the heap or on the garden.

Animal manures

Brassica stems

COMPOST MATERIALS

Material	1	2	3	Notes/comments
Bracken		2	3	Cut when green; do not collect when producing spores.
Comfrey leaves	1			See pages 88–9.
Brassicas (old plants)			3	Chop into small pieces with a sharp spade; do not add clubroot-infected roots.
Diseased material	-	-	-	See diseased plant material, pages 98–9.
Food scraps	1	2		Mix well with other ingredients; if scraps only are available, consider a worm compost system.
Feathers	1			Mix well with other ingredients; 15% nitrogen.
Glass				Will not compost.
Grass mowings, young	1			Do not use if weedkiller has been used within the last two mowings.
Grass mowings, long rough grass		2		Water well before adding if dry.
Hay		2		A good source of plant foods; soak well before adding if dry.
Hedge clippings				See Prunings, below.
Manure, with straw bedding (See also poultry manure)		2		Usually cow or horse. Composition will vary. Can act as an activator if fresh and the straw is well soaked with urine.
Manure with shavings			3	Usually horse. Use with caution; see page 54.
Manure, pet				May be used but with caution; see page 70.
Manure, poultry, no bedding	1			Very nitrogen-rich; do not obtain from intensive farms.
Manure, poultry, with bedding		2		Will also act as an activator if there is a high proportion of manure to straw. Straw and poultry manure together will make good compost.
Metal				Will not compost.
Nettles, old		2		A patch of nettles can be cut for composting twice a year.
Nettles, young	1			As above.
Plant and crop residues		2	3	See diseased plant material, pages 98–9.
Paper				Of little value in a compost heap; will soak up excess moisture. Tear up before use. Avoid coloured inks in any quantity.
Plastic				Will not compost.
Potato haulm		2		Blight-infected haulm can be composted; infected tubers should not be added to a compost heap.
Prunings, soft green		2		These can be added directly to the heap.
Prunings, woody			3	Chop small or shred before adding to a mixed nitrogen-rich heap (see pages 58–9). May have to go through a heap several times. Large quantities are best made into a separate heap which may take several years to decay.
Rhubarb leaves		2		Although poisonous to eat, these can be safely composted.
Sawdust			3	Small quantities may be added to a heap.
Seaweed	1			Fresh seaweed may be collected from the beach (see page 55). Encourages bacterial action; adds trace elements.
Straw			3	Useful for bulking up soggy heaps. Old or chopped straw is best. Soak first if dry.
Urine, human	1			Rich in nitrogen and potassium; dilute with around 3 parts water and water on to the heap.
Weeds, annual	1	2		Weed seeds may not be killed in a cool heap.
Weeds, perennial		2		Contain a lot of goodness so compost if possible. Kill them first by leaving in the sun to dry or make a separate heap which is left to compost for a longer period. Do not compost oxalis or celandine.

Building a compost heap

Building a heap

1 Collect together as much compostable material as possible; this should be a good mixture of tough and tender ingredients.

2 Add mixed materials to the compost container, watering it if dry. A dry heap will not compost.

Gathering material

Collect as much compostable material as possible, remembering that a mixture of soft and tough material is needed. Chop up large, tough items with a spade, shears or shredder. Very dry material must be soaked in water first.

Filling the container

If you have suitable stemmy materials, make a criss-cross layer about 15–30cm (6–12in) thick at the bottom of the container. This will encourage air to penetrate the heap.

Mix everything together first or add the different materials in layers of up to 20–25cm (8–10in) deep. The latter gives you an idea of how much of each material you have.

Grass mowings, which tend to settle into a dense, anaerobic mass, are best mixed with more open ingredients.

Adding moisture

The compost heap must have sufficient water to work. The ideal moisture content is difficult to describe; it is something you learn by experience. Weeds pulled shortly after rain when they are covered in a film of water will supply just the right amount of moisture. If necessary, water the ingredients as you make the heap.

Building up the heap

Spread the material right out to the edges of the container and firm it down gently. The idea is to allow a good supply of air in the heap, but not to have large gaps which would allow material to dry out. Larger, tougher items should be firmed down more than those that are soft and sappy. The best idea is to mix the two types.

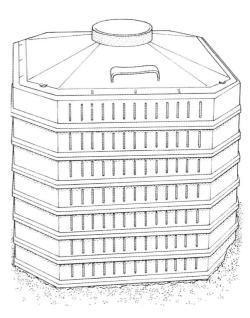

3 Gently firm down the contents of the container and cover with a square of old carpet or blanket if available. Replace the lid.

Cover the heap with a piece of hessian-backed carpet or other porous material and replace the lid.

If the container is now full, you have a number of options. You can either just leave it to compost or you can turn it once or twice. If there is still plenty of room in the container, however, you can fill it further by repeating the above process as more compost ingredients become available.

Once you have stopped adding new material to the heap, you can leave it alone until the compost is ready. Alternatively, remove everything from the container and examine what you find. If the heap was started many months before, you may find that the bottom layers are ready for use and can be removed. The remainder can be incorporated into a new heap to compost further.

4 When the container is full or you stop adding new material, simply leave the heap to compost. Turning will speed up the process.

If the heap looks too dry then add some more water or moist ingredients; if it looks too wet, add dry material. Mix everything together and refill the container. If you are using the container to start a new heap, cover this semi-decomposed heap with carpet or polythene.

When is compost ready?
Compost can be said to be ready as soon as the majority of the items you put into the container are no longer recognizable. Certain uses require a more mature product.

Starting a new heap
At some point you must decide to stop adding to this heap and start a new one. This could be when the container is full (though it may never fill completely as the ingredients reduce in volume as they decay or at the end of the season.

Worm composting 1

Worm composting is a very simple process, it takes up little space and it produces a quality end product.

Making worm compost is rather like keeping your own herd of animals to produce manure, but on an easily manageable scale! Compost worms are kept in a container and fed on kitchen waste and other compostable material. They convert this to worm manure, usually known as worm compost.

The benefits of worm composting

The benefits of worm composting are that it requires little space, time or effort, it is ideal for recycling kitchen waste, it is suitable even for patio gardens and balconies and it does not give off any unpleasant smells. It also produces a high-quality compost.

The worm's digestive system grinds and mixes food, concentrating plant nutrients and converting them into an available form. The worm casts produced (which make up the bulk of the compost) are also rich in humus and coated in a stabilizing gel, so they benefit the soil structure.

The effect of the worm compost on plants is thought to be due to the formation of plant growth hormones during the digestion process of the worm.

Garden or worm compost?

A worm compost system differs from a conventional compost system in that it works best with a regular supply of small quantities of material. A worm compost system cannot cope with any large quantities of material at one time.

Depending on your circumstances, you may rely on worm composting entirely for your garden or you may use a compost heap for the bulk of the material, with a worm system to supplement this and to cope with kitchen waste, especially during winter when it is particularly difficult to compost this waste in any other way.

Making worm compost

To set up a worm composting system you will need worms of the correct type, some bedding material, a supply of food and a container to keep everything in.

The worms

The worms used are known as "compost", "muck", "tiger" or "brandling" worms. Their official name is *Eisenia foetida*. They look similar to earthworms found in the soil but are darker red in colour, with a characteristic yellow banding. They live naturally in decaying organic matter such as compost and manure heaps rather than in the soil.

Sources of supply

The cheapest source of compost worms is a maturing compost heap, a pile of well-rotted manure or a working worm bin. The worms are easy to pick out by hand. If you look carefully, you may also find worm cocoons, tiny yellow lemon-shaped structures containing worm eggs. Collect these to add to your bin.

Compost worms can also be purchased by mail order, or bought in small tubs from fishing tackle shops. However, this latter source is more expensive.

Aim to start a worm compost bin with a minimum of 100 worms. The more there are at the outset, the quicker the system will get going and the less likely it is to fail. One of the most common causes of failure at the start is

Brandling worms

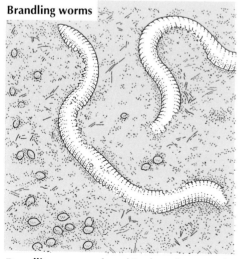

Brandling worms, found in decaying organic matter, are used to make worm compost. They have a distinctive dark red and yellow banding. Tiny yellow lemon-shaped egg cocoons produce several young worms.

giving the worms more food than they are capable of processing.

Providing the right conditions
Moisture A worm's skin must be moist for it to breathe, so the contents of a worm-composting container should be kept damp enough for the worms to thrive.

Air The container must be rainproof and well drained so that the contents do not become waterlogged and hence airless.

Warmth Worms are most productive at 18–25°C (64–77°F) and will continue to be active at 10–29°C (50–84°F). They will survive lower temperatures, but to keep the system active all year round the container should be insulated and/or kept in a warm place in winter. In summer it should not be allowed to get too hot.

Correct pH A pH of around 7 is ideal, although the worms will tolerate a pH of 5–9. Ground limestone can be used to raise the pH if the compost is too acid.

Worms will always move away from the light, so a worm-composting container should keep its contents dark.

Bedding material
When starting a worm compost bin you will need to provide bedding material for the worms to live in until they have produced some compost. Suitable materials include well-rotted compost, manure or leafmould. These can be mixed with equal parts of shredded paper or cardboard. A couple of handfuls of sand or ground limestone can be added to help the worms' digestion, though this is not essential. The bedding should be moist but not dripping wet.

Food for the worms
Compost worms can eat almost anything that will decompose. A varied diet is preferable, including items such as: annual weeds; vegetable peelings; tea leaves; coffee grounds; food scraps; crushed eggshells; citrus peel (not in large quantities); shredded newspaper; and half-rotted compost.

Materials that must be avoided are weeds with seeds, perennial weeds and diseased material. A worm compost system will not kill these.

Siting the container
A worm bin should be kept where it will not overheat in the sun nor get too cold in the winter. A frost-free shed or a sheltered, not too sunny spot in the garden is ideal. The bin may need to be insulated or moved into a warmer place in the winter.

If the bin is to be used primarily for kitchen waste, a position near the kitchen is sensible and the most convenient. As long as the worm bin is working well, there will be no smell.

Containers
Worm compost can be made in a variety of containers, home-made or purchased. The container should be seen as a home rather than a cage for the worms. If the conditions are right they will not try to escape.

To make a good worm bin, a container should keep moisture in and rain out; allow some air circulation; have good drainage; exclude light, flies and vermin; be insulated; and be mobile.

Worms like to feed near the surface. A container with a relatively large surface area will be able to deal with more food than one that is tall and thin.

Food for worms

Brandling worms can be fed almost anything that will decompose. They are particularly effective at processing vegetables scraps, tea leaves and other kitchen waste into worm compost.

Worm composting 2

Making worm compost

The best time to start a worm compost bin is in late spring and summer, when the warm temperatures activate the worms. A range of plastic, wooden and compressed paper bins are available, but it is more economical to make a worm bin by adapting a standard domestic plastic dustbin. Alternatively, recycle a wooden box or make one. Never use wood preservatives, as they may kill the worms. As there is no need for the container to have a base, unless you want to move it, you can use a conventional compost bin.

Using a plastic dustbin
You will need:
• A lidded plastic dustbin which has as wide a surface area as possible
• Coarse sand or gravel to fill the bin to a depth of approximately 7.5–10cm (3–4in)
• Boards, a circle of wood or some tough polythene to separate the compost and gravel
• Bedding material to make a layer about 7.5cm (3in) deep in the bin
• At least 100 worms
• One whole newspaper, soaked in water
• Approximately 1–2 litres (1¼–2½pt) chopped kitchen waste.

Feeding the worms

How much and how often you can feed a worm bin depends on how many worms there are, the temperature (and consequently how active they are) and the surface area of the worm bin. It is something that is learnt by experience. The most valuable hint is to err on the side of caution until you get to know the capacity of your worm bin. The worms are much more likely to be killed by overfeeding than by starvation.

A worm compost system can only process small quantities at any one time. The worms are unable to chew up kitchen scraps and feed instead on the soft bits that are beginning to decay. This is why a good working worm bin should never smell – because the worms continually eat the rotting material. If they are given more food than they can cope with, the material tends to putrefy, making the compost acid and smelly and the conditions unsuitable for the worms to function in. If large quantities are added, there is also the risk that it might heat up.

Collect a litre or so of suitable food; smaller quantities can of course be used. Chop up tough items such as raw potatoes, cabbage leaves, carrots and citrus peel. If you collect

Types of container

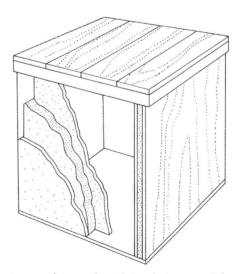

A wooden box with holes in the base makes a simple worm composting bin. Cover contents with wet newspaper or black polythene.

A worm box made with insulating material sandwiched between 2 sheets of oil-tempered hardboard can stand outside all year round.

vegetable waste in a plastic box or other similar container, put a newspaper in the bottom of the collection container to soak up excess moisture (this can also be added to the worm bin) and empty it regularly.

Put the food on the surface of the material in the container in a layer no more than 5cm (2in) deep. Do not cover the whole surface; leave an area for the worms to move to in case they do not like what you have given them. Cover the food with moist newspaper.

Alternatively, bury the food in small batches around the bin. Some people prefer this method as it puts the food out of sight, but it is then more difficult to gauge the rate of feeding.

When the previous addition of food has been well colonized by the worms, a new batch can be added, preferably in a different spot. Never add more food until you are sure that the worms will be able to cope with it.

An established working bin should be able to process the food waste from an average family of four. If necessary, start a second bin.

There is no need to worry about getting a "worm sitter" to look after your worms while you are on holiday. Feed them before you go in the usual way and they will survive quite happily until you return.

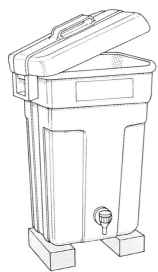

Commercially available plastic worm composting bins often have a tap to drain off liquid, which can be used to feed plants.

Problem solving

Check for the following common problems:

• **Worms congregating around the top of the bin** If there are only a few worms, do not worry. If there are large numbers, this indicates that the conditions within the bin are wrong.

• **Worm bin infested with tiny flies** These are likely to be fruit flies, introduced to the worm bin on the food scraps. Try to prevent the problem occurring by keeping the collecting container, the food in the bin and the bin itself covered. Check that conditions in the bin are suitable. Hoover up flies.

• **White thread-like worms in the bin** These are enchytraid worms, not young compost worms. Generally they do no harm and should be ignored, although a large numbers can indicate that conditions are too wet or acid.

• **Worm bin smells unpleasant** This indicates that the worms are not processing the food sufficiently quickly. Reduce feeding and check the pH, moisture content and temperature.

• **No worms to be found in the bin** The worms have either left (if this is possible) or died because conditions are not suitable. Check feeding, drainage and pH. Never use wood preservatives or insecticides on a worm bin.

• **Contents of the bin too wet** Check drainage holes are not blocked. Mix in shredded newspaper to soak up excess moisture. Avoid adding liquid when feeding worms.

If, after checking for all these symptoms, the worm compost is still not right, it may be that the contents of the bin is too acid. To remedy this, fork a handful of ground limestone or dolomite into the compost and reduce the quantity of citrus peel given. If a problem seems intractable, it may be worth emptying the worm bin and starting afresh.

When is it ready?

Over the months the worm bin will gradually fill up with rich compost, although the top layer will always consist of semi-rotted material as you continue to add food.

The speed at which the compost builds up depends very much on how much food is added, the number of worms present and the time of year. It is possible to make several full containers in a year, or you may find that you only make one annual batch which does not even fill the bin.

Worm composting 3

Extracting the compost

Compost can be removed from the bin when-ever it is available by simply digging some out with a trowel. This is fine if you only want a small quantity at once.

However, if you want to remove all the fin-ished compost from the bin it is best to do this in spring or summer so that you can get the bin going again quickly. If possible, keep the container full over the winter months because this gives the worms added insulation against the cold.

To empty the whole container, first remove the top layer, which will consist of food, half-rotted material and worms. Set this aside for starting the bin again.

Empty out the remaining contents, which should be finished compost, mixed with some worms. If you are not using the compost straight away, it can be stored in bags provided you spread it out to dry before bagging up.

There may still be a lot of worms mixed in with the finished compost. There is no need to remove them unless you want to use them to set up another worm compost bin or the com-post is to be used in pots and other containers, where their activities can disrupt the growing plants.

Extracting the worms

To separate the worms and compost, make use of the fact that worms will move away from heat, dryness and light. To do this, spread the compost out in a thin layer on a sheet of plas-tic or a similar material in a sunny spot. Place one or more folded-up wet newspapers on the compost to act as refuges for the worms. As the compost dries out in the sun, the worms will move into the cool, moist compost under the newspaper.

Alternatively, heap the compost up into small "molehills". Leave these for an hour or so and then scrape away the outer layer of each molehill, which should be worm-free. Repeat the process until the molehills are mostly worms.

Liquid feed

Some worm bins have a sump fitted with a tap to allow any liquid that has collected to be drained off and used as a liquid feed. The com-position of this liquid will obviously vary; use it diluted at a rate of at least 1 part liquid in 10 of water.

Wooden and other non-plastic bins are unlikely to produce excess liquid. The good-ness stays in the compost.

Types of container

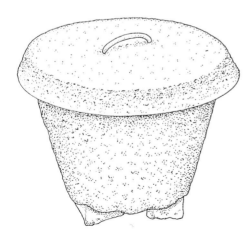

This worm compost container is made from recycled newspaper, waterproofed with bonding agents and resin.

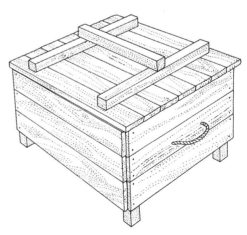

Alternatively, buy any of the commercially available wooden worm compost bins, such as this model.

Making worm compost

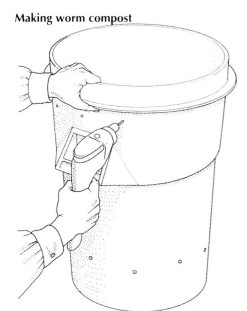

1 Drill holes 2.5cm (1in) and 7.5cm (3in) up from the base and around the top. Fill with 10cm (4in) of coarse gravel or stones.

2 Cover the gravel with boards or a perforated plastic sheet to separate gravel and compost.

3 Add 7.5cm (3in) or so of bedding material, along with the worms and some food. Cover with a wet newspaper.

4 Spread the finished compost out in the sun and the worms will collect under the wet newspapers.

Green manures 1

Green manuring is the practice of growing plants specifically to build and maintain soil fertility and structure. More usually thought of as a technique used by farmers, it can also be of great value in the organic garden.

Green manure crops are grown specifically for incorporating into the soil. They can look very attractive in the garden, making a positive contribution to its appearance.

Although green manuring can seem difficult to fit into the gardening year, it is well worth making the effort to include it.

The benefits of green manure
When soil is bare rain can wash out plant foods, damage the soil structure and, in extreme cases, cause erosion. A covering green manure crop breaks the force of the rain and allows it to penetrate the soil more easily. It also protects soil life from extremes of temperature and moisture. As the green manure plants grow, they take up plant foods that would otherwise be washed out of the soil. They are also useful in weed control because they help to smother weed growth.

Some green manures, such as grazing rye, are also particularly good at improving soil structure. Others – such as clover, which can take up nitrogen from the air – can add fertility to the soil.

How to green manure
Green manuring is simple. A suitable variety of green manure is sown, allowed to grow for a period of time, then, while still green, the crop is dug back into the soil. There the plants decompose, releasing nutrients for future plants to use.

The green manure plants are dug in when young and sappy, so there is no danger of nitrogen depletion.

Where to green manure
A green manure can be grown in any site in the garden where the ground is not required for other use for several weeks or more – for example, before a late-planted crop such as courgettes, or after the summer bedding has been cleared.

Green manures can also usefully be sown on recently cleared land to improve it before permanently planting it with other crops, or simply to keep it covered while planning what to do next. The performance of a green

Growing a green manure crop

1 Choose a green manure to suit the season. Either sow in rows or broadcast the seed over the ground. The plants will grow quickly to cover the soil.

2 When the land is needed, or when the green manure is beginning to mature (whichever comes first), dig the plants into the soil with a sharp spade.

manure crop can also give an indication of the fertility of the land. In the greenhouse, green manures can be used to help keep the border soil in good heart.

If you require a fine seedbed in the early spring, especially on heavy land, it is not advisable to grow a hardy green manure over the winter. This could mean digging in when the soil conditions are unsuitable.

One alternative is to grow a green manure variety that will be killed by the frost. Any residue left in the spring can be removed rather than incorporated.

Plants for green manuring
The plants used as green manures are usually agricultural crops, designed to cover the ground quickly and produce a good quantity of foliage. They can be annual, perennial or biennial, frost-hardy or tender, and between them they have a range of sowing times throughout the growing season. Some are for short-term use, reaching maturity in a few weeks, while others may be left to grow for a year or more.

Different green manures also vary in their soil requirements. Several green manures belong to the legume (pea and bean) family; these can take up nitrogen from the air. Those in the legume and brassica families are related to vegetable crops, an important factor to consider with crop rotations (see pages 46–9).

The majority of green manures will compete well with weeds.

LEGUMES
Alfalfa
(**Medicago sativa**)
Perennial
z 5
Sow from spring to mid-summer to grow for a few months, or, preferably, a year or two. Avoid acid and poorly drained soil. Once established, alfalfa can be cut two or three times a year. The foliage of this very deep-rooting plant is rich in plant foods. It can be cut for composting or for use as a fertility mulch.

Winter field beans
(**Vicia faba**)
Hardy annual
z 8
Sow from late summer to autumn to grow over winter. This plant is a good choice of green

3 Chop the foliage with the spade as you dig. If the crop is very bulky, make life easier by cutting it down and leaving it to wilt before digging.

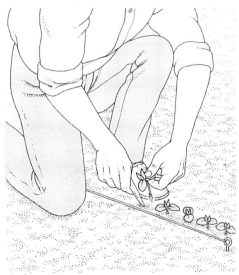

4 Allow up to a month or so depending on the season and plant maturity, for the green manure to decompose before any further sowing or planting.

Green manures 2

Crimson clover

Essex red clover

Fenugreek

Bitter lupin

manure for heavy land but do not use on waterlogged soil. It will not tolerate dry conditions, and it is not recommended as a weed suppressor.

Crimson clover
(*Trifolium incarnatum*)
Hardy annual
z 6
Sow early spring to late summer to grow for 2–3 months; it may survive the winter from a late sowing. Crimson clover prefers lighter soils. An added advantage of this type of green manure is that it produces an abundance of glorious crimson flowers which attract many insects especially bees.

Essex red clover
(*Trifolium pratense*)
Short-term perennial
z 6
Sow from mid-spring to late summer to grow for a period of several months to two years. Essex clover does best on good loam and does not like acid soils.

Fenugreek
(*Trigonella foenum graecum*)
Annual
z 8
Sow early spring to late summer to grow for 2–3 months. Small plants from a late sowing may survive the winter. Fenugreek does best

Alfalfa (see p. 81)

Winter field beans (see p. 81)

Buckwheat (see p. 84)

Alsike clover

on well-drained but moisture-retentive soil and it is one of the fastest-growing green manures. Although it is a legume, this type of green manure is unlikely to fix nitrogen in those areas where there is an absence of the appropriate strain of bacteria.

Bitter lupin
(*Lupinus angustifolius*)
Annual
z 4
Sow from early spring to early summer to grow for 2–3 months. This is one of the best green manures for light acid soil, and it is best sown in rows rather than broadcast. Bitter lupin is a poor weed suppressor.

Trefoil
(*Medicago lupulina*)
Biennial
z 5
Sow any time from early spring to late summer to grow for several months or up to a year or so. Trefoil prefers light, but not acid, soils. It will tolerate some shade and so is suitable for undersowing.

Winter tares
(*Vicia sativa*)
Hardy annual
z 5
Sow from early to late spring or mid- to late summer to grow for 2–3 months. Winter tares

Green manures 3

Mustard

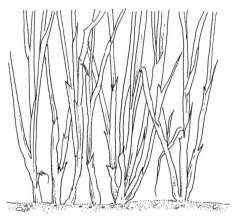

Grazing rye

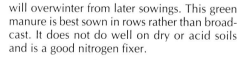

Phacelia

Winter tares (see p. 83)

will overwinter from later sowings. This green manure is best sown in rows rather than broadcast. It does not do well on dry or acid soils and is a good nitrogen fixer.

NON-LEGUMES
Buckwheat
(***Fagopyrum esculentum***)
Annual
z 3
Sow from spring to late summer to grow for 2–3 months. This is an attractive, frost-tender plant that will tolerate poor soils. Buckwheat is quick to grow, producing pink flowers that attract several types of insects, and hoverflies especially.

Mustard
(***Sinapis alba***)
Annual
z 6
Sow from spring to late summer to grow for up to eight weeks. It will not tolerate poor soil and goes to seed quickly in warm, dry weather. Fast-growing but susceptible to clubroot.

Phacelia
(***Phacelia tanacetifolia***)
Annual
z 6
Sow from early spring to late summer to grow for up to two months, or overwinter from a late sowing. It will survive a reasonable winter if

THE GREEN MANURING PROCESS

Sowing

First decide when you want to sow the green manure and when you will want to use the ground again. Then choose a suitable variety to suit the period, the soil type and your crop rotation where appropriate.

There is no need to feed the soil before sowing, although it will help the growth of a green manure where fertility is low.

Sow the green manure seed in rows or broadcast over the ground. The former method is preferable when conditions are dry, or where birds are likely to take the seed. Broadcasting is quicker and gives a more even cover but tends to use up more seed.

Digging in

Leave the green manure to grow until a few weeks before you want to use the ground again, or until the plants are beginning to mature, whichever comes first. Green manure foliage must be young and sappy when it is dug into the ground. For mustard, buckwheat, crimson clover, lupin, fenugreek, phacelia, winter tares and field beans, this means at or before flowering. If the plants go past this stage, remove them to the compost heap rather than digging them in.

Grazing rye should be dug in when you can feel the flower stem forming in the base of the plant. If it reaches this stage before you are ready to dig it in, simply cut the foliage down and leave it on the ground.

Alfalfa, clover and trefoil can be dug in whenever the foliage is fresh green and growing. If they are to be grown for more than one season, cut them down when flowering to encourage fresh new growth.

To dig in, take a sharp spade and turn the green manure into the top 15–20cm (6–8in) of soil, chopping the plants with the spade as you go. If there is a great bulk of foliage, this process may have to be repeated after a day or two. Alternatively, cut down the foliage and allow to wilt before digging in.

Alternatives to digging

Annual green manures can also be hoed, cut or mowed down, the foliage being left on the surface as a mulch.

Perennial green manures can be covered with a light-excluding mulch which can either be planted through or removed once the green manure is dead.

Sowing/planting after a green manure

If the soil is warm and the plants young and chopped, the land should be ready for use 2–3 weeks after incorporating the green manure. If the plant material is rather tough, and/or the soil is cold, leave 3–4 weeks. A fine tilth may take slightly longer to achieve.

Undersowing a green manure

Trefoil, a green manure that will tolerate some shade, can be sown under tall crops such as sweetcorn and Brussels sprouts. It will grow slowly until the crop is removed, when it will grow away strongly. This technique, known as undersowing, is useful for fitting a green manure into a tight rotation.

Sow the trefoil seed when the crop plants are 5–7.5cm (2–3in) high.

the plants are small and will tolerate most soils. It produces a mass of lavender blue flowers, loved by bees and hoverflies.

Grazing rye
(*Secale cereale*)
Hardy annual
z 5
Sow from late summer to late autumn to overwinter. Grazing rye is a cereal rye, not rye grass. It is one of the best green manures for overwintering, producing a mass of weed-suppressing foliage even in cold weather. Its extensive root system is very beneficial to soil structure. Grazing rye is not recommended for use where it would be followed by a direct-sown, small-seeded crop as it can inhibit germination.

Liquid feeds

Liquid feeds provide nutrients in a form that is readily available to plants. They do not really comply with the organic principal of feeding the soil-living creatures, but there are times when the use of a liquid feed is necessary. Vigorous, hungry plants growing in a restricted environment such as a pot, tub or growing bag, for example, will need a liquid feed to keep them adequately supplied with nutrients.

In the open garden liquid feeds may be used where the soil is poor, or applied as a foliar spray where soil conditions or root damage prevent sufficient uptake of nutrients by a plant's roots.

Liquid feeds are not an alternative to a good, rich potting mix or a regime of long-term soil improvement.

Using liquid feeds

Liquid feeds can be applied to the soil or to plant foliage (foliar feeding). Plants can take up more through the soil but a foliar application can be useful when root action is restricted.

Always dilute liquid feeds as instructed; an overdose can inhibit growth. A liquid of unknown analysis, such as that collected from a worm compost bin, should be used in a very diluted form (see page 78).

Liquid feeds should be applied to moist potting compost or soil. When feeding plants in the soil, it is a good idea to sink a plant pot into the ground near each plant and feed into this. This takes the liquid down into the soil, and also helps you to measure how much each plant is getting.

The rate of use of liquid feeds will vary with the feed, the fertility of the potting compost or soil, the size of the pot, the type of plant, its stage of growth and the growing conditions. A vigorous tomato plant in full fruit production will, for instance, require a great deal more feeding than a few bedding plants planted in a large tub.

Sources

Proprietary organic liquid feeds are available – fish emulsion, plant extracts and liquid animal manures, for example. Where possible, purchase only those carrying a recognized organic symbol.

It is very simple to make your own liquid feeds using easily available ingredients.

Home-made liquid feeds

Comfrey leaves make a liquid high in potash, with reasonable levels of nitrogen and phosphate. It is particularly good for greedy fruiting plants such as tomatoes and peppers, but can also be used more generally. Its nitrogen levels may be slightly low for plants growing in a very restricted environment, such as a hanging basket, which need a lot of feeding.

Using liquid feed

1 To liquid feed a plant, sink a plant pot in the soil next to it.

2 Pour the liquid feed into this to help it to penetrate down to the plant roots.

Ingredients

Nettle leaves (*Urtica dioica* z 3) make a good general liquid feed, a little low on phosphate, but supplying magnesium, sulphur and iron. Nettles collected in spring contain the highest levels of nitrogen, potash and phosphate. The main disadvantage of this product is its smell. Both comfrey and nettle liquids, being slightly alkaline, are not recommended for use on acid-loving plants.

Liquid feeds can also be made from various types of animal manures. Their analysis varies depending on the manure. Sheep manure is said to make the best, but cow, horse or goat is also suitable.

Equipment

Liquid feeds can be made by steeping comfrey leaves, nettle leaves or animal manure in water.

You will need: a plastic container of any size, with a lid; comfrey leaves – 3kg (6⅝lb) per 45 litres (12gal) water or nettle leaves – 1kg (2¼lb) per 10 litres (2¾gal) water, or animal manure – 4.5 litres (1⅛gal) tied in a sack per 54.5 litres (14⅔gal) water. A tap, such as that on a water butt, is useful but not essential.

Procedure

Place the container in a site where the smell it may produce will not cause a nuisance. Fill the container with ingredients as listed above and replace the lid. The sack of manure can be suspended on a length of rope. Leave for two weeks for nettle and manure liquids, four weeks for comfrey liquid.

Comfrey and manure liquids are used without further dilution. Nettle liquid should be diluted with 10 parts water. Any residue from these liquids can be added to a compost heap.

Comfrey concentrate

Comfrey leaves can also be used to make a concentrated liquid feed (see pages 88–9). This can be stored for a longer period than the dilute form and it does not need such a large container. Also, it does not smell so much.

Seaweed extract

Seaweed extract is a plant growth stimulant rather than a supplier of plant foods. It contains trace elements and other compounds which promote healthy growth. It has been shown to have remarkable effects on plant growth and pest and disease resistance, though where growing conditions are good it seems to have little effect.

Seaweed extract does not contain the major plant foods and seaweed products on the market sold as liquid feeds, rather than as a plant stimulant, are likely to have had their nutrient value boosted with chemical fertilizers.

Making liquid feed

1 Tie the manure up in a sack and suspend it in a barrel of water.

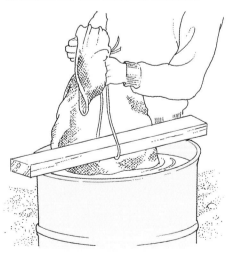

2 After a couple of weeks the liquid will be ready to use to feed plants.

Comfrey

Russian comfrey (*Symphytum* x *uplandicum*) z 5

Russian comfrey is a vigorous, deep-rooted, herbaceous perennial. It is grown to provide a supply of cut foliage rich in plant foods, especially potash. Comfrey leaves can be added to a compost heap as an activator, applied to the soil around plants to provide nutrients and used to make a liquid feed.

Bocking 14 is the variety of Russian comfrey most commonly grown for garden use. It has large, hairy leaves and purple, tubular flowers produced on tall stems. Plants may reach a height and spread of up to 1m (3¼ft). Its substantial tap root can reach 3m (10ft) underground. This crop can be harvested up to five times during the growing season and it will still grow strongly again.

Growing comfrey

Bocking 14 does not set seed and is propagated by offsets or root cuttings. Plants and cuttings may be purchased during the growing season; they are not sold when the plants are dormant. For an average garden, start with around six plants.

Choose a permanent site for your comfrey bed, preferably in full sun. It is not advisable to move comfrey too often as every bit of root left in the ground will regrow.

Planting

Spring is the best time for planting but any time during the growing season will do. Before planting, remove all perennial weeds and feed the soil well with manure or nitrogen-rich fertilizer. Plant the comfrey at a spacing of 60–100cm (2–3½ft) each way. Offsets should be planted with the growing point just below the surface of the soil and root cuttings approximately 5cm (2in) deep.

Maintenance

Mulch comfrey with animal manure every couple of years, or feed it with a pelleted poultry manure and mulch with leafmould. In the first year, remove the flower stems but do not harvest the foliage.

Cutting comfrey

Once they are established, comfrey plants can be cut four or five times a season. They will yield approximately 2kg (4½lb) per plant at each cutting.

Cut approximately 5cm (2in) above soil level when the foliage is around 60cm (2ft) high, before the flower stems start to show. It is advisable to wear garden gloves when handling comfrey as in some cases the hairy leaves can irritate the skin.

To allow sufficient regrowth before the winter, the last cut should take place no later than early autumn.

Using comfrey

Comfrey leaves, rich in nitrogen and low in fibre, decay quickly to a black liquid. They have a variety of uses.

Cultivating comfrey

Russian comfrey is a vigorous, deep-rooted herbaceous perennial with purple flowers. Its leaves are rich in nitrogen and potassium.

Russian comfrey is propagated vegetatively using offsets or root cuttings. Offsets are planted with the tip just below the soil surface.

COMFREY CONCENTRATE

Comfrey leaves can be used to make a concentrated liquid and a dilute form (see page 87). The concentrate can be stored for longer than the dilute form and does not smell so strongly. Use it diluted with 10–20 parts water. A 45 litres (10gal) container should produce about 2.5 litres (4½pt) of liquid, but smaller quantities can be made in a large plastic drinks bottle.

Analysis of comfrey concentrate Nitrogen (N) 79mg/litre; Phosphorus (P) 26.4mg/litre; Potassium (K) 205mg/litre.

Requirements A plastic container such as a water butt with a cover; some bricks; comfrey leaves; a collection vessel, minimum size about 1 litre (1¾pt). If making the liquid outdoors, use a vessel with a narrow neck to keep the rain out.

Procedure Drill a hole about 6mm (¼in) in diameter in the bottom of the container. Put the container on a pile of bricks and pack in the comfrey leaves tightly. Replace the lid and put the collection vessel under the hole. Alternatively, cut the bottom off a plastic bottle and stuff it full of comfrey leaves. Remove the cap and invert the bottle in a container. After 2–3 weeks a dark liquid will start to drip from the container, and this may continue for a week or more.

Store the liquid in a cool dark place. Do not seal tightly as it can ferment in warm weather. Add the residue – the tougher fibres in the leaves – to the compost heap.

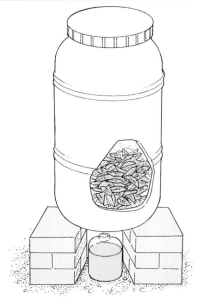

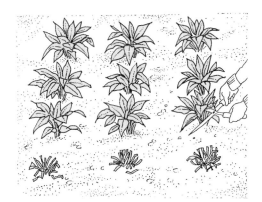

Comfrey plants can be cut several times during the growing season. The leaves are used as a mulch or to make a liquid feed.

• As a compost activator – mix comfrey leaves with more fibrous compost ingredients to add goodness and start the composting process.
• For a liquid feed – comfrey leaves make a rich liquid feed, suitable for tomatoes.
• As a fertility mulch – use comfrey leaves to mulch-hungry feeders such as blackcurrants, potatoes and tomatoes. Do not use on acid-loving plants.
• To feed potatoes – place a layer of comfrey leaves 2.5–5cm (1–2in) deep in the bottom of a potato trench and cover the leaves with soil before planting potatoes.
• As a growing media ingredient – when they are mixed with 2–3 year-old leafmould, comfrey leaves decay to form comfrey leafmould (see page 57), which makes an excellent base for growing media (see pages 160–5).

Introduction

The organic approach

The healthy growth of plants may be disrupted by a pest or disease attack, a nutrient deficiency or a disorder caused by climatic or environmental conditions.

The organic approach to coping with plant problems should be a long-term one, involving a "whole-garden strategy". The easiest way of dealing with a problem, after all, is to prevent it occurring in the first place.

There are also more instant techniques available which can be used to deal with problems as they arise; these should be used in conjunction with the longer-term strategy. For some problems, of course, there is no cure.

If you follow the steps below, the majority of plants will remain hale and hearty with little further attention. There will, unfortunately, be times when the system fails and more specific action is required.

Preventing problems

• **Encourage nature** (see pages 8–17)
The aim in an organic garden is not to eliminate pests and diseases entirely but to keep them at a level where they do little or no harm, creating an environment, both above and below ground, that encourages healthy plant growth and where beneficial creatures thrive while pests and diseases are actively discouraged.

The first step in an organic pest and disease management strategy is to create a garden environment in which the natural predators and parasites of pests and diseases thrive. The work of these creatures – ladybirds, beetles, bluetits and many more – often goes unrecognized, but without it we would soon be overrun. They cannot always achieve the level of control that we would like so other measures may also be required, but they should always be given a chance to do their bit.

Encourage predators and parasites by providing them with suitable food, shelter and breeding sites and, of course, not killing them with harmful sprays.

• **Know your friends** (see pages 18–23)
Having encouraged beneficial creatures into the garden it is important to recognize them so that they are not killed in the mistaken belief that they are pests. Most gardeners are familiar

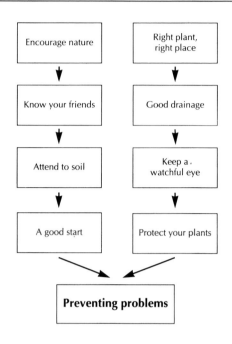

Preventing problems

In order to prevent problems happening in the first place, adopt the "whole-garden strategy". This entails selecting vigorous plants and growing them in the right place, making sure your soil is healthy, and always keeping an eye out so that you can act quickly if there is a problem.

with the distinctive markings of the adult ladybird, for example, and know it for a friend – yet they might easily take the ladybird larva for a pest instead.

• **Attend to the soil** (see pages 160–1)
Build up a healthy, well-structured soil in order to provide plants with a balanced diet and a regular water supply. Such plants will be less susceptible to attack, and more able to resist problems that do arise. The key to building a healthy soil is the addition of organic matter in the form of compost, animal manures and other materials.

A good start

Give plants a good start in life. Buy the best you can, sow and plant correctly, and in the right conditions. Poor planting can result in reduced growth and poor performance throughout the life of a plant.

• Right plant, right place (see page 32)
Get to know your soil type and the prevailing conditions in your garden and then choose plants to suit them. This is a much more successful strategy than buying the plants first and then trying to keep them growing in conditions that are less than appropriate.

Grow resistant varieties (see page 92) where regular problems occur, especially if there is no other way of dealing with the pest or disease.

• Good gardening (see pages 46–9 and 94–5)
Use crop rotation and other good gardening techniques to keep plants growing steadily and to avoid pest and disease build-up.

• Keep a watchful eye
Take a regular walk around your garden and get to know what is going on. Keep an eye out for pests and diseases and nip problems in the bud before they have a chance to get out of hand.

Protect your plants (see pages 106–8)
Use protective barriers, traps and scaring devices to keep pests and diseases at bay.

What to do when problems arise
• Identify the cause
A lot of time and energy can be wasted in trying to control a problem if it has not been correctly identified in the first place. Do not jump to conclusions: remember that poor growing conditions can cause as much damage as pests and diseases and that not every creepy-crawly is a pest – indeed, it could well be a friend.

The A-Z directory (see pages 110–41) will help with the identification of pests, diseases, disorders and deficiencies of vegetables, fruit, ornamentals and lawns.

• Find out more (see pages 96–103)
Having identified the cause of a problem, find out more about it. Knowing the habits of a pest or disease, and the underlying causes of a disorder or deficiency, can make planning a control strategy easier and more successful. Knowing more also helps you to assess the severity of a problem, so you know whether instant action is or is not necessary.

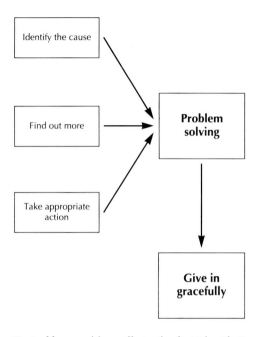

To tackle a problem efficiently, first identify it is and then find out more about it. When you have all the relevant facts at your fingertips, take the appropriate action to solve it. There are times, however, when a solution cannot be found, in which case it is best to give in gracefully and try and avoid future problems.

• Action options (see pages 104–9)
There is a range of options available for dealing with specific problems associated with specific plants. There are many control methods: action could involve removing the culprits by hand, altering a care regime, waiting for natural controls to take over, trapping, introducing a biological control agent or, if essential, using a pesticide spray.

Give in gracefully
Not every problem has a solution, and there are times when the best option is to give in gracefully, while planning for success in future seasons.

Prevention is better than cure
Having tried to deal with a problem, you will have discovered that prevention is easier, and much more effective, than cure.

Preventing problems 1

Choosing plants

Give a plant a good start and it will grow health-ily and strongly and be more likely to withstand most problems. Choose plants and cultivars that are suited to your garden conditions. These will thrive where others might fail to prosper: a rose or honeysuckle planted in poor, dry soil up against a house may suffer from mildew; an apple tree next to a pond is likely to be prone to scab; and hostas may suffer from slug damage if planted in a dark, wet corner whereas a fern will thrive. Fruit types and varieties can be chosen to suit many different locations, and there are even some vegetables that will grow in the shade. Always think about the situation in which a plant is to grow (soil type, shade or sun, expo-sure and aspect) before buying or planting.

Resistant cultivars

Plants vary in their susceptibility to pests and diseases and those that show some resistance are a valuable means of preventing a specific, recurring problem such as blackspot on roses, or one that has no cure such as cucumber mosaic virus. Use resistant cultivars as part of an overall pest and disease management strat-egy; they are less susceptible but not altogeth-er immune to attack. Although examples of disease resistant cultivars and varieties are given below, the range changes all the times so con-sult catalogues for an up-to-date selection.

Plants and planting material

Buy the healthiest plants available. Young, vig-orous plants will establish more quickly than those that are old and pot-bound. Bare-root plants should have a good fibrous root system. While bedding plants in flower may look more attractive, those not yet in flower are in fact a better buy because the plants will be able to put

---

RESISTANT CULTIVARS

FRUIT

Apple *Scab:* 'Discovery', 'Sunset', 'Ashmead's Kernel'; *powdery mildew:* 'Sunset', 'Blenheim Orange'; *canker:* 'Newton's Wonder'
Blackcurrant *Powdery mildew:* 'Ben Sarek', 'Ben Nevis'
Gooseberry *American gooseberry mildew:* 'Invicta', 'Greenfinch'
Pear *Scab:* 'Jargonelle', 'Dr Jules Guyot'
Raspberry *Spur and cane blight:* 'Malling Admiral'; *aphids:* 'Malling Joy', 'Leo', 'Glen Moy'; *viruses:* 'Malling Promise', 'Malling Jewel'
Strawberry *Botrytis:* 'Red Gauntlet'; *powdery mildew:* 'Red Gauntlet', 'Cambridge Favourite'; *ver-ticillium wilt/red core:* 'Rhapsody', 'Troubadour'

VEGETABLES

Brussels sprout *Powdery mildew:* 'Saxon', 'Rampart'; *ringspot:* 'Cor Valiant', 'Rampart'; *white blister:* 'Saxon'
Calabrese (B) *Club root:* 'Harmony'; *downy mildew:* 'Harmony', 'China Pride'
Carrot *Carrot root fly:* 'Flyaway'
Chinese cabbage *Club root:* 'Trixie'; *downy mildew:* 'Emperor'; *virus:* various
Corn salad *Mildew:* 'Jade'
Courgette/marrow *Cucumber mosaic virus:* 'Supremo', 'Defender', 'Bush Champion', 'Petita', 'Burpee Hybrid' (cucumbers); 'Tiger Cross' (mar-row); *downy and powdery mildews:* 'Slice King', 'Burpless', 'Tasty Green'

Kale *Club root:* 'Tall Green Curled'
Leek *Rust:* 'Autumn Mammoth', 'Verina'
Lettuce *Botrytis:* 'Avondefiance'; *downy mildew:* 'Dynasty', 'Musette', 'Avondefiance'; *root aphid:* 'Lakeland', 'Avondefiance', 'Little Gem'; *virus:* various
Onion *Downy mildew/white rot:* 'Norstar'
Parsnip *Canker:* 'Tender and True', 'Cobham Improved Marrow'
Pea *Wilt:* 'Hurst Green Shaft', 'Sugar Snap', 'Kelvedon Wonder'; *powdery mildew:* 'Kodiak', 'Oregon', 'Sugar Pod'
Potato See page 128
Spinach *Downy mildew:* 'Bergola'
Swede *Club root/powdery mildew:* 'Marian'
Tomato *Tobacco mosaic virus:* 'Estrella', 'Shirley', 'Dombito', 'Pixie'; *verticillium wilt:* 'Estrella', 'Pixie'; *fusarium wilt:* 'Estrella', 'Shirley', 'Pixie'; *green back:* 'Estrella', 'Shirley'.

ORNAMENTALS

Antirrhinum *Rust:* 'Rust Resistant Mixed', 'Coronette Mixed'
Aster *Wilt:* 'Carousel Mixed', 'Starlight Rose'; *powdery mildew:* various
Hollyhock *Rust:* various
Pyracantha *Scab:* various
Rose *Blackspot:* 'Alec's Red', 'Elina', 'Remember Me', 'Anne Harkness'; *powdery mildew:* various; *rust:* 'Sweet Magic', 'Maigold', 'Joseph's Coat', 'Wedding Day'

Interplanting

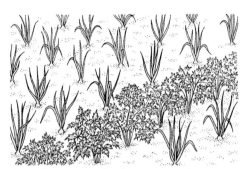

Alternate rows of cabbages and French beans will help to reduce aphid and rootfly damage. Plant out when both types of plant are the same size.

Grow four rows of onions to one of carrots to repel carrot root fly. However, the effect lasts only while the onion leaves are growing.

all their energy into settling in before flowering. Bulbs should be firm and show no sign of mould. Always buy certified virus-free seed potatoes, and fruit trees and bushes where available.

Inspect all new plants for pests and disease, especially those destined for the greenhouse, as this is the way that many greenhouse problems are brought in. Keep plants in quarantine for a while if you are unsure.

Seeds should be as fresh as possible. Old seed may produce plants lacking in vigour; the faster a seedling grows away, the less it is at risk. Older seed may of course be used, but it may need extra care.

Sowing and planting (see page 166–7)
The care with which plants are sown and planted has a great effect on their future performance.

Timing to avoid pests
Sowing times can be adjusted in order to avoid the periods when certain pests and diseases are most active.

The pea moth lays its eggs on pea flowers in early to mid-summer. Peas sown early (late winter) and late (late spring) should avoid damage from this pest as they will flower outside its period of activity. The carrot root fly lays its eggs around seedling carrots in late spring to early summer. Sow in early to mid-summer to avoid this generation of the pest.

Powdery mildews are worse when the soil is dry. Sow peas early and swedes and turnips late

so they are not trying to grow during the height of the summer.

Interplanting for pest control
A monoculture – that is to say, rows and rows of the same plant grown together – is paradise for a pest or disease, because once it has discovered one suitable host plant, every way it moves it will encounter another one equally suitable. Monoculture does not encourage the good mixed population of creatures that is desirable in an organic garden. It is generally a good idea to mix plants up as much as possible as long as individual crops do not suffer as a result of this.

Eliminate some of the division between fruit, flower and vegetable garden. Vegetables can look good in an ornamental border; lettuce, beetroot, carrots, rhubarb, chard and courgettes, for example, all have very attractive foliage. Interspersed among unrelated ornamentals, they are less likely to be discovered by any pests or diseases.

This method of growing can require more attention – making sure that plants do not overwhelm each other and that there are spare plants to fill in the gaps where a vegetable has been harvested, for example – but it can be fun and is a way of growing both flowers and crops in a small garden. Fruit trees and bushes are also attractive, and a few flowers in the vegetable garden can liven up a plot while also attracting beneficial insects that can help with pest control.

Preventing problems 2

Breaking the cycle
A pest such as cabbage mealy aphid or white-fly or a disease such as leek rust can become established where there are suitable host plants all year round. To break the cycle of reinfection, remove all susceptible plants at one time of the year before planting out more.

For example, in early spring, dig up all over-wintered Brussels sprouts, broccoli and other related plants. Bury them in a trench about 30cm (1ft) deep, chopping up tough stems with a sharp spade. This will get rid of the mealy aphids and whitefly that winter on these plants. Wait a week or two before planting out more brassicas, making sure of course that these are pest-free.

Rotation (see pages 46-9)
As a general rule, never follow a plant with another of the same type.

Fruit trees and roses are prone to replant disorders, known as rose sickness in the case of the latter. If an apple tree is planted where an old one has recently been removed, it may grow poorly or even die. Try replacing the soil or adding good quantities of organic matter or, better still, plant it on a new site altogether.

A watchful eye
All diseased plant material should be removed as soon as it is noticed. Where appropriate, put it straight into a plastic bag so that disease spores are not wafted around.

Pests such as aphids, slugs and caterpillars are mostly easy to spot and can be removed by hand. If you keep a close eye on your garden, you should be able to identify and curtail problems before they get out of hand.

Water and watering (see page 167)
Too much or not enough water can damage plant growth, as can an irregular, fluctuating supply. A poorly drained soil can encourage root problems such as *Phytophthora* and violet root rot and red core in strawberries, but growing on raised beds can help. If the problem is severe, installing drains or planting a bog garden to take advantage of the moisture may be the only answers.

Wilting is an obvious sign of water shortage, but other side-effects can occur before this.

Powdery mildews and potato scab, for example, are much more severe where plants are short of water. The answer is to improve the water-holding capacity of the soil by adding organic matter (see pages 50–7). You can also time the sowing of particular vegetables to avoid the dry months.

Most established plants in the open garden should not need regular watering. However, if there is a period of very dry weather, they will need extra water to grow well.

Summer plants in a greenhouse are likely to need regular and copious watering, especially those in growing bags. Vigorous fruiting plants such as tomatoes should never be allowed to go short, even for a brief period, otherwise they may get blossom end rot.

Winter digging
While winter digging is not good for soil structure and fertility, it has its uses. For example, winter digging will expose pests such as root fly, millipedes and slugs, which spend the winter in the soil, to predators such as birds.

Soil pH (see pages 34–5)
Altering the pH of a soil can help in the control of certain diseases that thrive in particularly acid or alkaline conditions. For instance, raising the pH of an acid soil can help reduce the level of club root infection. Potato scab, on the other hand, thrives in more alkaline conditions, so increasing the acidity of the soil by adding organic matter such as grass mowings is one means of reducing the effects of this disease.

Plants that have a particular requirement for an acid or alkaline soil may grow very poorly and show severe mineral deficiencies where the pH is not appropriate. It is possible to alter the soil pH if it is close to the required conditions, but if the pH of your soil is very different, select plants that are suited to your soil and grow any acid- or alkaline-loving plants in isolated pots filled with the required growing media.

Good airflow around plants
Diseases thrive in the moist air around overcrowded plants. Encourage a good airflow by thinning seedlings, using the correct spacing, and pruning (see pages 168-9). Good ventilation is particularly important in a greenhouse, even during cold weather (see pages 184–5).

COMPANION PLANTING (see page 27)

Companion planting is the growing of specific combinations of plants to the benefit of one or both. While there is evidence to show that plants can have an effect on each other, there is little practical advice as to how to make specific combinations work. Onions can protect carrots from the carrot root fly, but only when there are four rows of onions to one row of carrots. The effect only lasts as long as the onion leaves are growing; when they stop and the bulbs start to form the carrots are again at risk.

One combination that has been studied is that of brassicas interplanted in alternate rows with an unrelated crop such as dwarf beans. The level of mealy aphid and cabbage root fly damage is significantly reduced, the mixture of plants confusing the pests. But for this to work, the plants must be a similar size when young and fill the gaps between plants and rows as quickly as possible. This means raising both crops in pots and planting them out when they are the same size. Sow a fairly compact cultivar of cabbage about three weeks before the beans. Make sure that the beans have grown at least their first true leaves before transplanting both in alternate rows 25cm (10in) apart.

The whitefly cycle

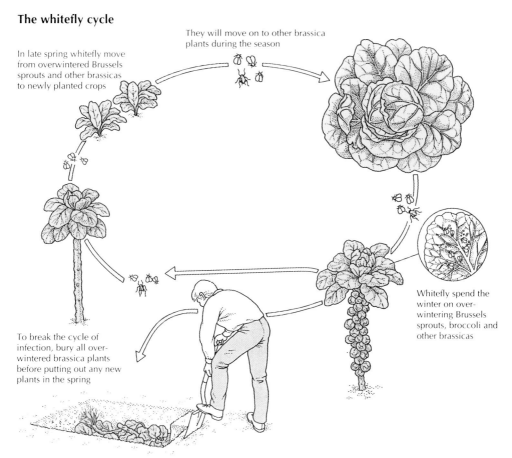

They will move on to other brassica plants during the season

In late spring whitefly move from overwintered Brussels sprouts and other brassicas to newly planted crops

Whitefly spend the winter on over-wintering Brussels sprouts, broccoli and other brassicas

To break the cycle of infection, bury all over-wintered brassica plants before putting out any new plants in the spring

Understanding the problem 1

PESTS

Despite our best endeavours, plants may suffer from a pest, disease or virus. Adverse environmental conditions and shortages of plant foods, known as physiological disorders and mineral deficiencies respectively, can also cause unwanted symptoms.

"Pest" is the term given to any creature that affects a plant in a way we do not approve of. But a creature that is a pest in one situation may not be seen as such in another, for the aim in organic gardening is to keep pests at a manageable level (that is to say, at a level where they are no longer regarded as a pest) rather than to eradicate them completely.

Whatever the problem, it is important to identify the cause correctly. Similar symptoms can have very different causes. For example, the red blisters that appear on the leaves of red and white currants in early summer are caused by a pest, known as the redcurrant blister aphid. These pale yellow aphids can be seen initially on the underside of affected leaves, but symptoms will remain after they have moved on. Similar red blisters on peach leaves in the spring, on the other hand, are caused by a disease – peach leaf curl.

Having identified the cause of a problem, now find out more about it: whether the problem is a pest or disease, it is useful to know when it first appears, when it leaves, how it spreads, the range of plants it will attack, how and where it survives the winter and what level of infestation or infection can be tolerated.

This information will help in planning a control strategy. Some pests and diseases, for example, are devastating and may spread to many plants in the garden; others may not be nearly as bad as they look and may restrict their activities to a few specific plants. In the case of mineral deficiency, knowing the underlying cause can help correct the problem in the long term.

Creatures that can be pests

Many different creatures such as birds, mammals, insects, molluscs, mites and eelworms can act as pests. They vary considerably in habits, habitats, lifecycles and appearance.

Some pests (slugs, for example) look more or less the same from birth to death – they just get larger. Others, insects in particular, go through several very different stages of growth, so it is not always obvious that the different stages are related. They may have different common names and the different stages are not all necessarily capable of causing damage. For example, the leatherjacket is a garden pest, but its adult form, the crane fly (daddy-longlegs) does not harm plants. On the other hand, both vine weevil larvae and adults are pests.

Plant hosts

Some pests, such as slugs and certain aphids, attack many plants. Others, such as the lily beetle and potato eelworm, restrict their activities to one or a few plants. Successive generations may stay on the same plant or move to more of the same species or to different plants. The move may be governed by the growth stage of the pest or the time of year.

Although we tend only to notice pests when they are damaging our garden plants, they may of course also be living on other garden plants, weeds and wild plants. These colonies can act

Peach leaf curl

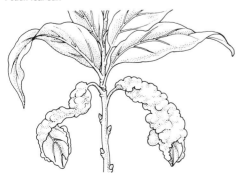

Currant blister aphid

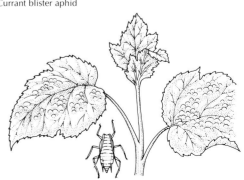

as a useful food reserve for beneficial creatures, keeping their numbers up when other food supplies have been removed.

Spread and survival
Pests may walk, crawl or fly to find another host plant; others are transported in infected soil and in or on plants. Some come from a great distance, blown on wind, transported in soil on our footwear or on purchased plants.

In the absence of a suitable host, some pests will leave the garden; others, such as the potato cyst eelworm, can survive in the form of tough "resting bodies" which can live for 20 years in the soil waiting for a suitable host plant.

Pests may survive the winter on plants, in the soil, in greenhouse staging and many other nooks and crannies, indoors and out.

Periods of activity
Some pests are active all year, except in cold weather. Others are active in certain seasons or during the "pest" stage of their life cycle.

Symptoms and identification
If the pest is visible, identification is relatively easy – but remember that the presence of a creature does not mean that it is necessarily the guilty party. Often, symptoms are all we have to go on because the pest is too small to see or it has already moved on.

Holes in foliage, stems or roots, or plants disappearing completely, are caused by pests with biting or rasping mouth parts: caterpillars, beetles, earwigs, fly maggots, sawfly larvae, midge larvae, woodlice, slugs and snails, rabbits and other mammals. Curled leaves and

---

THE BLACK BEAN APHID (BLACKFLY)

In late spring, female blackfly appear on the shoots of young broad beans. They feed and produce wingless females. If left unchecked, they spread down the stem and on to pods. The plant matures, producing less nutritious sap. This triggers the production of aphids with wings, which move on to other beans or to their summer hosts, French and runner beans, dahlias, poppies and nasturtiums. The process is repeated.

Blackfly will continue to colonize these plants throughout the summer. In early autumn, when the food supply is finished, aphids, known as "autumn migrants", are produced. These fly off to overwintering plants such as *Euonymus europaeus*, *Philadelphus* and *Viburnum opulus*. At the same time, winged males are born. These fly to the overwintering plants to mate with the females, who then lay eggs on stems and winter buds. The shiny black eggs will survive the winter.

In the spring, the eggs hatch. The young, wingless aphids feed and multiply until late spring, when winged offspring are produced. These fly to broad bean plants to repeat the cycle.

---

distorted growth are caused by creatures that feed on plant sap, either by piercing the plant tissue (for example aphids, capsid bugs, leaf hoppers, mites, whitefly, scale insects) or by living within the plant (eelworms), for instance.

Crane fly/leatherjacket

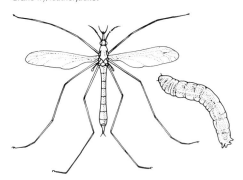

Vine weevil

Understanding the problem 2

DISEASES
Disease symptoms are caused by fungi, bacteria and viruses. They are parasitic organisms, that is to say, ones that take their food from other living creatures. They are mainly microscopic (invisible to the naked eye). They tend to be known by the symptoms they produce, such as "white rot" or "downy mildew", rather than by the name of the causal organism.

Fungal diseases
The majority of plant diseases are caused by fungi (though the majority of fungi do not cause diseases). Fungi consist mainly of microscopic threads, invisible to the naked eye, that grow through plant tissue. We only notice the more conspicuous reproductive structures such as toadstools and bracket fungi of some species.

Fungi are plants, but they do not contain chlorophyll – the pigment that allows green plants to make their food. This is why they must take food from other plants, living or dead.

Plant hosts
Similar disease symptoms such as rust, grey mould and powdery mildew may be found on a variety of plants, which leads to the common belief that a disease on one type of plant will rapidly spread to others. This is not always so. Some diseases like grey mould can behave in this way; in many cases (with powdery mildews and rusts, for example), the similar symptoms are caused by different species of fungi on different plants and they do not cross-infect.

Spread and survival
Fungi spread from plant to plant mainly in the form of spores, which grow to form new fungi. Spores can be spread by wind, rain or contaminated soil. Some fungi (honey fungus, for instance) will grow through the soil to find another suitable host.

The majority of disease-causing fungi can live on both dead and living plants, so dead plant material can act as a source of further infection. A few, including rusts and powdery mildews, can survive only in living plants.

Fungi can survive the winter in live plants (which do not always exhibit symptoms), in crop debris and as spores or "overwintering bodies" in the soil. In the absence of a suitable host plant, some, including club root and white rot,

produce very tough resting bodies which can survive in the soil for 20 years or more. This makes them particularly problematic to control.

Disease symptoms
The effects of fungal diseases are many, ranging from mild to life-threatening. Some are localized, damaging a restricted area, while others are systemic, meaning they spread throughout the plant.

Typical symptoms include death of plant tissue (spots); abnormal increase in tissue (cankers, scabs); change in colour such as silvering or yellowing (silver leaf); wilting (wilts, foot rots); wet rots (damping off); powdery and fluffy moulds (mildews, grey mould).

Bacterial diseases
Bacteria are tiny, simple organisms. They cause few diseases but those they do cause are important and/or difficult to control. Some of the most common symptoms include soft rots, leaf spots, cankers and galls.

Bacteria are spread in soil water, in and on planting material, and by wind and rain. They are unable to break through a plant's "skin", so their main point of entry is through a wound caused by another organism or by mechanical damage such as pruning.

Virus diseases
Viruses are even smaller than bacteria, only a few hundred thousandths of a centimetre long. They can only multiply within other plant cells. However, despite these limitations, viruses are responsible for some of the worst plant diseases and, unfortunately, once a plant is infected the virus moves throughout the plant and nothing can cure it.

• **Plants affected** Viruses are named after the plant that they were initially, or are most commonly, found in. This can lead to confusion as the virus is not necessarily restricted to this type of plant; the cucumber mosaic virus, for example, can be found in over 400 different species of plant. However, not all viruses are so adaptable.

• **Spread and survival** Because they are so small, viruses rely on other creatures for their spread. The majority are moved from plant to plant by aphids or eelworms. Cuttings taken from infected plants will also be infected.

Rose blackspot – break the cycle

In spring and summer, blackspot infection appears on rose leaves and twigs

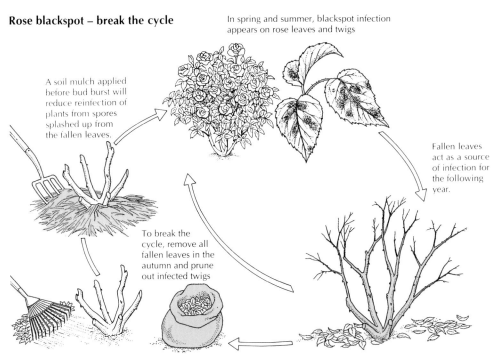

A soil mulch applied before bud burst will reduce reinfection of plants from spores splashed up from the fallen leaves.

Fallen leaves act as a source of infection for the following year.

To break the cycle, remove all fallen leaves in the autumn and prune out infected twigs

A few viruses are distributed in pollen and seed, while others rely on humans. We can transfer some viruses (tobacco mosaic virus in particular) on hands and secateurs.

We also bring viruses into the garden in infected plants, which may not show obvious symptoms. This is the reason why it is advisable to buy plants and planting material such as potato tubers that are certified virus-free.

• **Symptoms and identification** Viruses are almost impossible for the amateur to identify precisely. What is important to know is when symptoms are caused by a virus rather than by a disease, pest or deficiency.

Viruses can stunt growth and reduce cropping considerably. Obvious symptoms include mottling, mosaic and other patterns on leaves; growth may also be malformed and flowers streaked.

Some of these symptoms may be confused with mineral deficiencies. A virus is initially likely to appear on one or two plants only, whereas a deficiency is more likely to affect a whole row. Viral symptoms may come and go, especially in hot weather. A cool, dull day is the best time to look for them.

• **Virus control** Once a plant is infected with a virus, the virus will spread through it. Unfortunately, there is no cure; the only answer is to try to prevent infection in the first place. Although viruses can attack a wide range of plants, and cause many different symptoms, the methods of prevention are similar for all.

VIRUS CONTROL

• Control the agent which spreads the virus or prevent it from reaching susceptible plants
• Grow virus-resistant cultivars
• Where appropriate, break the cycle by removing all susceptible plants
• Practise crop rotation
• Buy certified virus-free planting material where available, for example fruit, potatoes, bulbs and some ornamentals (see page 92)
• Dig up and burn or dispose of infected plants
• Grow new plants from seed

Understanding the problem 3

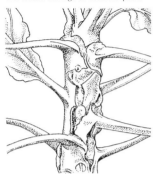

Herbicide damage to brassica plant

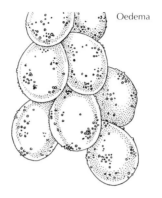

Oedema

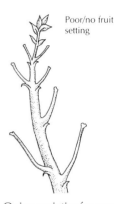

Poor/no fruit setting

DISORDERS

Plant disorders are problems caused by environmental conditions such as low temperature, day length or herbicide spray drift. They can also result from shortages of particular plant foods; these are known as mineral deficiencies and are dealt with on pages 102–3.

Bolting

Bolting is the term used when a plant flowers prematurely. It can be caused by adverse temperature, day length, root disturbance at transplanting or shortage of water. Bolting is mainly a problem with vegetables that are normally picked before they produce a tough flowering stem. Similar adverse conditions may cause annual flowers to run to seed too quickly without producing a good display.

The following plants are prone to bolting:

Beetroot Low temperatures encourage bolting. in beetroot. Choose 'bolt-resistant' varieties for early sowings.

Celery/celeriac Low temperatures, root disturbance and water shortage can trigger bolting. Keep young plants at a minimum of 12°C (54°F), even when planted out. Raise plants in modules to avoid root disturbance. Incorporate organic matter into the soil before planting, mulch well and water if necessary.

Chinese cabbage Low temperatures and increasing day length can trigger bolting. Keep plants at a minimum of 10°C (50°F). Sow at the appropriate time for the variety (check instructions on the seed packet). Many must be sown in midsummer or later to prevent bolting.

Spinach Grow in spring and autumn to avoid long days and dry weather that can encourage bolting.

Overwintering onions Onion varieties for overwintering will tend to bolt in spring if the plants are too large when winter starts. Follow the recommended timing of sowing or planting precisely.

Poor or no fruit set

Poor pollination will result in a poor crop of fruit, beans, tomatoes, courgettes and other fruiting crops. This may be due to cold, wet and windy weather conditions preventing the work of pollinating insects, frost killing the flowers or lack of pollen.

Providing windbreaks and choosing later-flowering varieties can help to solve the first two problems. Lack of pollen may be due to several causes. With apples, pears, sweet cherries and some plums, another variety of the same fruit, flowering at the same time, is required to provide pollen. In the case of courgettes and other cucurbits, it may be that the pollen-providing male flowers are not open at the same

POLLINATION

Remove petals from an open male flower. Rub its pollen on to the centre of a female flower – which has a tiny courgette at the base.

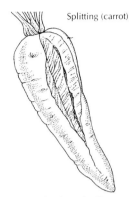
Splitting (carrot)

Bolting (Chinese cabbage)

Frost damage (strawberry flower)

time as the female flowers. This often happens early in the season. If necessary, these flowers can be pollinated by hand if bees are not doing the job adequately.

Water shortage and high temperatures can also reduce fruit set, especially in the case of runner beans and tomatoes.

Poor flowering can be caused by overfeeding and hard pruning, which can encourage a plant to grow vigorously at the expense of flowering. The answer is to stop feeding and alter the pruning regime.

If a large fruit tree is growing too vigorously, sowing grass around it to compete for food can be helpful. Alternatively, the problem may just be lack of flower buds because of inappropriate pruning or perhaps bullfinch damage (see pages 168-9 and 134).

Narrow leaves and distorted growth
Hormone weedkillers can cause distorted growth on tomatoes, cucumbers, cabbages, sprouts and other brassicas, sweet peas, and vines in particular.

This can happen even in a garden where no weedkillers are used. The spray may drift in from another garden, or herbicide residues in straw or grass mowings may be the source. There is no cure.

Oedema
The presence of small warty growths on stems and the underside of leaves is a condition known as oedema. It occurs mainly on eucalyptus, ivy-leaved pelargoniums, peperomia, camellia, brassicas and vines.

The cause is an excess of water in the plant. Stop watering and new growth should not be affected. In the greenhouse, increase ventilation and restrict watering to the morning only. Removing affected leaves only exacerbates the problem.

Split fruit, vegetables and bark
Splitting of fruit, such as tomatoes, and vegetables such as carrots and cabbages, as well as the bark of trees, is caused by an irregular supply of water. Heavy rain after a drought, for example, will cause very rapid growth which leads to splitting.

Increasing the water-holding capacity of the soil by adding organic matter and mulching are ways of helping to reduce the risk of this disorder occurring.

Frost damage: brown or shrivelled leaves
Sudden browning of leaves overnight of strawberries, potatoes and a wide range of unrelated plants is usually caused by frost. Other signs of frost may not be visible the morning after the frost because the worst of the damage is only apparent after a spell of good growing weather.

During cold, frosty weather, valuable plants can be protected overnight with a covering of straw, sacking or horticultural fleece, all of which should be sufficient to protect the plants.

Leaves yellow between veins, bark peels, foliage discoloured and shoots dying back
The above symptoms, which will vary with different type of plant and the severity of the condition, are caused by poor root action due to waterlogging. Plants that regularly suffer from any of these symptoms should be moved to a drier site.

Understanding the problem 4

MINERAL DEFICIENCIES

A plant that is short of food may grow poorly and exhibit a range of symptoms on leaves, stems and fruit including discoloration and growth distortion. This condition is known as a mineral or nutrient deficiency and can be caused by a number of factors.

A shortage in the soil

A mineral deficiency can develop as a result of a shortage of a particular nutrient in the soil. This can be rectified simply by applying the missing mineral to the plant or the soil. Where appropriate, the soil structure should be improved in order to help it retain the added nutrients.

Sources of plant foods to correct various mineral deficiencies are given under each specific deficiency described below. Short-term materials should have an effect in the season in which the deficiency is noticed. While they will improve new growth, they will not cure existing symptoms. The soil should then be improved by using the longer-term materials and cultural practices.

Induced deficiencies

Deficiencies can also develop on soils that are not short of plant foods but where something is making the nutrients unavailable to plants. In this case, correct the particular adverse condition (or simply wait for it to pass).

Causes of induced deficiencies

The following are all causes of induced deficiencies:
• Heavy soils are usually rich in plant foods, but if the soil structure is poor and drainage impeded, then these plant foods will unfortunately not be available to the growing plant.
• A sudden period of cold weather, checking plant growth and activity of soil life, can cause a temporary deficiency in both. This will hopefully disappear when the temperature rises again.
• Shortage of water in the soil can reduce nutrient uptake.
• Adding uncomposted tough material to the soil can reduce the available nitrogen supplies temporarily. This is commonly known as nitrogen depletion.
• Excessive or insufficient liming or fertilizer

application can make certain nutrients unavailable to plants. This can also be the case if the soil is too acid. It is important to identify a deficiency and its cause correctly rather than adding extra food "just in case".
• Root damage, whether by pest, disease or waterlogging may make a plant unable to take up the food it requires.

Individual deficiencies

Mineral deficiencies are not easy to diagnose; the symptoms may be confused with those caused by viruses, disorders or other factors. If a problem occurs regularly and diagnosis is unsure, a commercial soil analysis may be needed to establish the cause.

Boron The most likely cause is over-liming, making boron unavailable to plants; high nitrogen use can exacerbate the problem. Symptoms are typically distortion and blackening of leaves, together with cracked and/or corky areas on stems and midribs.
Prevention/treatment
Short term – rake in borax at 3g per sq m.
Cultural – correct soil conditions.

Calcium Calcium deficiency is usually the result of disruption in the supply of calcium to the plant rather than a soil deficiency. It can be caused by a shortage of water, which slows the transport of calcium, or by excessive use of potassium or magnesium fertilizers. Two common conditions caused by this deficiency are blossom end rot in tomatoes (see page 128) and bitter pit in apples (see page 133).
Prevention/treatment
Short term – none.
Longer term – limestone and gypsum will supply calcium if soil is deficient.
Cultural – maintain conditions that allow steady, uniform growth throughout the season. A steady water supply is essential.

Iron This deficiency is almost always a result of a naturally high soil pH (over 7.5), which reduces the availability of this element to plants. The symptoms of deficient plants include yellow between the leaf veins, or all over, giving a very bleached look. Perennial crops are much more susceptible to this deficiency; annuals seldom show symptoms.

Iron deficiency is sometimes confused with manganese deficiency, but it is completely different.
Prevention/treatment
Short term – chelated (sequestered) iron.
Cultural – do not grow acid-loving plants on alkaline soil. Improve soil structure.

Magnesium One of the more common deficiencies, especially on sandy soils and in wet weather. Soil compaction, waterlogging and water stress all aggravate the condition. Excess application of potassium fertilizers can make magnesium unavailable to plants. The typical symptom is yellowing between the leaf veins, on the older leaves first, giving a mottled appearance. Symptoms may be confused with virus or natural ageing.
Prevention/treatment
Short term – foliar feed every two weeks with a 2 per cent solution of 10 per cent Epsom salts. Longer term – reduce use of potassium fertilizers if appropriate; add dolomite limestone if pH allows.
Cultural – improve soil structure.

Manganese Most likely to occur on soils with a high pH (over 7.5) and/or poor drainage and/or high organic matter levels. The typical symptom is yellowing between the leaf veins on the youngest leaves first. Manganese deficiency can often be confused with both iron or magnesium deficiency.
Prevention/treatment
Short term – spray deficient plants with manganese sulphate dissolved in water at 50g (2 oz) in 11.5 litre (2½ gal) water, two or three times at two-week intervals.
Cultural – always check pH before liming.

Nitrogen Only likely on poor and neglected soils low in organic matter or in pot-bound plants. A nitrogen deficiency can be induced by nitrogen robbery. Typical symptoms, which appear on the oldest leaves first, are poor, spindly growth and pale yellow leaves; these may turn reddish-purple. Similar symptoms may also be caused by root damage and phosphorus deficiency.
Prevention and treatment
Short term – liquid feeds; grass mowings.
Longer term – animal manures; compost; blood,

Mineral deficiency

Potassium deficiency causes the scorching of leaves, which may also start to curl, as seen on this bean plant.

fish and bone meal; hoof and horn.
Cultural – grow legumes; green manuring; improve soil organic matter levels.

Phosphorus Most common in areas of high rainfall, especially on acid soils and during cold spells. Symptoms include poor growth, especially in young plants. Leaves may also develop a dull blue tinge.
Prevention/treatment
Short term – none.
Longer term – bone meal; bone flour; rock phosphate.
Cultural – lime soil to raise pH if appropriate.

Potassium Most likely on light, sandy, peaty, or chalky soils. Plants that require a lot of potash, such as tomatoes, beans and fruit, may show deficiencies on more fertile soils. Typical symptoms, which appear on older leaves first, are scorching round the edge of leaves, which may curl up or down.
Prevention/treatment
Short term – comfrey liquid manure; comfrey leaves; wood ash.
Longer term – seaweed meal; garden potash.
Cultural – improve soil structure.

Taking action 1

BIOLOGICAL CONTROL

An important aspect of organic gardening is the encouragement of natural predators and parasites to keep pests and diseases in check (see pages 18-23). These naturally occurring pest controllers can be bought as commercially produced "biological control agents". The use of such agents is known as biological control. The agents are all tiny or microscopic, and are very specific in their action.

Biological control agents are available to help control a range of pests and one disease. They include: parasitic wasps that kill their prey by laying their eggs in them; predatory mites that eat other mites; and microscopic nematodes that infect pests with lethal diseases.

The majority of biological control agents are only suitable for use in a conservatory or greenhouse as they require warm conditions to be effective. Some are available for outdoor use. *Trichoderma* and *Bacillus thuringiensis* (Bt) are two biological control agents that differ somewhat from the others in their mode of use. *Trichoderma*, a fungus that will repel other fungi, is used to control silver leaf (see page 136)

BIOLOGICAL CONTROL AGENTS

Pest: **Whitefly**
Predator/parasite: *Encarsia formosa*
Type: Parasitic wasp
Opt. temp: 18–25°C (64–77°F)

Pest: **Red spider mite**
Predator/parasite: *Phytoseiulus persimilis*
Type: Predatory mite

Pest: **Mealybug**
Predator/parasite: *Cryptolaemus montrouzieri*
Type: Predatory beetle
Opt. temp: 20–25°C (68–77°F); humidity 70%

Pest: **Aphid**
Predator/parasite: *Aphidius matricariae/Aphidoletes aphidimyza*
Type: Parasitic wasp/predatory midge larva
Opt. day temp: 21°C (70°F); min. night temp: 16°C (61°F)

Pest: **Vine weevil grubs**
Predator/parasite: *Heterorhabditis megidis*
Type: Pathogenic nematode.
Opt. soil temp: 14–25°C (57–77°F); min. 10°C (50°F)

Pest: **Slugs**
Predator/parasite: *Phasmarhabditis hermaphrodita*
Type: Pathogenic nematode
Opt. soil temp: 15°C (59°F); minimum 5°C (41°F)

*Also suitable for outdoor use

---

and also as a wound paint (see page 168). *Bacillus thuringiensis* (Bt) is a bacterium used for caterpillar control. It is applied to plants in the same way as more conventional sprays (see page 109).

Level of control

The aim of biological control is to reduce pest levels and related damage rather than to eliminate them completely. In some cases this can be achieved with one application; sometimes a further batch of biological control agents may have to be introduced.

Sources of supply

Most biological control agents are purchased by mail order as they have a limited shelf life.

Tips on using biological control

(*Note that these guidelines are not applicable to all biological control agents*)
Watch out for the first appearance of the pest. Biological control is most effective where the agent is introduced when the pest level is low. There is no advantage in introducing the agent before pests are present. If pest levels are high, try to reduce them using non-chemical means before introducing the agent. If you plan to use biological control, do not use any persistent pesticides. Some can still harm the agents up to ten weeks after spraying.

As soon as the pests are seen, order the relevant biological control agents. Before ordering, check the following:

• That you have not used a pesticide that will harm the agent within the last ten weeks. If necessary ask your supplier for details.

• That you can meet the required conditions of temperature (minimum and maximum), humidity and daylight.

• The delivery date. Often, the package containing the agents must be opened on arrival. Try to use the agents as soon as they are delivered. Read the instructions carefully before opening the container. Some may be stored in a fridge if delay in using them is unavoidable.

If you should need to use a pesticide to control other pests or diseases, use one that will not harm the natural predator or parasite.

HETERORHABDITIS MEGIDIS FOR VINE WEEVIL CONTROL (in pots outdoors)

This is a microscopic nematode used on soil or compost in pots where vine weevil action is suspected. It is most effective when applied in late summer or early autumn when the soil or compost temperature is over 10°C (50°F). It comes in a sachet containing millions of nematodes and can be stored for up to six weeks in the fridge but is best used fresh. To use, mix the contents of the sachet with water and apply to moist soil or compost.

ENCARSIA FORMOSA FOR WHITEFLY

As soon as you see the first whitefly in the greenhouse order a supply of *Encarsia formosa* (parasitic wasps). There must be plants in the glasshouse and make sure you have not used any chemicals within the past two months that could harm the wasps. The night-time temperature inside should be over 15°C (59°F) and the daytime temperature 20–26°C (68–79°F).

Remove any yellow sticky traps before introducing the wasp and only open the package in the greenhouse. If essential, the box can be stored unopened for one day in the fridge and no longer.

The box should contain small cards, each bearing a cluster of tiny black "scales". These are parasitized young whitefly, containing pupae of the *Encarsia* wasp. Hang these cards up on infested plants out of the sunlight.

Within a few days the wasps should have emerged. Hold a card up to the light; if wasps have hatched, you will see a tiny hole in the back of each blackened scale. You are unlikely to notice the wasps themselves. Within a couple of weeks you should be able to find blackened scales on the underside of leaves. This shows that the wasps are doing their work. Do not remove leaves from plants that show blackened scales underneath because you will be removing new supplies of wasps.

Biological control

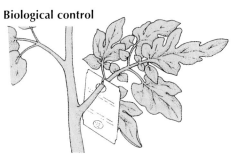

Cards bearing *Encarsia* larvae are hung on plants; wasps hatch out and control whitefly.

Nematodes for controlling vine weevil larvae are watered on to individual pots.

For aphid control, *Aphidoletes* cocoons mixed with vermiculite are left under a pot to hatch.

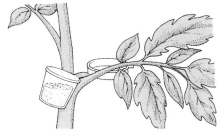

Predatory spider mites are provided in small tubs; they soon climb out to search for prey.

Taking action 2

BARRIERS AND TRAPS

The age-old technique of netting plants against pests or using other forms of barriers to protect them can be most effective. Traps can be used in the garden to reduce pests in a small area and to monitor new arrivals so that the timing of an appropriate spray or introduction of a biological agent can be made accurately. The use of traps to catch pests or devices to scare them off can also help to reduce damage to plants.

Rabbit fencing (see page 113)

A wire mesh or electric fence is the only effective method of keeping rabbits out of a garden.

Tree guards and shelters

Newly planted trees can be protected from grazing animals, and the weather, by the use of tree shelters – tall, thin cloches that are placed over individual plants.

Spiral tree guards wrapped around the trunk of young trees will protect them from rabbits and deer which may otherwise strip their bark in winter.

Scaraweb

This proprietary product consists of a cord composed of thousands of threads of rayon which are teased out into a "spider's web". It is placed over fruit trees and bushes to protect buds from bird damage in the winter.

Fruit cage

Grouping soft fruit plants together within a fruit cage can be an efficient method of protecting the ripening fruit from birds. Proprietary fruit cages are available in various sizes, and the sides of the cage should be covered with netting which has a mesh size 12–18mm (½–¾in). Cover the top of the cage with 18mm (¾in) netting. The top netting should be removed when fruiting has finished and not replaced until after blossom has set. This allows access for pest-clearing birds and pollinating insects and also avoids the danger of snow bringing down the roof.

Netting

Individual fruit trees and bushes can be protected from birds by draping netting over them. This is much simpler where the plants are trained against a wall.

Strawberries can be covered with a low netting, supported on posts about 40cm (16in) high. A glass jar or plant pot placed upside down on top of each post will prevent it pushing through the netting. For individual rows, the netting can be draped over wire cloche hoops.

Vegetables can be protected in the same way, varying the height of the netting as appropriate.

Crop covers

Very fine mesh materials are available that can be used to protect plants against smaller pests such as flea beetle, carrot root fly and cabbage caterpillars. These covers are very lightweight and some can be placed directly over a growing crop without the need for any framework for support. These covers have an advantage over traditional cloches in that they allow air and rain to penetrate, so you do not have to remove them every time you want to water the crops or let in air to avoid overheating.

When using a crop cover, it is important to put it in place before the pest is present – usually as soon as a crop is sown. They can, if necessary, be left in place for the life of the crop. Be sure to check regularly for weeds and diseases, both of which can thrive in the sheltered environment.

Wherever possible, remove covers as soon as the plants can look after themselves. Choose a still, overcast day to reduce the shock and replace covers at night for a while until plants are hardened off.

Horticultural fleece A fine, lightweight, spun polyester material which is placed directly over a crop. The fleece should be cut to the size of the plot to be covered, allowing at least an extra 30cm (1ft) all round, depending on the height the plants will reach before the cover is removed. The material is held down by covering the edges with soil or using proprietary pegs made for the purpose. It should be pulled fairly tight, the excess material being held at the edges; this must be released as the plants grow. Horticultural fleece also gives some protection against frost.

Environmesh A fine mesh plastic material that can be used in the same way as fleece or to cover tunnel cloche hoops. It is longer lasting than fleece but does not give as much protection against the weather. Other materials of a similar nature are available.

Root fly barriers

Cabbage root fly Cabbages and other members of the brassica family can be protected from the cabbage root fly by the use of small squares of carpet underlay.

Cut 13cm (5in) squares of rubbery carpet underlay. Make a slit to the centre. Lay the squares around newly planted brassicas, making sure that they lie flat on the soil. The underlay, which will stretch as the plant grows, will prevent the cabbage root fly from laying its eggs in the soil around the roots.

Carrot root fly A 75cm (30in) high barrier erected around a plot of carrots can give considerable protection against the carrot root fly. The barrier can be made of polythene, clear plastic or fine mesh netting (the best in windy areas) supported by four sturdy corner posts. It should be erected as soon as the carrots are sown.

Bottle cloches

Cloches to cover individual small plants can be made from plastic drinks bottles. These can give protection against many pests, including slugs.

Use the biggest size of bottle available to give the plants room to grow. Cut the bottom off, using a sharp serrated knife or scissors. Remove the screw tops for ventilation.

Pheromone baited traps

Some proprietary traps use synthetic pheromones (sex hormones) to attract specific moth pests into a trap from which they cannot escape. They can be used against the codling moth and the plum moth. On their own they may reduce pest damage to an acceptable level; alternatively, by indicating the presence of a pest, they can help to time a spray effectively.

Sticky yellow traps

Yellow plastic cards covered with a non-drying glue are available for use in houses and greenhouses. They will trap a variety of pests including whitefly. This may be sufficient to control the pest; alternatively, they can be used to indicate the presence of a pest so that the appropriate biological control agent can then be introduced in time.

Barriers and traps

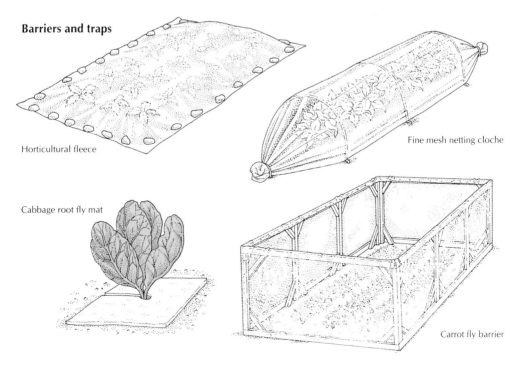

Horticultural fleece

Fine mesh netting cloche

Cabbage root fly mat

Carrot fly barrier

Taking action 3

Grease bands

A band of grease can help to protect fruit trees and ornamentals from winter moths and ants – pests that climb up the trunk of the tree. A proprietary fruit tree grease should be used. This can be applied directly to older trees in a 10cm (4in) band around the trunk, 1–2m (3¼–6½ft) above ground. In the case of young trees, where the bark can be damaged by the grease, a proprietary paper-based grease band should be used in the autumn.

If the plant has a stake, either apply the band above the point where the stake is attached or grease band the stake too.

Glue bands

A non-drying glue is available that can be used to make a sticky barrier on pots and legs of greenhouse staging which will act against vine weevil, ants and woodlice. Where applicable, wrap a strip of wide PVC tape around first then smear it liberally with the non-drying glue. This can then be removed easily at the end of the season.

Slug traps See page 111.

Scaring and repelling devices

Various devices for scaring and repelling larger pests such as cats, rabbits and moles are available. Most are not that effective but may be worth a try if you have a persistent problem.

BEST SPRAYING PRACTICE

- Choose an appropriate spray product, having first identified the problem.
- Only use sprays for those applications mentioned on the product label.
- Follow label instructions precisely.
- Only make up the quantity you need.
- Never store made-up spray.
- Use a good-quality sprayer.
- Spray only the relevant areas.
- Spray in still weather to prevent drift.
- Never spray where bees are working. If it is essential to spray a plant in flower, do this in the evening when bees have returned to their hives.
- Always store pesticides in their original container in a safe, cool, dark place.

Barriers and traps

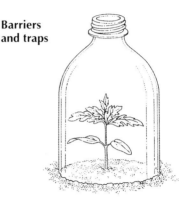

A mini cloche, made from a plastic bottle, will protect young plants from pests and from the weather.

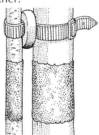

A grease band applied to a tree trunk and stake will prevent the wingless female winter moths from climbing up into the tree.

A sticky yellow trap is useful for whitefly control.

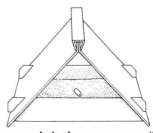

A pheromone-baited trap attracts codling moth.

ORGANIC PESTICIDE SPRAYS

A few sprays may be used to control pests and diseases in an organic garden. They should never be used on a regular basis, but only when necessary to prevent a particular problem getting out of hand. They may be less harmful or persistent than other pesticides, but they can still harm creatures other than those you want to kill. If regular spraying is required to keep a plant healthy, consider replacing it with a sturdier plant.

Traditionally, organic gardeners used a selection of home-made concoctions such as boiled rhubarb leaves to control pests and diseases. The use of such preparations is now illegal; all materials used as a pesticide must now be registered as such.

All the normal precautions to safeguard the environment should be taken when using the sprays described here. Read the label before you buy and use pesticides safely.

Bacillus thuringiensis (Bt)
This is a powder containing spores and protein crystals of the bacterium *Bacillus thuringiensis*, a naturally occurring disease of caterpillars. It is applied as a spray to protect brassicas and other plants against butterfly and moth caterpillars.
Cautions: Bacillus thuringiensis can kill a wide range of caterpillars; avoid spray drift to non-target plants.

Derris (rotenone)
A liquid or powder made from the roots of derris plants, for use against small pests including aphids, spider mite, sawfly larvae, raspberry beetles, or as directed on the product label.
Cautions: Poisonous to fish and some beneficial creatures including ladybirds, anthocorid bugs and worms.

Pyrethrum
Pyrethrum is made from pyrethrum *Chrysanthemum cinerariaefolium* flowers. It usually also contains piperonyl butoxide to increase efficacy. Use against aphids, small caterpillars, flea beetle or as directed on product label.
Cautions: Poisonous to fish and to some beneficial insects.

Insecticidal soap
A mixture of potassium salt soaps for use against aphids, whitefly, red spider mite and slugworm or as directed on the product label. Insecticidal soap is totally non-persistent so is suitable for spot spraying where biological control agents are used.
Cautions: It can harm beneficials, including ladybirds if they are sprayed directly. Some plants are sensitive to soap.

Bordeaux mixture
A mixture of copper sulphate and quicklime, Bordeaux mixture is used to prevent disease spread. It can be used against potato blight and a range of fruit diseases.
Cautions: Harmful to some plants; toxic to fish. Do not use on plants under stress.

Sulphur
Sulphur is sold as a dust or spray to prevent and control disease. Its main use is against powdery mildews and apple scab.
Cautions: Harmful to predatory mites and some other beneficial insects. Several varieties of apple and gooseberry are sensitive to sulphur.

Soft soap
This old-fashioned soap of vegetable origin is used as a "wetter" to help sprays to stick to waxy leaves of plants like brassicas and peas. It has some mild pesticide activity.

Aphids/Slugs/Snails

APHIDS

Aphids are one of the most widespread and prolific pests of fruit, vegetables, ornamentals and houseplants. Small, soft-bodied creatures with long legs, they are often known as green-fly or blackfly, although they come in a wider range of colours than green and black. There are over 500 species of aphid in Britain. Some will feed on hundreds of unrelated plants; others restrict their activities to a very limited selection. Some will stay on the same plant all year round, while others migrate to different hosts at certain times of year (see Blackfly lifecycle, page 97).

Aphids feed by sucking sap out of the plant. Their numbers can build up very quickly, weakening growth, distorting leaves and young shoots. Those that feed on roots, such as lettuce root aphids, can kill a plant.

The indirect effects of aphid feeding can be more serious. They are one of the main means of transmitting viruses in the garden and greenhouse. They also exude a sticky honeydew – the excess sugars and water from their diet of sap – which provides a site for unsightly black sooty moulds to grow. The wounds caused by aphids can allow disease entry.

Finding out more about the habits of a particular aphid – knowing when it is likely to be where and whether it is going to spread or not – can help you to devise a control strategy.

Prevention and treatment
• Encourage natural enemies such as bluetits, hoverflies, lacewings, ladybirds, spiders,

COMMON SPECIES OF APHID
Woolly aphid (*Eriosoma lanigerum*)
A common pest of apples, crab apple, cotoneaster and pyracantha. It may seriously disfigure young plants and allow canker into older trees.
Lettuce root aphid (*Pemphigus bursarius*)
This aphid feeds on the roots of lettuce. Once the effects of its feeding are visible, it is too late to save the plant. Other species occur on auricula and pinks.
Cherry blackfly (*Myzus cerasi*)
These black aphids infest ornamental and fruiting cherries in the spring, distorting leaves and shoots. Quantities of sticky honeydew are produced, on which black moulds grow. Cherry blackfly does not attack broad beans.

earwigs, anthocorid bugs and parasitic wasps into your garden. Give them a chance to work.
• In the winter, hang up pieces of fat over roses and in fruit trees to attract bluetits which will eat overwintering aphid eggs.
• Give plants the best growing conditions possible. Those that are struggling are always more susceptible to attack.
• Do not overdo nitrogen fertilizers. The soft growth they produce is very attractive to aphids.
• Use crop rotation to prevent build-up of root aphids.
• Grow resistant varieties where available such as lettuce, raspberries and flowering cherry.

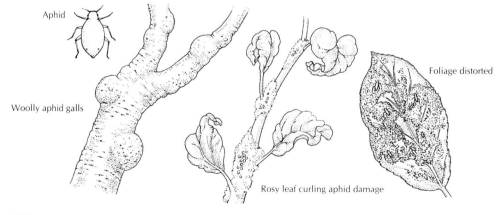

Aphid

Woolly aphid galls

Foliage distorted

Rosy leaf curling aphid damage

• Autumn-sown broad beans are less attractive to blackfly in the spring than the less tough spring-sown plants.
• Inspect vulnerable plants regularly and squash any aphids or pick off infested shoots and leaves.
• Scrape off woolly aphid colonies as noticed. Prune out and burn branches if damaged.
• Pick out the tops of broad bean plants once they have reached the required size.
• Break the cycle of infection by removing all susceptible plants at one time of year and burying them in a trench.
• If total control is essential, grow plants under horticultural fleece.
• Biological control agents can be used in the greenhouse (see pages 104–5).
• Spray affected area with derris, pyrethrum or an insecticidal soap.

SLUGS AND SNAILS
(*Deroceras reticulatum, Arion hortensis, Arion ater, Milax* spp. and *Helix aspersa*)

Slugs and snails are common and widespread pests that cause considerable damage to strawberries, seedlings and many types of vegetable and ornamental plants.

There are many slugs ranging in colour from pinkish-fawn to black. The majority are approximately 3–4.2cm (1¼–1¾in) in length, although one species grows up to 15cm (6in).

Typical symptoms include seedlings eaten or failing to come up and irregular holes in roots, stems, bulbs, tubers, fruit and leaves of many plants. Damage is usually worse in warm, damp conditions, especially in spring and autumn.

Look out for characteristic slime trails to confirm diagnosis or go out into the garden with a torch at night and see them.

There is no single simple method of dealing with slugs and snails. The best you can aim for is to reduce their numbers and to protect plants as long as they are vulnerable.

Prevention and treatment
• Encourage natural enemies, including frogs, toads, birds, beetles and centipedes.
• Ensure quick germination and growth of seedlings. Never sow or plant into cold soil.
• Use sturdy, vigorous transplants that have been grown in modules or pots.
• When sowing seeds, water the bottom of the drill then cover with dry soil.
• Water transplants in the morning so there is no film of water left on the soil or leaves by the evening.
• Where snails are a particular problem, do not plant vulnerable plants near walls covered with ivy or other climbers, piles of logs and other similar situations where snails may lurk.
• Grow varieties of potato less susceptible to slugs; harvest all tubers by early autumn.
• Soil dug in the autumn allows slugs to move down into the soil to hibernate. If you must dig, do it in the cold of winter for maximum disruption of slugs and eggs.
• Protect seedlings and young plants with plastic bottle cloches.
• Remove slugs from areas of new seedlings or transplants. Slugs will congregate under roof tiles, lettuce leaves, wet newspaper or a pile of comfrey leaves laid on the soil; they can then

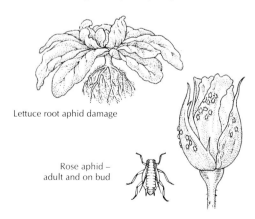

Lettuce root aphid damage

Rose aphid – adult and on bud

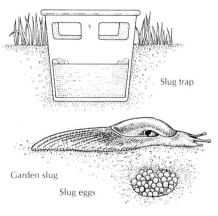

Slug trap

Garden slug

Slug eggs

General pests

be collected up and disposed of as you see fit. It is worth starting this before plants are introduced into the area.

• Lay a continuous ring of comfrey leaves around an area of susceptible plants. This seems to act as a decoy, but is said to be ineffective after mid-summer.

• Go out at night with a torch and remove slugs and snails from plants.

• Use slug traps in areas of new seedlings and transplants.

• Use a method of biological control (see pages 104–5).

GENERAL PESTS
(See pages 104–8 for information on control methods)

Ants

Ants can be disruptive but they rarely cause any serious or direct damage to plants.

Typical symptoms: Plants in pots and bare ground grow poorly where ants have tunnelled underneath; heaps of dry soil appear in lawns where ants are present. Aphid problems are exacerbated when ants move them to different feeding sites around a plant and defend them from predators.

Prevention and treatment: Little can be done to banish ants from the garden, although it is possible to protect individual trees and pots with grease bands as used for codling-moth control. Pots and greenhouse staging, popular refuges for these insects, can also be protected with a non-drying glue; regularly check that these barriers have not been breached.

Birds

Birds are generally welcome in the garden for their decorative and harmonious qualities, but some can cause severe damage to fruit, flowers and vegetables.

Typical symptoms: Fruit buds are eaten; holes are pecked in pea pods; leaves of brassicas are pecked and torn; crocus petals are torn; and fruit is eaten.

Prevention and treatment: Cover plants with net or Scaraweb or grow them in a cage. Where birds are not such a problem, try various scaring devices, changing the type every so often as soon as the birds soon get used to the different methods.

Earwigs (*Forficula auricularia*)

These creatures are useful pest controllers, but they can also damage fruit, seedlings and some flowers.

Typical symptoms: Ragged holes in the petals of chrysanthemums, dahlias and other ornamental flowers and also in young leaves and buds. Earwigs are often found nestling in cavities in fruit but the insects themselves rarely initiate such damage.

Prevention and treatment: tidy up unnecessary debris where earwigs could breed and hide. Earwigs tend to congregate under materials such as planks of wood or sheets of cardboard laid on the soil or in straw-filled flower pots on top of a cane. They can then be collected up and disposed of.

Leatherjackets (*Tipula* spp.)

Leatherjackets are fat, greyish-brown larvae up to 5cm (2in) long. The juvenile form of the crane fly, they feed on plant roots and are mainly a pest of lawns, where they create yellow patches, especially during dry weather. The activity of starlings and other birds searching for leatherjackets can further damage the lawn; young plants growing in newly dug grassland are also at risk.

Typical symptoms: Plants turn yellow, wilt and die; yellow patches appear in lawns.

Prevention and treatment: First confirm the presence of leatherjackets, as these symptoms can have other causes. Regular cultivation and weed control should gradually clear these pests from plots and borders. On lawns, water the grass well, then cover it with thick cardboard or black plastic overnight. This will bring the leatherjackets to the surface, from where they can be collected. On cultivated land, trap them by covering well-watered ground with lawn mowings, topped with cardboard or plastic. Leave for several days before collecting up the pests and disposing of them.

Millipedes (*Blaniulus guttulatus* and others)

These slow-moving, many-legged creatures feed mainly on dead plants or they extend wounds caused by other creatures in roots, tubers, corms and bulbs.

Typical symptoms: Seedlings, especially of peas and beans, germinate poorly and pieces are eaten away.

Prevention and treatment: Encourage their natural enemies, which include birds, hedgehogs and ground beetles. Cultivate land regularly to disturb the millipedes and expose them to predators.

Moles (*Talpa europaea*)
The activities of these beautiful and hard-working creatures – tunnelling and the production of molehills – undermine and disturb plants.
Typical symptoms: Plants wilt or grow poorly for no apparent reason. Tunnels are found under plants; mounds of soil appear in beds and lawns.
Prevention and treatment: Many gadgets making a sound or vibration in the soil are said to repel moles but they rarely have any effect. Trapping, carried out by an expert, is really the only effective answer.

Rabbits (*Oryctolagus cuniculus*)
These creatures can cause severe damage to a wide variety of fruit, vegetables and ornamental plants.
Typical symptoms: Many plants are grazed; young shoots and leaves are eaten; bark is often stripped away from young trees. Rabbit droppings are visible.
Prevention and treatment: Trunks of individual trees and shrubs can be protected with spiral tree guards. Tree shelters, used for young trees, will also keep rabbits at bay. Fencing is the most practical way of protecting a garden. Use wire mesh netting, maximum mesh size 3cm (1¼in), approximately 1m (3½ ft) high. The bottom 15cm (6in) should be bent out at an angle of 90° so that it lies flat on the ground, pointing away from the garden. Bend the top 15cm (6in) out at an angle of 45° to prevent the rabbits from climbing over. A simpler though more costly alternative is to use an electric fence, and there are special designs available specifically for rabbit control.

Scale insects (*Coccus hesperidum* and others)
These small, limpet-like creatures are widespread pests of ornamental plants, especially in greenhouses.
Typical symptoms: Sticky honeydew is produced on which black moulds grow. A severe infestation can weaken growth and make the plant look unsightly.

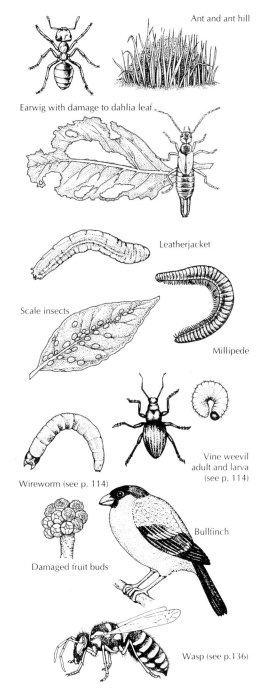

Ant and ant hill

Earwig with damage to dahlia leaf

Leatherjacket

Scale insects

Millipede

Wireworm (see p. 114)

Vine weevil adult and larva (see p. 114)

Damaged fruit buds

Bullfinch

Wasp (see p.136)

113

General pests/General diseases

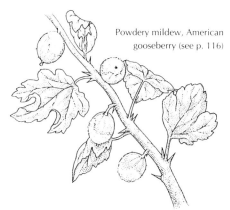

Powdery mildew, American gooseberry (see p. 116)

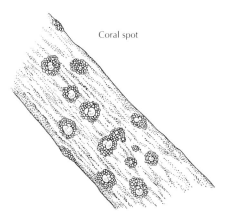

Coral spot

Prevention and treatment: Always examine new plants for scales before introducing them into the garden or greenhouse because this is the main way in which scales are spread. Where scales are present, and the leaves of the plant are tough enough, gently rub the creatures off the plant using a soft cloth or toothbrush and insecticidal soap. Try a test run on an individual leaf first if you are unsure if the plant will take this kind of treatment. The only effective time to spray this pest is when the juvenile scales, tiny mobile creatures known as "crawlers", are present. Outdoors, this is usually during late spring to early summer, but indoors, it can be almost any time of the year. To do this, use a magnifying glass to help identify the presence of crawlers and then spray affected areas with insecticidal soap.

Vine weevil (*Otiorhynchus sulcatus*)

The vine weevil larvae are serious pests that can affect a wide variety of plants, especially those grown in containers. The adults do some damage, but this is generally much less serious.
Typical symptoms: Plants wilt suddenly and, if watered, do not recover. This is because the roots have been eaten away by the larvae. Plump, creamy-white, brown-headed larvae, up to about 1cm (½in) long, are found in the soil around the plant. The adult vine weevil feeds at night, making irregular holes and notches in plant foliage.
Prevention and treatment: Check the compost of new plants for the presence of vine weevil larvae; destroy any that are found. As the adult vine weevil cannot fly, individual pots and greenhouse staging can be protected with a

band of non-drying glue. If a wilting plant is caught in time, it can be potted up into clean soil and may recover.

A biological control agent, the parasitic nematode *Heterorhabditis megidis*, can be used against this pest (see page 105).

Wireworm (*Agriotes* spp.)

These slender, shiny brown, tough beetle larvae live in the soil and feed on the stems, tubers and roots of many plants. They are a particular problem on newly broken ground.
Typical symptoms: Plants may not thrive; knitting needle-type holes can be seen in tubers.
Prevention and treatment: Thorough cultivation and weed control should reduce the problem in newly cultivated ground. Lift potatoes by early autumn to limit damage. In small areas, such as a greenhouse, trap wireworm in pieces of potato or carrot spiked on a stick and remove them regularly.

GENERAL DISEASES

Coral spot (*Nectria cinnabarina*)

More usually associated with dead wood, this distinctive disease can cause die-back on currants, gooseberries, apples and many other woody plants.
Typical symptoms: Bright pink pustules appear on dead twigs and branches; branches also die back.
Prevention and treatment: Clear up dead twigs and branches. Prune out infected wood, cutting back at least 15cm (6in) into healthy wood. Disinfect secateurs after use.

Honey fungus

Grey mould
on strawberry

Downy mildews (*Peronospora* spp., *Bremia* spp.)

Downy mildews are not of great importance in a garden except, at times, on lettuces and onions. Some species of downy mildew are quite specific in the plants they affect. Crucifer downy mildew affects brassicas, watercress and wallflowers; onion downy mildew affects onions and shallots; spinach downy mildew affects spinach, spinach beet and beetroot; lettuce downy mildew affects lettuce. Other downy mildews are rarely a problem.

Typical symptoms: Yellow patches on leaves, with corresponding patches of purplish mould underneath. When the mould is wiped off, the leaf underneath is yellow. (This distinguishes downy mildews from powdery mildews, to which they are not related.) Seedlings may die, plants grow poorly; onions may rot in store. Downy mildews are most common in cool damp weather.

Prevention and treatment: Grow resistant varieties if available. Use as long a crop rotation as possible. Encourage good ventilation between and within plants and clear up infected plants and debris to remove sources of infection.

Grey mould (*Botrytis cinerea*)

An ubiquitous and important disease causing many different symptoms on a wide range of plants including blackcurrants, strawberries, blackberries, gooseberries, lettuce and many ornamentals. Grey mould thrives in cool, damp and crowded conditions.

Typical symptoms: All symptoms are usually associated with a distinctive fluffy grey mould. Flowers, buds and soft fruits rot; a cloud of spores may rise when disturbed. Lettuces develop a reddish-brown stem rot resulting in the tops of the plants being detached from the roots. Gooseberry, and sometimes raspberry and blackcurrant, branches may die back with no other symptoms.

Prevention and treatment: As grey mould is generally very common on dead and dying plant material, good hygiene is essential. Ventilation in greenhouses and thinning and pruning of plants to allow for good air flow also play an important role. Grey mould is a weak pathogen and usually infects through a wound already made by something else, therefore try to avoid damaging plants that could allow entry in the first place. Cut out and burn branches showing die-back; if symptoms persist, remove and dispose of the whole plant.

Honey fungus (*Armillaria mellea*)

This is an extremely serious disease of all woody and some herbaceous plants. Some plants are less susceptible to honey fungus, and these include ash, beech, box, elaeagnus, hawthorn, holly, larch and laurel, as well as ivy, yew and clematis.

Typical symptoms: affected plants die suddenly. The bark near the base of the stem pulls away easily, revealing a white fungal sheet smelling of mushrooms.

Prevention and treatment: Do not leave stumps of old trees and shrubs in the ground where honey fungus is known to be a problem. Remove and burn infected plants, including as much of their root system and associated soil as possible. Replace with plants that are less susceptible to the disease.

General diseases/Seedlings

Powdery mildews (*Erysiphe* spp., *Sphaerotheca* spp., *Podosphaera* spp.)

Powdery mildews cause some of the most common and serious diseases of fruit, vegetables and ornamentals. Some species of mildew are quite specific in the plants they attack, for example: crufier powdery mildew attacks brassicas, especially swedes and turnips; cucurbit powdery mildews attacks courgettes, cucumbers, marrows and pumpkins; pea powdery mildew attacks peas and lupins; American gooseberry mildew attacks gooseberries and blackcurrants; apple powdery mildew attacks apples, pears and quince; rose powdery mildew attacks roses; strawberry powdery mildew attacks strawberries; and vine powdery mildew attacks vines. As well as this, there are many indistinguishable powdery mildews that affect asters, clematis, aquilegia, honeysuckle, hawthorn, and other ornamental plants. Powdery mildews are most common in warm dry weather and on dry soils.

Typical symptoms: A powdery white coating on almost any part of the plant. Individual powdery patches may spread and coalesce. Blossom may wither and fail and leaves drop prematurely. Infected parts may be distorted and die back, while the whole plant is weakened. Gooseberry fruit develops a brown-coloured, felt-like coating.

Prevention and treatment: Grow resistant cultivars if they are available, for instance, roses, strawberries, gooseberries, currants and asters. Do not grow susceptible plants up against a house wall or in any situation where the soil is likely to dry out. Sow turnips and swedes late and peas early to avoid any periods of dry weather, and improve soil structure and use mulches to help ensure the plants have a regular supply of water. Do not apply nitrogen fertilizer too liberally. Pick off and prune out infected leaves and shoots as appropriate, and remove and destroy all infected plant debris. Use a sulphur spray, except on plants that are "sulphur shy", such as several varieties of gooseberry and apple.

Sclerotinia (*Sclerotinia sclerotiorum*)

This is a widespread disease infecting many types of vegetables and ornamentals, including carrots, parsnips, bulbs, corms and tubers in store. It is worst in cool, damp conditions.

Typical symptoms: Plants suddenly wilt and fall over. Stems of susceptible plants and bulbs, tubers, corms and roots in store develop a brown rot, often associated with a distinctive snowy-white, cottony mould.

Prevention and treatment: Good hygiene and ventilation can help to reduce the risk of this disease. Where it develops, carefully remove and destroy (do not compost) infected plants. Do not grow susceptible plants on infected land for three years.

Violet root rot (*Helicobasidium brebissonii*)

A distinctive disease, violet root rot affects root crops, asparagus and celery. It can also infect many ornamental plants and weed species. It is most commonly found on plants growing on wet, acid soils.

Typical symptoms: Plants grow poorly; a purple felty coating develops on roots, tubers, bulbs and corms.

Prevention and treatment: Correct pH and drainage before planting if necessary. If the disease appears, remove and destroy (do not compost) infected plant material. Do not grow susceptible plants on the same land for at least three years. Vegetables that are not susceptible to this disease include peas, Brussels sprouts, cabbages, cauliflowers and sweet corn.

Wilts (*Verticillium, Fusarium* spp.)

A common and widespread group of diseases, wilts cause similar symptoms on fruit, vegetables (especially legumes, tomatoes and cucurbits) and ornamentals.

Damping off seedlings in seed tray

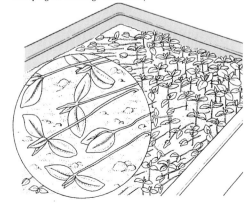

Typical symptoms: Wilting, often starting at the lower leaves, with some recovery at night to begin with. A dark discoloration can be seen in the stem if cut through above ground level.
Prevention and treatment: Where appropriate, earth up plants showing early symptoms of the diseases. Remove all infected plants and associated soil but do not compost. Do not grow susceptible plants on infected land for at least six years.

SEEDLINGS (including YOUNG PLANTS) (See also page 125)

It is never easy to identify the cause of seed and seedling failure. Conditions that encourage pests and diseases of seedlings and young plants are those that do not favour plant growth. The best strategy therefore is to give plants a good start so that they grow away quickly, strongly and healthily.

Bean seed fly (*Delia platura*)
This pest affects beans of all types.
Typical symptoms: Seeds fail to emerge and become infested with small white maggots. Losses can be considerable, especially in cold wet seasons when germination is slow.
Prevention and treatment: Raise plants indoors; encourage quick early growth of direct-sown plants. Cover with fleece or polythene.

Cutworm (*Noctua* spp.; *Agrotis* spp.)
This pest affects young vegetable plants, especially lettuces and brassicas.

Typical symptoms: Young plants suddenly wilt; the top may be severed from the roots. Fat caterpillars, which may curl up into a crescent shape when disturbed, are sometimes found in the surrounding soil, or on plants at night.
Prevention and treatment: Dig over the site where cutworm has been a problem to encourage birds to eat the pests. Protect individual plants with collars applied when transplanting. These can be made from tins with the top and bottom cut off, sections of plastic drainpipe or the inner tubes from toilet paper rolls. Push the collar a few centimetres down into the soil. Where there is cutworm damage, search the soil around plants and remove any caterpillars. Also examine plants at night and pick off the culprits.

Damping off (*Pythium* spp., *Rhizoctonia* spp. and others)
This affects the seedlings of many plants.
Typical symptoms: Seedlings topple over, usually soon after germination, due to the base of their stems withering.
Prevention and treatment: Do not sow into cold, damp soils. A heated propagator will help avoid this problem in a greenhouse. Sow thinly to avoid overcrowding and allow good ventilation. Do not overwater (see also page 167).

Downy mildews
Downy mildews affect the seedlings of brassicas, especially cauliflower, and of lettuce.
Typical symptoms: White furry growth on the underside of leaves and poor growth.
Prevention and treatment: See page 115.

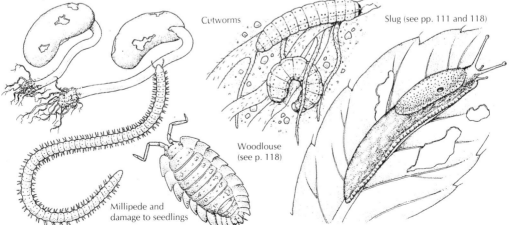

Cutworms

Slug (see pp. 111 and 118)

Woodlouse (see p. 118)

Millipede and damage to seedlings

Seedlings/Brassicas

Mice

Mice will make substantial inroads into peas, beans and sweet corn.

Typical symptoms: Seeds are eaten; individual holes where mice have tunnelled towards the seed appear in the soil. If the seed has germinated it may still be eaten, the shoot itself being left untouched. Damage by mice is worst from autumn to early spring.

Prevention and treatment: Raise early sowings of peas and beans indoors in boxes, pots or gutters (see page 125) and transplant them when the soil has warmed up. Avoid autumn and early spring sowings. Use mousetraps.

Millipedes (*Blaniulus guttulatus* and others)

Millipedes attack most seedlings but particularly peas and beans.

Typical symptoms: Poor emergence and survival of seedlings. Millipedes can be seen in the soil.

Prevention and treatment: See pages 112-13.

Poor soil structure

A cloddy seedbed, or one where the soil forms a hard dry crust, will prevent seedlings from emerging.

Typical symptoms: Seedlings fail to emerge in spite of otherwise good conditions and absence of pests.

Prevention and treatment: Hoe and rake to form a fine seedbed before sowing. Cover seed drills with a mixture of soil and leafmould or similar rather than replacing the existing soil. Improve the structure of the surface soil generally by applying mulches of organic matter.

Slugs (*Arion hortensis* and others)

Slugs may eat seedlings before, as well as after, they emerge above the soil surface. Slime trails may be seen.

Typical symptoms: Poor emergence of seed if attacked underground; above ground, leaves and growing points are eaten.

Prevention and treatment: See pages 111–12.

Wire stem disease (*Thanatephorus cucumeris*)

Wire stem disease affects seedlings of the brassica family.

Typical symptoms: The base of the stem shrinks to a thin "wire". Some seedlings may topple over and some larger plants grow poorly.

Prevention and treatment: Sow seed into good soil; do not overwater.

Woodlice (*Oniscus asellus* and others)

Woodlice can destroy young seedlings and cause damage to young plants by eating the stems and leaves. This tends to be a particular problem with seedlings grown in a greenhouse.

Typical symptoms: Irregular holes appear in leaves and stems may also be chewed or even eaten through at ground level.

Prevention and treatment: Clear up any debris and clutter that provide shelter for the insects. Encourage natural controls including beetles, toads, centipedes and spiders. Do not mulch susceptible young plants, and destroy any woodlice you find congregating under pots, planks, stones and any other nooks and crannies around the garden.

VEGETABLES
(See also Seedlings, page 117–18)

BRASSICAS and related crops
Including: *Brussels sprouts, broccoli, cauliflower, cabbage, calabrese, Chinese cabbage, kale, radish, swede, turnip and Oriental greens*

Blossom (pollen) beetle (*Meligethes aeneus*)

Typical symptoms: Heads of calabrese are grazed by these small beetles which are black and shiny.

Prevention and treatment: Protect plants with a lightweight cover like horticultural fleece. This must be done before any flower buds appear.

Bolting

Typical symptoms: Plants (especially Chinese and spring cabbage) flower prematurely.

Prevention and treatment: See page 100.

Boron deficiency

Typical symptoms: Cauliflower curds show brown patches when cut.

Prevention and treatment: See page 102.

Cabbage root fly (*Delia radicum*)

Typical symptoms: Seedlings and young plants grow poorly and are easily pulled from the ground. Small white maggots eat the roots.

Prevention and treatment: Encourage natural enemies such as centipedes, ground beetles and birds. Protect plants with a lightweight cover, a cabbage root fly mat (see page 107) or by inter-cropping with beans. Earthing up infested plants can encourage new root growth if the plant is not already too far gone. Winter-dig the soil after an infested crop to expose pupae to birds.

Cabbage whitefly (*Aleyrodes proletella*)
Typical symptoms: Plants become infested with tiny white flies which fly up when disturbed. Leaves may be sticky and covered with a black, sooty mould.
Prevention and treatment: Break the cycle (see page 95) by removing all overwintered brassi-ca plants before planting out new ones. Bury old plants in a trench 30cm (1ft) deep or in a compost heap. Pick off lower leaves infested with young whitefly "scales" on the underside. If the problem is severe spray with insecticidal soap, preferably on a cold day when the white-fly are less active.

Caterpillars
The caterpillars that affect brassicas are those of the small white butterfly (*Pieris rapae*), the large white butterfly (*Pieris brassicae*) and the cabbage moth (*Mamestra brassicae*).
Typical symptoms: Leaves have irregular holes or are stripped down to the veins. Caterpillars may be also present.
Prevention and treatment: Encourage natural enemies such as wasps and protect plants with a lightweight cover (see page 106). Inspect unprotected plants, especially seedlings, regu-larly, and remove any caterpillars found. Look out particularly for caterpillars of the small white butterfly: these are well-camouflaged and green-ish in colour. They tend to lie along the veins of the leaves and so are difficult to spot. Spray with *Bacillus thuringiensis* if hand-picking is not a practical option.

Club root (*Plasmodiophora brassicae*)
Typical symptoms: Plants grow poorly and may wilt and/or develop reddish-purple coloration. Roots are swollen and deformed or rotted to a slimy, smelly mess.
Prevention and treatment: Club root can survive in the soil for 20 years in the absence of a suit-able host plant, so it is worth trying to keep the

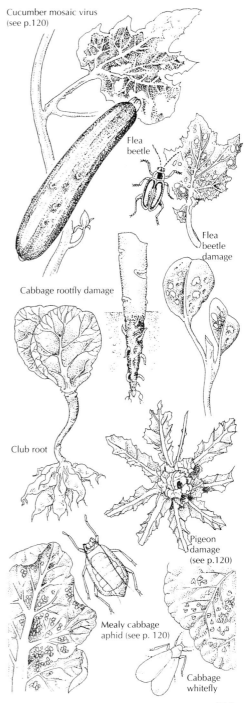

Cucumber mosaic virus (see p.120)

Flea beetle

Flea beetle damage

Cabbage rootfly damage

Club root

Pigeon damage (see p.120)

Mealy cabbage aphid (see p. 120)

Cabbage whitefly

Brassicas/Cucurbits/Beetroot

ground club root-free. Never bring infected soil or plants into the garden. To make conditions less suitable, improve drainage on wet soils and lime soil to a pH of 6.5 to 7 before growing brassicas. Use as long a rotation as possible. Where club root is present, grow resistant varieties where available. Kale, sprouting broccoli and spring cabbage may crop despite infection. Raise transplants in large pots, and/or plant into a trench of clean soil to allow some roots to develop free of disease. Dig up and dispose of infected plants but do not compost them.

Crucifer downy mildew (*Perenospora parasitica*)
Typical symptoms: Yellow patches appear on upper surface of the leaves with mould growing below in damp weather. Seedlings may be stunted or killed.
Prevention and treatment: See page 115.

Crucifer powdery mildew (*Erysiphe cruciferarum*)
Typical symptoms: Powdery white coating found on leaves and other parts of plants may eventually spread and kill plants.
Prevention and treatment: See page 116.

Flea beetle (*Phyllotreta* spp.)
Typical symptoms: Small holes appear in the leaves of seedlings and young plants. Chinese cabbage is particularly susceptible to these small, shiny beetles and even larger plants can be eaten.
Prevention and treatment: Protect plants with a lightweight cover. Keep seedlings and young plants well watered in dry weather and, if the problem is severe, spray with derris.

Hormone weedkiller damage
Typical symptoms: Stems develop warty abnormal outgrowths.
Prevention and treatment: See page 101.

Mealy cabbage aphid (*Brevicoryne brassicae*)
Typical symptoms: Leaves are discoloured and distorted, with colonies of "floury" grey aphids.
Prevention and treatment: See pages 110–11.

Nitrogen deficiency
Typical symptoms: Leaves show yellow or purplish colouring and may be reduced in size; there is no root damage.
Prevention and treatment: See page 103.

Pigeons
Typical symptoms: Leaves are pecked and torn, especially in winter.
Prevention and treatment: See page 112.

Slugs
Typical symptoms: Leaves are eaten and slime trails are present.
Prevention and treatment: See pages 111–12.

CUCURBITS and related crops
Including: *marrows, courgettes, cucumbers, squashes and pumpkins*

Cucumber mosaic/Zucchini yellow mosaic virus (ZYMV)
Typical symptoms: A yellow mosaic pattern appears on leaves and the plants grow poorly; fruits are puckered and deformed. Symptoms caused by ZYMV are usually much more severe.
Prevention and treatment: There is no cure. Remove infected plants as soon as symptoms are seen and burn or dispose of diseased plants outside the garden. Where cucumber mosaic is a regular problem, grow resistant varieties. There are as yet none resistant to ZYMV.

Fruit bitter
Typical symptoms: Cucumber fruit tastes bitter, even when young.
Prevention and treatment: Do not use excessive amounts of nitrogen fertilizers and maintain an even water supply. Prevent pollination of greenhouse varieties by removing the male flowers before they open or grow varieties that produce female flowers only.

Fruiting poor
Typical symptoms: Very few or no fruit are produced.
Prevention and treatment: See page 100.

Powdery mildews (*Erysiphe cichoracearum, Sphaerotheca fuliginea*)
Typical symptoms: A powdery white coating appears on leaves, especially in dry weather and at the end of the season.
Prevention and treatment: See page 116.

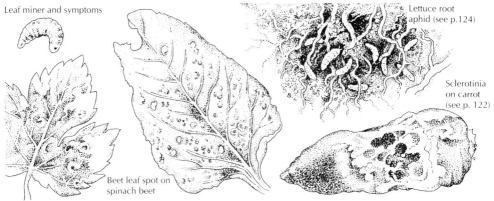

Leaf miner and symptoms

Lettuce root aphid (see p.124)

Sclerotinia on carrot (see p. 122)

Beet leaf spot on spinach beet

Red spider mite, glasshouse (*Tetranychus urticae*)

Typical symptoms: Leaves are lightly mottled and tiny greenish mites can be seen on the underside, although a magnifying lens may be needed to spot them. Silken webbing may be present when infestation is in an advanced stage. Red spider mite is mainly a problem in greenhouses, but it can also occur outside in hot, dry weather.

Prevention and treatment: Mist plants with water twice a day in warm weather and use a biological control (*Phytoseiulus persimilis*). Also clean the greenhouse thoroughly in autumn (see pages 184–5).

Sclerotinia (*Sclerotinia sclerotiorum*)

Typical symptoms: Plants rot at soil level; a white cottony mould may also be present on affected plants.

Prevention and treatment: See page 116.

Whitefly, glasshouse (*Trialeurodes vaporariorum*)

Typical symptoms: Small white flies on underside of leaves. Black sooty mould may be present on upper sides.

Prevention and treatment: Use yellow sticky traps to monitor the presence of whitefly in the greenhouse. Reduce whitefly numbers by using a portable vacuum cleaner to suck up adults disturbed by shaking the plants. If this does not work, spray with insecticidal soap. Alternatively, introduce the biological control agent *Encarsia formosa* as soon as the first whitefly are seen. Clean out the greenhouse thoroughly in autumn (see pages 184–5).

BEETROOT and related crops
Including: *spinach, spinach beet and Swiss chard*

Beet leaf miner (*Pegomya hyoscyami*)

Typical symptoms: Blotchy brown blisters are visible on the leaves of affected plants. Once the plants are established this pest is not a great problem on beetroot where the leaves are not eaten.

Prevention and treatment: Where leaf miner is a recurrent problem, spinach, spinach beet and Swiss chard can be covered with horticultural fleece or other fine cover. Encourage quick early growth of beetroot. Squash larvae within leaves or remove infested leaves. Winter-dig soil after an attack to expose pupae to birds.

Beet leaf spot (*Cercospora beticola*)

Typical symptoms: Small circular pale brown spots appear on the leaves of beetroot and spinach beet. However, beet leaf spot does little harm.

Prevention and treatment: To prevent this disease developing within a crop, take the following measures: increase potash levels in the soil if low; use a crop rotation; thin plants early to allow a good airflow around the leaves. Once it has occurred, remove infected leaves at once and clear up all crop debris. Never save seed from infected plants.

Black bean aphid (*Aphis fabae*)

Typical symptoms: The plants are infested with small black insects; the leaves may be distorted and sticky.

Prevention/treatment: See pages 110–11.

121

Beetroot/Celery/Carrots/Lettuces

Bolting
Typical symptoms: The plants produce flower stems prematurely.
Prevention and treatment: Use beetroot varieties resistant to bolting if sowing early in the season. Sow spinach in autumn and spring; avoid the long days of summer which encourage bolting. (See page 100.)

Spinach downy mildew (*Peronospora farinosa*)
Typical symptoms: Yellow patches on the leaves; a grey mould may appear underneath in damp weather.
Prevention and treatment: See page 115.

Viruses
Typical symptoms: Leaves show unusual colouring including red and yellow coloration and green or yellow mottling; they may be tough or crumpled.
Prevention and treatment: See page 99.

CELERY AND CELERIAC

Bolting
Typical symptoms: Plants produce flower stems prematurely.
Prevention and treatment: Raise plants in modules to avoid root disturbance. Keep young plants at a minimum temperature of 12°C (54°F), even when planted out. Ensure that the crop does not go short of water.

Boron deficiency
Typical symptoms: Leaf stalks split and show discoloured brownish patches.
Prevention and treatment: See page 102.

Carrot root fly (*Psila rosae*)
Typical symptoms: Plants collapse and the base of stem and roots are tunnelled by small white maggots.
Prevention and treatment: See page 107.

Celery leaf miner (*Euleia heraclei*)
Typical symptoms: Leaves develop brown blotchy "mines" which contain small larvae. These later dry to give a scorched look.
Prevention and treatment: Where celery leaf miner is a recurrent problem, protect affected plants with a lightweight cover (see pages 106–7). Pick off infested leaves or squash the larvae within them.

Downy mildew (*Peronospora nivea*)
Typical symptoms: Pale yellow spots appear on the leaves; grey mould may develop on the underside in damp weather. This mildew may also infect parsnips.
Prevention and treatment: See page 115.

Grey mould (*Botrytis cinerea*)
Typical symptoms: Leaf stalks are rotted and grey mould is present.
Prevention and treatment: See page 115.

Leaf spot (*Septoria apicola*)
Typical symptoms: Leaves develop small brown spots with black pinheads in them. Symptoms of this disease are seen on the oldest leaves first.
Prevention and treatment: Seed and crop debris are the main sources of infection, so always clear away infected plants and those that have finished cropping. Never save seed from an infected plant. Thin plants early to allow a good airflow.

Sclerotinia (*Sclerotinia sclerotiorum*)
Typical symptoms: Leaf stalks rot at the base. Also, a white fluffy mould may be present.
Prevention and treatment: See page 116.

Slugs
Typical symptoms: Irregular pieces are eaten out of stems. Slime trails may be seen.
Prevention and treatment: See pages 111–12.

Splitting
Typical symptoms: Leaf stalks split but show no discoloration.
Prevention and treatment: See page 101.

Violet root rot (*Helicobasidium brebissonii*)
Typical symptoms: Roots and tubers are covered with dark purple strands; they may also rot. The upper part of the plant may become stunted and discoloured.
Prevention and treatment: See page 116.

Viruses
Typical symptoms: Irregular yellow patterns appear on leaves.
Prevention and treatment: See page 99.

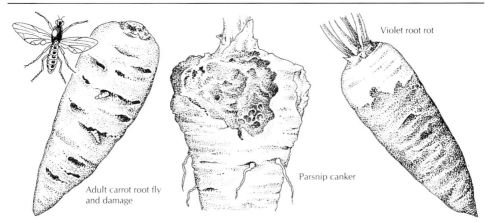

Violet root rot

Adult carrot root fly and damage

Parsnip canker

CARROTS, PARSLEY AND PARSNIPS

The following may attack all three crops unless otherwise stated.

Carrot root fly (*Psila rosae*)
Typical symptoms: Seedlings may fail to grow. On older plants, leaves may show red or yellow colouring and growth may be stunted. Often the only symptom on carrots is the surface tunnelling of the roots; small yellowish larvae may be seen in these tunnels.
Prevention and treatment: Once a crop is infested nothing can be done about it. The most successful method of avoiding attack is to grow the crop under a cover or to sow to avoid the main egg-laying period of the fly, that is, early (late winter to early spring) or late (early summer). Other methods include growing on a windy site intercropping with onions (see page 95) and growing within a carrot root fly barrier (see page 107). Use a crop rotation and winter-dig where carrot root fly has been a problem. Sow seed thinly to avoid the need for thinning out later. (See also resistant cultivars, page 92.)

Carrot willow aphid (*Cavariella aegopodii*)
Typical symptoms: Carrot leaves are infested with small green aphids.
Prevention and treatment: See pages 110–11.

Parsnip canker (various fungi)
This disease affects parsnips only.
Typical symptoms: Small brown spots appear on leaves; the roots develop orange-brown patches on the "shoulder".
Prevention and treatment: Grow resistant varieties of vegetables. Use a crop rotation and drain or avoid wet soils. Small roots produced by using a spacing of approximately 7.5–10cm (3–4in), are less prone to canker.

Splitting
Typical symptoms: Roots split.
Prevention and treatment: See page 101.

Violet root rot (*Helicobasidium brebissonii*)
Typical symptoms: A network of purple strands appear on roots; root tissues are affected by brownish rot. Above ground plants may become stunted or yellowed.
Prevention and treatment: See page 116.

LETTUCES

Aphids (various species)
Typical symptoms: Leaves are infested with pink or green aphids; the leaves may be sticky.
Prevention and treatment: See pages 110–11.

Cutworm (*Noctua pronuba* and other moth larvae)
Typical symptoms: Plants wilt suddenly; stems are eaten through at ground level. Large, fat caterpillars may be found in surrounding soil.
Prevention and treatment: See page 117.

Grey mould (*Botrytis cinerea*)
Typical symptoms: Heads of lettuce rot; a fluffy grey mould is present.
Prevention and treatment: see page 115.

Lettuce downy mildew (*Bremia lactucae*)
Typical symptoms: Yellow patches appear on

Lettuces/Peas/Beans

leaves; white mould may develop underneath in damp conditions. The patches turn brown and angular with age.
Prevention and treatment: See page 115.

Lettuce root aphid (*Pemphigus bursarius*)
Typical symptoms: Plants wilt suddenly; growth may be stunted. Small, pale aphids are seen on the roots surrounded by a white powdery wax.
Prevention and treatment: The most effective way to avoid this pest is to grow resistant varieties. See also pages 110–11.

Slugs and snails
Typical symptoms: Leaves are eaten at night; slime trails are visible.
Prevention and treatment: See pages 111–12.

Viruses and deficiencies
Typical symptoms: Yellow marbling or other unusual patterns on leaves.
Prevention and treatment: See page 99.

Wireworm (*Agriotes lineatus*)
Typical symptoms: Seedlings and larger plants grow poorly.
Prevention and treatment: See page 114.

PEAS, BEANS and related crops
Including: *broad beans, French beans, runner beans, clover* and *vetches*

All peas, beans and related crops are susceptible unless otherwise stated.

Bean root aphid (*Smynthurodes betae*)
This affects runner, French and broad beans.

Typical symptoms: Poor growth and crop. Small creamy-brown aphids associated with a white waxy powder are found on roots.
Prevention and treatment: Use crop rotation. See also pages 110–11.

Birds (especially jays)
Typical symptoms: Triangular pieces pecked out of broad bean and pea pods.
Prevention and treatment: See page 112.

Black bean aphid (*Aphis fabae*)
This aphid is found on broad beans, and on French and runner beans. It also attacks beetroot and spinach beet and ornamentals including nasturtiums, poppies and dahlias.
Typical symptoms: Colonies of small black aphids are visible on main growing shoots. These may spread down the plant and on to the pods, stunting growth and reducing the crop.
Prevention and treatment: Autumn-sown broad beans are less susceptible to attack. Pick out and destroy infested growing shoots; spray with insecticidal soap if the attack is severe. (See also pages 110–11.)

Broad bean rust (*Uromyces viciae-fabae*)
Broad beans and peas are affected.
Typical symptoms: The underside of leaves and the stems develop rusty-brown pustules. Broad bean rust is spectacular but rarely serious.
Prevention and treatment: Avoid damp, sheltered sites. Clear up and compost all crop debris.

Chocolate spot (*Botrytis fabae*)
Broad beans, field beans and winter tares are affected by chocolate spot.

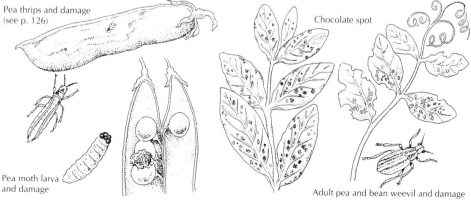

Pea thrips and damage (see p. 126)

Chocolate spot

Pea moth larva and damage

Adult pea and bean weevil and damage

Typical symptoms: Small chocolate brown spots are visible on leaves and stems. The spots may blacken and merge in damp conditions.
Prevention and treatment: To reduce the incidence of chocolate spot, avoid growing broad beans in damp, sheltered sites with poorly drained soil. Increase soil potash levels if they are low. Autumn-sown broad beans are more susceptible. If the crop is infected, clear up and compost all debris once the beans have been picked.

GROWING PEAS IN A GUTTER
(See also pages 117–18)

To avoid damage by mice, pea seeds can be grown in a piece of guttering in a greenhouse and transplanted once they are big enough.

Take a length of plastic guttering about 1m (3½ft) long and fill it with moist compost. Sow the pea seeds in the compost in two rows about 5cm (2in) apart and leave around 5cm (2in) between each seed. If mice are also present in the greenhouse, it may be necessary to hang the guttering from the roof.

When the pea seedlings are approximately 5cm (2in) high, harden them off and then transplant them into the open ground. To do this, make a channel in the soil the same size and shape as the gutter. Water the guttering well and leave it for an hour or two, then place one end of the guttering at the end of the prepared channel and gradually slide the row of peas out from the gutter onto the soil. Firm in gently and water well.

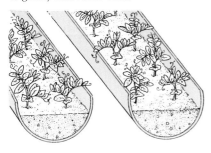

Foot and root rots (Various fungi)
Typical symptoms: The plants collapse; roots and/or base of the stem are rotted.
Prevention and treatment: See page 129.

Mice
Peas and broad beans are eaten by mice.
Typical symptoms: Seeds are removed from the soil, leaving a small hole above the site of the seed. Seedlings may also be disturbed and seeds removed.
Prevention and treatment: See page 116.

Pea and bean weevil (*Sitonia lineatus*)
This weevil affects broad beans, peas, clover and vetches.
Typical symptoms: Greyish-brown weevils feed on the leaves, creating a characteristic scalloped edge. Seedlings may fail to thrive if attacked when young. The symptoms cause little harm to older plants.
Prevention and treatment: Where this pest is a problem, avoid early sowings, which will be slow to get started. If small plants are severely affected, treat with derris.

Pea moth (*Cydia nigricana*)
The pea moth affects peas only.
Typical symptoms: Peas are eaten in the pod by small, black-headed caterpillars. The pea moth lays its eggs on pea flowers and the larvae move into the pods when they are very small, so no external damage is visible.
Prevention and treatment: Sow peas either early or late so that they are not in flower when the pea moth is laying its eggs (normally early to mid-summer). Alternatively, cover plants with a fine mesh material while they are in flower. This should not reduce cropping. Winter-dig plots where infested plants were growing.

Pea powdery mildew (*Erysiphe pisi*)
Pea powdery mildew affects peas only.
Typical symptoms: White powdery patches are visible on leaves and pods, especially in dry conditions.
Prevention and treatment: See page 116.

Poor pod set
This is a problem of runner beans.
Typical symptoms: Flowers fail to set pods.
Prevention and treatment: See page 100.

Peas/Beans/Onions/Potatoes

Thrips (*Kakothrips robustus*)
Thrips affect peas only.
Typical symptoms: Leaves and pods show a characteristic silver sheen and the pods may also be distorted. Thrips, also commonly known as thunder flies, are mainly a problem in hot, dry weather conditions. Yellow larvae and yellow-brown adults are present on affected plants in late spring/early summer.
Prevention and treatment: Ensure that plants do not go short of water during spells of hot, dry weather. Winter-dig plots where infested plants have been growing.

Virus
Typical symptoms: Unusual yellow patterns appear on the leaves of infected plants. Plants may be stunted and growth generally poor; also, plants may develop distorted leaves, flowers and pods.
Prevention and treatment: See page 99.

Wilt (various fungi)
Typical symptoms: The plants wilt, oldest leaves first. When the stem is cut through a dark streak is visible.
Prevention and treatment: See page 116.

ONIONS and related crops
Including: *shallots, leeks, garlic* and *chives*

Onion downy mildew (*Peronospora destructor*)
Typical symptoms: Leaves yellow and die from the tip down.
Prevention and treatment: See page 115.

Onion fly (*Delia antiqua*)
Typical symptoms: Leaves wilt; small white maggots are found in roots and bulbs. Young plants may die; infested bulbs rot.
Prevention and treatment: Where onion fly is a recurring problem, protect plants with a lightweight cover. Crop rotation, winter-digging infested land and removing infested plants as soon as the onion fly is noticed can help to limit its effects.

Leek rust (*Puccinia allii*)
This affects leeks, chives and occasionally other related crops.
Typical symptoms: Distinctive bright orange pustules develop on leaves in summer and early autumn. A severe infection may kill young plants.
Prevention and treatment: This disease is more likely to occur where soil potash supplies are inadequate, poor drainage is a problem, and where nitrogen is applied excessively. Immediate action is not necessary as the disease often disappears of its own accord in the autumn. If leek rust is a recurrent problem, break the cycle of infection with uninfected plants.

Neck rot (*Botrytis allii*)
Neck rot affects onions only.
Typical symptoms: Onions in store develop a soft rot that starts in the neck. Grey mould may be present.
Prevention and treatment: Use a minimum three-year crop rotation. To avoid infection, clear up all crop debris and avoid damage to plants while weeding. Never bend green onion

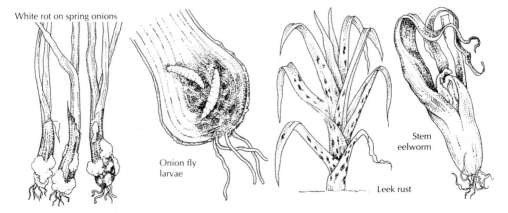

White rot on spring onions

Onion fly larvae

Stem eelworm

Leek rust

tops over; leave them to die down naturally. Dry bulbs well before storing. Never save seed from an infected plant.

Stem eelworm (*Ditylenchus dipsaci*)
This pest also attacks a wide range of fruit, ornamental plants, weeds and other vegetables such as French and runner beans.
Typical symptoms: Leaves swollen and distorted; the base of the plant swells prematurely. Plants grow poorly and may die.
Prevention and treatment: Avoid bringing infested plants into the garden. Where the pest attacks, remove infested plants (do not compost) and do not grow another susceptible plant on the site for two to three years. Brassicas and lettuce are not susceptible.

White rot (*Sclerotium cepivorum*)
This disease affects onions, garlic and leeks.
Typical symptoms: Leaves die back; root growth is poor. A fluffy white mould develops on the base of onion bulbs and the neck of garlic.
Prevention and treatment: White rot can survive in the soil for 20 years or more in the absence of a host crop so it makes sense to avoid bringing infected plants or soil into the garden. Where the disease occurs, dig out infected plants with a good spadeful of soil and dispose of it in the dustbin. There is no cure for this disease, but leeks may produce a crop on infected land where onions and garlic fail.

POTATOES

Blackleg (*Erwinia carotovora*)
Typical symptoms: Leaves roll; individual stems grow poorly. Stems turn dark brown just above and below ground and rot in wet weather. Tubers may rot to a foul-smelling mess in the ground or may rot in store. Seed tubers are one of the main sources of infection. There is little spread between plants except in wet soils.
Prevention and treatment: Grow less susceptible varieties such as 'Wilja', 'Marfona', 'Pentland Crown' and 'Romeo' and avoid poorly drained land. Always harvest every tuber at the end of the season and compost potato foliage in a hot compost heap. If blackleg is a recurrent problem, do not mulch potatoes as this can exacerbate it. Check tubers in store regularly.

Common scab (*Streptomyces scabies*)
Typical symptoms: Tubers have rounded, corky, scabby patches on the skin, but the crop is otherwise usable.
Prevention and treatment: Scab is most common on light, dry and alkaline soils. Add organic matter to improve the soil and check the pH. Grass mowings in the potato trench will make conditions more acid. Spread a layer 2.5–5cm (1–2in) thick along the bottom of the trench, cover with 2.5cm (1in) of soil then plant as usual. Watering the crop as the plants meet between the rows can also reduce the incidence of scab. Varieties such as 'Wilja' and 'Pentland Javelin' are less susceptible to the disease.

Frost
Typical symptoms: Foliage of plants turns brown, wilted and shrivelled overnight; severe frosts may also cause the scorching of shoots. Symptoms do not spread (unless there happens to be another frost).
Prevention and treatment: See page 101.

Magnesium deficiency
Typical symptoms: Leaves turn yellow between veins on older leaves first giving a marbled effect. Magnesium deficiency is common on light, acid, sandy soils especially in when the weather is wet.
Prevention and treatment: See page 103.

Potash deficiency
Typical symptoms: The oldest leaves are affected first; the leaf margins turn brown, with a scorched look and may curl at the edges. Plants generally unhealthy.
Prevention and treatment: See pages 100–1.

Potato blight (*Phytophthora infestans*)
Typical symptoms: Brown blotches appear on top of leaves in damp weather; white mould may develop underneath. The disease spreads very rapidly in warm, humid conditions, destroying all foliage. Tubers may rot in store.
Prevention and treatment: Where blight is common, grow less susceptible varieties such as 'Wilja' and 'Cara'. Early varieties are more likely to produce a reasonable crop before blight appears. Earthing up or mulching plants can reduce damage to tubers, which results from blight spores being washed into the soil from

Potatoes/Tomatoes

infected leaves. Check regularly for blight symptoms from mid-summer. If it is seen to be spreading, cut off all foliage to ground level and compost it in a hot heap. Blight spores can survive for around three weeks in the soil; delay harvesting for this period to avoid infecting the tubers as they are lifted. Always check stored tubers regularly. Bordeaux mixture may slow down the spread of the disease if it is applied early enough, but it is of little use if the weather is wet.

Potato cyst eelworm (*Globodera* spp.)
Typical symptoms: Affected plants grow poorly and die down early; the leaves yellow and the crop is small. With the aid of a magnifying lens, pinhead-sized cysts may be seen on roots in mid-summer. There are two types of cyst eelworm: one has yellow cysts, the other brown or white.
Prevention and treatment: Cyst eelworm eggs can survive in the soil for 15 years or more, so it is worth taking measures to avoid introducing it into the garden. Always use certified seed potatoes. Crop rotation can help to prevent pest build up in the soil. If the soil is infested, grow resistant varieties such as 'Cara', 'Penta', 'Pentland Javelin' and 'Sante'. Most resistance is to the more common yellow cyst eelworm; a few, such as 'Sante', are also resistant to the brown or white cyst type. Increasing organic matter in the soil, growing early varieties and using the no-dig method will also help to improve the crop (see pages 38–41).

Powdery scab (*Spongospora subterranea*)
Typical symptoms: Potato tubers develop irregular brown crater-like depressions and occasionally canker-like growths.
Prevention and treatment: Use a long crop rotation and avoid poorly drained soils. Do not grow 'Pentland Crown', which is particularly susceptible to this disease.

Slugs
Typical symptoms: Holes or extensive galleries are evident in tubers.
Prevention and treatment: Do not grow varieties that are prone to slug damage. Examples of these include 'Maris Piper', 'Desiree' and 'King Edward'. Harvest all tubers by the end of the summer because it is during the early autumn

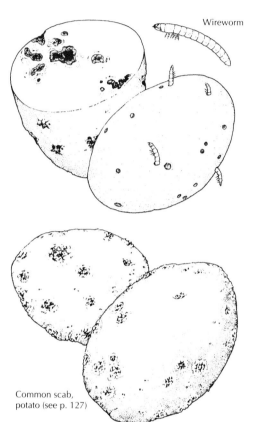

Wireworm

Common scab, potato (see p. 127)

that the most severe slug damage is caused. See also pages 111–12.

Wireworm (*Agriotes lineatus*)
Typical symptoms: Often confused with eelworm, this much larger pest makes knitting needle-sized holes in potato tubers.
Prevention and treatment: See page 114.

TOMATOES

Blossom end rot
Typical symptoms: A circular, sunken, dark-coloured patch can be found at the blossom end of affected tomato fruits. These symptoms are due to a shortage of calcium in the fruit and this deficiency is caused by an irregular supply of water.
Prevention and treatment: Ensure that plants are never short of water, especially those grown in pots and growing bags. See also page 167.

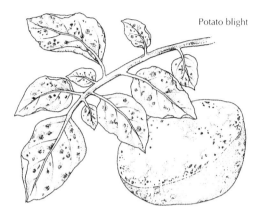

Potato blight

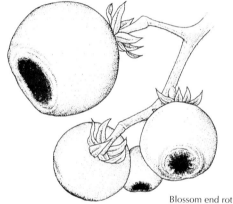

Blossom end rot

Cold nights
Typical symptoms: Leaves curl up; growth otherwise normal. This is a harmless condition caused by wide differences in day and night temperatures.
Prevention and treatment: Protect tender plants.

Foot and root rots (various fungal diseases)
Typical symptoms: Plant wilts and the foliage may become yellowed. The stem base and/or roots rot.
Prevention and treatment: Correct conditions such as poor soil structure or drainage that could stress plants. Use a crop rotation. Greenhouse tomatoes may be saved by earthing up stems with clean soil or compost. Remove and burn badly infected plants.

Fruit splitting
Typical symptoms: Tomato fruits split.
Prevention and treatment: See page 101.

Hormone weedkiller damage
Typical symptoms: Leaves are narrow and twisted; stems twist in a spiral. Fruit may be hollow and seedless.
Prevention and treatment: See page 101.

Magnesium deficiency
Typical symptoms: Orangish-yellow colour develops between leaf veins, on the lower leaves first.
Prevention and treatment: See page 103.

Potato blight (*Phytophthora infestans*)
This is the same disease that attacks potatoes.
Typical symptoms: Dark patches appear on the leaves and the stems may collapse. A tough, dry, brown rot can develop on the fruit, although this may not become obvious until after it has been picked.
Prevention and treatment: There is little that can be done against this disease. In a greenhouse, increased ventilation may help to reduce the spread. Bordeaux mixture may be used to protect plants (see page 128).

Red spider mite, glasshouse (*Tetranychus urticae*)
Typical symptoms: Leaves turn yellowish-bronze and die off. With the aid of a magnifying lens, tiny yellowish-green mites can be seen on the underside of leaves. A severe attack may cause the leaves to wither and die.
Prevention and treatment: Give plants good growing conditions. Do not let the soil or the atmosphere in the greenhouse become too dry. The biological control agent *Phytoseiulus persimilis* can be introduced to control this pest (see page 104). Check new plants before bringing them into the greenhouse (see pages 184–5); clean the greenhouse out thoroughly every autumn.

Virus diseases
Typical symptoms: Symptoms including stunting, distortion or unusual coloration of leaves.
Prevention and treatment: See pages 98–9.

Whitefly, glasshouse (*Trialeurodes vaporariorum*)
Typical symptoms: Leaves are covered in small white insects that fly up when disturbed. Whitish-green scales are visible on the underside of leaves.

129

Tomatoes/Soft fruit

Black sooty moulds and sticky deposits may be present.
Prevention and treatment: Use sticky yellow traps (see page 107) to monitor the appearance of whitefly in the greenhouse; take action as soon as they are seen. Suck up the adult flies using a portable vacuum cleaner or spray with insecticidal soap. The biological control agent *Encarsia formosa* can be introduced (see page 105). Always check new plants for whitefly before bringing them into the greenhouse.

Wilts (various fungal diseases)
Typical symptoms: Leaves wilt but may recover at night initially. Brown streaks are visible in the stem if it is cut well above soil level.
Prevention and treatment: See page 116–17.

SOFT FRUIT
Including: *raspberries, blackberries, strawberries, gooseberries* and *currants*
American gooseberry mildew (*Sphaerotheca mors-uvae*)
American gooseberry mildew affects gooseberries and currants.
Typical symptoms: A white powdery coating on leaves and on shoots, which may die back; a brown felty cover on gooseberry fruits.
Prevention and treatment: See page 116.

Aphids (various species)
Gooseberries, currants, raspberries, blackberries and strawberries are all affected by various species of aphids.
Typical symptoms: Leaves and shoots are infested with tiny insects of varying colours. Leaves may be blistered, distorted, sticky and blackened. Shoot growth may also be distorted. Symptoms may persist after pests have flown.
Prevention and treatment: See pages 110–11.

Big bud mite/gall mite (*Cecidophyopsis ribis*)
This affects blackcurrants. The fact that they can transmit reversion virus (see page 132) is more important than any direct damage they cause.
Typical symptoms: Buds are round and swollen in winter.
Prevention and treatment: Remove and burn all swollen buds in the winter. Where infestation is severe, cut out all wood and burn it. Never plant new stock near infested plants. Grow resistant cultivars 'Foxendown' and 'Farleigh'.

Bullfinches
Typical symptoms: Fruit buds are eaten in winter and early spring.
Prevention and treatment: See page 106.

Cane blight (*Leptosphaeria coniothyrium*)
This affects raspberries, blackberries and hybrid berries.
Typical symptoms: Canes wither or fail to grow; they may be pulled easily out of the soil.
Prevention and treatment: Prevent damage to canes by cane midge and wind rock as this can be a source of entry for cane blight. Cut out and burn infected canes as soon as they are noticed. Disinfect secateurs after use. Do not plant new stock in the same site.

Cane midge (*Resseliella theobaldi*)
Blackberries, raspberries and hybrid berries are affected by cane midge.
Typical symptoms: Tiny orange larvae are found in cracks in new canes. The damage caused is usually light, but it can be an entry point for cane blight.
Prevention and treatment: Remove mulch and lightly cultivate the soil around the base of the canes in winter. If the problem is severe, spray the base of the canes with derris as directed, usually in late spring, repeating two weeks later.

Cane spot (*Elsinoe veneta*)
Raspberries, blackberries and hybrid berries are susceptible to cane spot.
Typical symptoms: Purple spots on canes, leaves and blossom stalks. Severe infections cause distortion and death.
Prevention and treatment: Remove and burn infected canes. Spray with Bordeaux mixture as directed, usually fortnightly from bud burst to petal fall. Grow resistant varieties on a new site.

Common green capsid (*Lygocoris pabulinus*)
This affects gooseberries and currants.
Typical symptoms: Irregular holes develop in young leaves.
Prevention and treatment: Tolerate the problem, which is rarely severe.

Coral spot (*Nectria cinnabarina*)
Typical symptoms: Pink pustules appear on dead wood. Branches die back.
Prevention and treatment: See page 114.

Gooseberry sawfly (*Nematus ribesii*)
Gooseberry sawfly attacks gooseberries primarily but also feeds on red and white currants.
Typical symptoms: Leaves are eaten; the whole bush may be stripped to leaf veins in a very short period. Large numbers of pale green, black-spotted caterpillars may be present.
Prevention and treatment: Inspect bushes regularly and remove any eggs and caterpillars found. Concentrate in particular under the leaves in the centre of the bush. The times to do the inspection are mid-spring, early summer, mid-summer and early autumn. If hand-picking does not control the problem, spray with derris. Plants grown as cordons or fans make hand-picking or spraying much easier and a lot more effective.

Grey mould (*Botrytis cinerea*)
All soft fruit is susceptible to grey mould.
Typical symptoms: Affected plants suffer from a poor crop and rotting fruit with patches of fluffy grey mould. On currants and gooseberries, the only symptom is that the branches die back.
Prevention and treatment: See page 115.

Phytophthora root disease (*Phytophthora* spp.)
This affects blackberries, raspberries and hybrid berries.
Typical symptoms: Canes die back progressively. Roots die but do not decay.

Prevention and treatment: Avoid planting susceptible fruit in wet and waterlogged soils. If the disease appears, dig up and burn infected canes. Disinfect tools and put the site down to grass.

Powdery mildews (*Sphaerotheca macularis*)
Raspberries, blackberries, hybrid berries and strawberries are all susceptible to this.
Typical symptoms: A white powdery coating appears on the leaves. The flowers may be distorted and the fruit inedible.
Prevention and treatment: See page 116.

Raspberry beetle (*Byturus tomentosus*)
Blackberries, raspberries and hybrid berries are attacked by raspberry beetle.
Typical symptoms: Fruits are malformed and may contain small, white larvae.
Prevention and treatment: Remove all mulches and lightly cultivate the soil around the canes in winter. If the problem is severe, spray with derris as directed on the container (usually at petal fall and when the first pink fruit appears).

Red spider mite, glasshouse (*Tetranychus urticae*)
This greenhouse pest can also attack fruit outside during a hot summer. It affects strawberries, raspberries and currants.
Typical symptoms: Leaves turn yellowish-bronze and may become withered or crisp. Use a magnifying lens to see tiny yellowish-green mites on the underside of leaves.

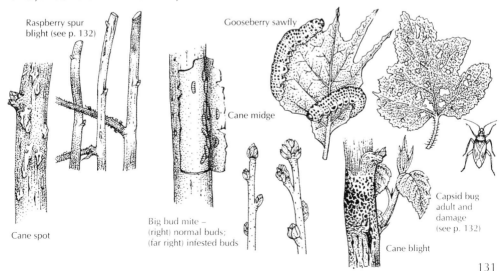

Raspberry spur blight (see p. 132)

Gooseberry sawfly

Cane midge

Cane spot

Big bud mite – (right) normal buds; (far right) infested buds

Capsid bug adult and damage (see p. 132)

Cane blight

Soft fruit/Top fruit

Prevention and treatment: Ensure that plants have an adequate water supply. *Phytoseiulus persimilis*, a biological control agent, can be used to control red spider mite (see page 104). At the end of the season, cut off all strawberry leaves and remove mulches. Prune currants and raspberries as appropriate.

Reversion virus
This is a very common disease of garden blackcurrants.
Typical symptoms: The number of flowers and the size of the main veins on the primary leaves are reduced. Cropping is sparse.
Prevention and treatment: Control is not easy. Keeping big bud mite levels down can help as this pest transmits the disease. When planting new stock, always buy good-quality plants and remove any diseased bushes first.

Slugs and snails
These pests attack strawberries as well as several foliage plants
Typical symptoms: Large pieces are eaten out of the fruit; slime trails are visible.
Prevention and treatment: See pages 111–2.

Spur blight (*Didymella applanata*)
Spur blight affects raspberries, blackberries and hybrid berries.
Typical symptoms: Purple patches appear on stems around the buds; these patches turn silver in winter.
Prevention and treatment: Keep canes thinned as appropriate by pruning. It is also important to burn infected canes. Where spur blight is a problem, spray with Bordeaux mixture as directed on the container (usually when canes are approximately 10cm (4in) tall). Resistant varieties are available.

Strawberry red core (*Phytophthora fragariae*)
This affects strawberries only.
Typical symptoms: Symptoms of strawberry red core are most obvious in mid-summer. Patches of stunted plants appear; the outer leaves are brown and stiff and the inner ones are small and red. Roots rot, with a red central core.
Prevention and treatment: Strawberry red core can last for up to 12 years in the soil, so always plant new strawberry plants in a new site. Infected land is best isolated by putting it

down to grass; no curative measures are available. Never grow strawberries on poorly drained land.

Vine weevil (*Otiorhynchus sulcatus*)
Strawberries are affected by vine weevil.
Typical symptoms: Plants suddenly wilt and die; fat white grubs with brown heads are found in the soil.
Prevention and treatment: See page 114.

TOP FRUIT
Including: *apples, pears, quinces, cherries, plums, damsons, peaches, almonds, apricots and nectarines*

All tree fruit are susceptible to the following pests, diseases and common problems unless otherwise stated.

Aphids (various species)
Typical symptoms: Leaves and young shoots are infested with pink, green, black or brown aphids. Leaves may be distorted or tightly curled and sticky to the touch. Growth of young shoots may be reduced or distorted.
Prevention and treatment: See pages 110–11.

Apple canker (*Nectria galligena*)
This affects apples and pears (also hawthorn and poplar).
Typical symptoms: Twigs and branches show cracks around the base and wrinkled, discoloured, sunken patches. Spurs, shoots and branches may die.

Prevention and treatment: Grow varieties that are less-susceptible to this disease. Avoid poorly drained sites and overfeeding as both conditions will make trees more susceptible to canker. Inspect apple and pear trees regularly and cut out any canker immediately it is seen. Burn diseased wood.

Apple and other capsid bugs (*Plesiocoris rugulipennis, Lygocoris pabulinus* and others)
Apple, pear, plum and damson are susceptible to capsid bugs.
Typical symptoms: Tattered holes appear in young leaves; fruits are distorted and/or with raised bumps or scabs.
Prevention and treatment: Damage caused by

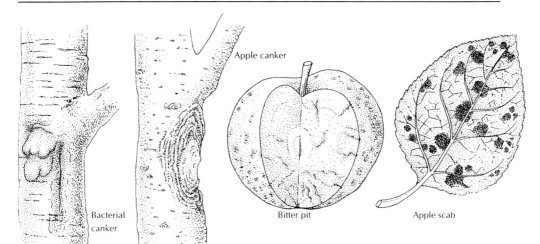

Apple canker

Bacterial
canker

Bitter pit

Apple scab

capsid bugs is rarely severe. Little can be done other than to keep trees growing well.

Apple powdery mildew (*Podosphaera leucotricha*)
This affects apples and pears.
Typical symptoms: Powdery white coating on leaves, flowers and twigs.
Prevention and treatment: See page 116.

Apple sawfly (*Hoplocampa testudinea*)
Apple sawfly affects apple fruitlets.
Typical symptoms: The damage caused by sawfly larvae is similar to that of the codling moth but occurs earlier in the season. A large cavity is eaten in the fruit; this cavity is filled with the droppings of the larvae, known as "frass". The fruit may fall early. Fruit that does mature may show a characteristic ribbon scar.
Prevention and treatment: Remove and compost all fruits that fall early. If there is a regular severe problem, spray with derris liquid as directed on the container, usually at petal fall.

Apple scab (*Venturia inaequalis*); pear scab (*Venturia pirina*)
These affect apples and pears respectively.
Typical symptoms: Dark greenish-brown blotches on leaves and fruit. When infection is severe, leaves may fall early and fruit become cracked or corky. (Note that adverse soil conditions can also cause black blotches on pear leaves.)
Prevention and treatment: Grow resistant varieties, especially in wet areas. Do not grow susceptible plants in damp areas or close to water.

Keep the tree open by pruning to allow good air flow. Collect up all fallen leaves in the autumn or run a mower over them to speed up decomposition. Prune out infected twigs, which will show blistered swellings. These measures will help reduce reinfection in spring.

Bacterial canker (*Pseudomonas morsprunorum*)
This affects plums, cherries and peaches.
Typical symptoms: Leaves have small round "shot" holes. Shallow depressions (cankers) appear on branches, often on one side of the branch only. If the canker girdles the branch, growth beyond it will die.
Prevention and treatment: Do not grow Victoria plum, which is particularly susceptible. Avoid wounding trees when staking and tying as the disease enters through wounds. Prune out and burn or dispose of diseased wood, cutting back into healthy wood as soon as it is noticed. If the disease persists, spray with Bordeaux mixture in late summer and early and mid-autumn.

Bitter pit (calcium deficiency)
This affects apples, especially 'Bramley' and 'Newton Wonder'. It is most frequent on young, vigorously growing trees.
Typical symptoms: The fruit becomes pitted and brown spots appear scattered through the flesh, which may also show "glassiness" – a translucency. These symptoms are caused by a shortage of calcium in the fruit, but this is rarely due to a calcium deficiency in the soil, rather an

Top fruit

imbalance of calcium with other elements.
Prevention and treatment: Check the pH of the
soil and add lime if it is much lower that 6.5.
Do not overfeed with nitrogen.or potash, both
of which can reduce the availability of calcium.
Maintain a regular supply of water to the tree
by improving soil structure, mulching and
watering when necessary. When bitter pit is a
recurring problem, use the fruit as soon as it is
ripe or preserve it by freezing or bottling. The
condition develops further in stored apples.

Brown rot, blossom wilt, spur blight and wither tip (*Monilinia fructigena; M. laxa*)

This affects most tree fruit (also ornamental
Prunus species).
Typical symptoms: Blossom wilts; fruit spurs
may die after flowering; fruit develops soft
brown patches with concentric rings of white
pustules. Dehydrated fruit will hang on tree all
winter.
Prevention and treatment: The fungus infects
through wounds caused by weather, birds,
insects and rubbing branches. Prune well, thin
the fruit and try to repel birds. Remove all mummified fruit; prune out all infected wood, burn
or dispose of it and treat the cuts with
Trichoderma paste.

Bullfinches

Typical symptoms: Buds removed in winter;
poor blossom and bare lengths of stem in spring.
Prevention and treatment: See page 106.

Codling moth (*Cydia pomonella*)

Apple and pear are susceptible to codling moth.
Typical symptoms: Codling moth caterpillars
tunnel to the fruit's core; it may be rendered
inedible. The caterpillar usually leaves before
the damage is discovered as there is generally
no obvious sign of its presence on the outside
of the fruit.
Prevention and treatment: Encourage blue tits
into the garden as these are effective predators
of the codling moth. To protect fruit, hang
pheromone traps in the trees to catch male
moths (see page 107). The traps should be in
place from late spring to late summer, or during early autumn in a dry year. However, traps
alone may be insufficient to control codling
moths, in which case use them to indicate the
presence of the moths so that spraying can be
timed effectively: the young caterpillars must
be killed before they can enter fruit. To ensure
this, spray with derris seven to ten days after the
moths are caught.

Coral spot (*Nectria cinnabarina*)

This affects all top fruit.
Typical symptoms: Masses of bright pink
pustules appear on dead wood. Branches may
die back.
Prevention and treatment: See page 114.

Fireblight (*Erwinia amylovora*)

This affects apple and pear trees (also other related ornamentals).
Typical symptoms: Dead blossoms and dark
brown leaves hang from affected branches giving the appearance of having been scorched by
fire. A mature tree can be killed in as little as six
months.
Prevention and treatment: Pear varieties that
flower in summer are much more prone to infection than those that flower early. Prune out
infected branches immediately, cutting at least
45cm (1½ft) into the healthy wood. If this procedure does not save the plant, dig it out and
burn or dispose of it.

Honey fungus (*Armillaria mellea*)

This affects all top fruit.
Typical symptoms: Trees die suddenly. The bark
near the base of the trunk pulls away easily,
revealing a white sheet of fungal growth of
mushrooms.
Prevention and treatment: See page 115.

Peach leaf curl (*Taphrina deformans*)

This affects peaches, almonds and nectarines.
Typical symptoms: Red blisters appear on leaves
in early summer; infected leaves turn brown and
fall prematurely. Regular attacks will reduce the
vigour of the tree.
Prevention and treatment: Do not plant susceptible trees in cool, damp situations, especially near a pond. Small trees and those grown
against a wall can be covered with a structure
to keep the rain off. This will prevent the transfer of disease spots from the bare wood to the
developing leaves and it should be kept in place
from early spring until all the leaves have developed. Where practical, remove and burn or
dispose of affected leaves as soon as they are

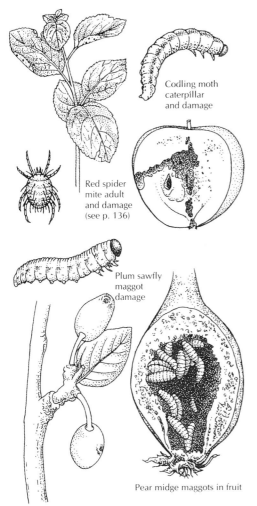

Codling moth caterpillar and damage

Red spider mite adult and damage (see p. 136)

Plum sawfly maggot damage

Pear midge maggots in fruit

noticed. Spray with Bordeaux mixture as directed on the container, usually in mid- to late winter, just before leaf fall. If regular spraying is required, consider growing species of top fruit other than peaches, almonds and nectarine and instead concentrate on those not prone to this disease.

Pear and cherry slugworm (*Caliroa cerasi*)
This affects pear and cherry along with almond, hawthorn, rowan and related trees and shrubs.
Typical symptoms: The upper surface of the leaves is grazed so that only the skeleton remains. Small, shiny black, slug-like larvae may be seen.

Prevention and treatment: Where pests are seen, remove them by hand. If this is not practical, spray with derris or insecticidal soap. In winter, lightly cultivate the soil under infested trees. This will expose overwintering pupae to predators. Remove mulches and replace with new material in the spring.

Pear midge (*Contarinia pyrivora*)
This pest attacks pear trees only.
Typical symptoms: Small fruitlets become swollen and distorted and they blacken. Such fruit fails to develop normally; when it is cut open, small larvae may be found inside.
Prevention and treatment: Grow early- or late-flowering pear varieties which should not be flowering when the midge is laying its eggs. Pick off all affected fruitlets and collect up all fallen fruit as soon as it is noticed. Destroy immediately. Lightly cultivate the soil around the trees in summer or autumn to expose midge cocoons. Remove and compost mulches in autumn; replace with fresh material in the spring.

Plum fruit moth (*Cydia funebrana*)
Plum and damson are susceptible to this insect.
Typical symptoms: Small white or pink caterpillars eat into the fruit in mid- to late summer. The fruit rots and/or ripens early.
Prevention and treatment: Collect up and destroy affected fruits as soon as the presence of this pest is noticed, before the caterpillars leave them.

Plum rust (*Tranzschelia prunispinosae*)
This affects plums, apricots, peaches, almonds and nectarines (also *Anemone* species).
Typical symptoms: Bright yellow spots appear on the leaves from mid-summer. The leaves turn yellow and may fall early.
Prevention and treatment: Pick up and remove all fallen leaves in the autumn. If they are made into leafmould, do not use this on susceptible trees. Remove anemones in the vicinity if the problem is severe.

Plum sawfly (*Hoplocampa flava*)
Plum sawfly affects plums and damsons.
Typical symptoms: Creamy-white sawfly larvae eat into developing fruit. Holes in the damaged fruit exude a sticky "frass". The fruit may fall prematurely, severely reducing the crop.

Top fruit/Ornamentals

The level of attack may vary considerably from year to year.
Prevention and treatment: Remove and compost all fruit that falls early. Where this pest is known to be a problem, spray with derris as directed on the container, usually when the petals fall.

Poor fruiting

This affects all tree fruit.
Typical symptoms: Various factors can be responsible for poor fruiting, frost being an important cause.
Prevention and treatment: See page 100.

Red spider mite, fruit tree (*Panonychus ulmi*)

Apples, pears, plums and damsons are susceptible to this pest.
Typical symptoms: Leaves are speckled, bronzed and dried up; they may fall prematurely. With the aid of a magnifying lens, tiny mites may be seen under the leaves.
Prevention and treatment: Encourage the activities of typhlodromid mites and anthocorid bugs, the natural enemies of this pest. Where mites are present in small numbers, remove all infested leaves. If the infestation is severe, spray with derris or insecticidal soap – though this can be counter-productive as the sprays can harm natural predators.

Silver leaf (*Chondrostereum purpureum*)

This affects plums, damsons, cherries, apples, apricots (also hawthorn and other rosaceous trees and shrubs).

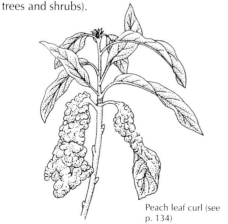

Peach leaf curl (see p. 134)

Typical symptoms: Silvery sheen appears on the leaves; symptoms may be confined to a single branch initially. Infected wood shows a dark brown discoloration within when cut through and may die back in late summer.
Prevention and treatment: Do not prune susceptible trees between early autumn and late spring; the disease will gain entry through pruning cuts more easily when the tree is not actively growing. Natural recovery is quite common. If the disease persists, cut out and burn or dispose of infected wood.

Wasps, common (*Vespula vulgaris*)

Apples, pears, damsons and plums are attacked.
Typical symptoms: Large holes are found in ripening fruit in summer and early autumn.
Prevention and treatment: Tolerate damage if possible; at other times of the year, wasps are useful predators of caterpillars and other pests. Wasps very often extend damage to fruit caused by diseases, disorders or pests such as birds. Dealing with these problems may reduce wasp damage. If essential, trap wasps in jars containing a little jam, some water and detergent.

Winter moths (*Operophthera brumata, Alsophila aescularia, Erannis defoliaria*)

Apples, pears, plums and damsons are susceptible to winter moths.
Typical symptoms: Young leaves, flowers and buds are eaten by "looper" caterpillars. These tend to drop to the ground when disturbed.
Prevention and treatment: Apply tree grease or grease bands to trees and stakes from mid-autumn to late spring (see page 108). These will prevent the female moths from making their way up into the tree. In spring, check trees regularly and remove any caterpillars found. If the problem is severe, spray with derris at bud burst.

Woolly aphid (*Eriosoma lanigerum*)

This affects apple, crab apple and other related ornamental plants.
Typical symptoms: Conspicuous tufts of white "cotton wool" appear on stems and branches of trees. This "wool" is protecting colonies of aphids. Infested stems and branches may develop hard, irregular, woody swellings which can split open, allowing diseases such as canker to infect the tree.
Prevention and treatment: See pages 110–11.

ORNAMENTALS
Including *flowers in general, roses and bulbs, corms* and *tubers*
(See also Seedlings, pages 117–18)

FLOWERS

Aphids (various species)
Young shoots and blooms of most plants can become infested with different aphid species. The large lupin aphid on lupins and black bean aphid on nasturtiums can be particularly damaging. However, most herbaceous plants grow vigorously enough to overcome attacks.
Typical symptoms: Leaves and shoots become infested with tiny insects of varying colours. Leaves may be blistered, distorted, sticky and blackened; shoot may be distorted. Symptoms may persist after the pests have flown.
Prevention and treatment: See pages 110–11.

Caterpillars (various species)
Typical symptoms: Irregular holes are eaten in leaves. Caterpillars may or may not be seen. Check at night to confirm that the damage is not caused by slugs or earwigs.
Prevention and treatment: Examine plants regularly and remove caterpillars. If this is not practical, spray pests with derris.

Earwigs
Earwigs attack ornamental plants, especially chrysanthemums, clematis, dahlias, delphiniums and pansies.
Typical symptoms: Ragged holes are eaten in the flower petals.
Prevention and treatment: See pages 19–20 and 106–7.

Leaf miners (various species)
Leaf miners attack chrysanthemums and calendula; also other plants.
Typical symptoms: Silvery snaking "mines" appear in the leaves.
Prevention and treatment: Pick off affected leaves or squash the larvae within the leaves. Weed out groundsel and sow thistles, which can harbour the pests.

Lily beetle (*Lilioceris lilii*)
This pest attacks lilies and fritillaries.
Typical symptoms: Bright red beetles and their plump red and black larvae eat the foliage in late spring and summer. Beetles and larvae can cause considerable damage.
Prevention and treatment: Check lilies regularly in spring and remove any beetles and larvae that are found. Spray pests with derris.

Powdery mildew (various species)
Powdery mildew is found on asters, calendula, chrysanthemums, forget-me-nots, lupins, sweet peas, violas and other plants.
Typical symptoms: A white powdery coating appears on leaves and stems.
Prevention and treatment: See page 116.

Rusts (various species)
Rust affects antirrhinums, cornflowers, sweet Williams, hollyhocks; also other types of ornamental plants.
Typical symptoms: Leaves are infected with yellow, rusty or brown pustules.
Prevention and treatment: Grow resistant varieties of antirrhinum. If hollyhock rust is a recurring problem, treat hollyhocks as biennial rather than perennial plants. Do not overfeed sweet Williams with nitrogen. Remove diseased plant material; herbaceous plants that get rust every season should be removed, as the disease will be living within the plant.

Slugs and snails
Typical symptoms: Irregular holes are eaten in the foliage of bedding and herbaceous plants, especially during wet weather in spring and autumn. Slime trails are visible.
Prevention and treatment: See pages 111–12.

Ornamentals: Roses/Bulbs

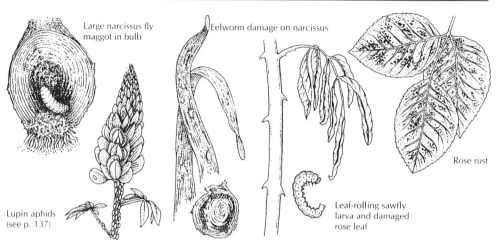

Large narcissus fly maggot in bulb

Eelworm damage on narcissus

Rose rust

Lupin aphids (see p. 137)

Leaf-rolling sawfly larva and damaged rose leaf

Solomon's seal sawfly (*Phymatocera aterrima*)

This pest affects Solomon's seal only.

Typical symptoms: The foliage of affected plants is shredded; greyish-white caterpillars with black heads are found on the plants.

Prevention and treatment: Regularly check all flowering plants as this is when the sawfly lays its eggs. Remove the caterpillars before they cause severe defoliation.

Virus, cucumber mosaic

Cucumber mosaic virus affects many ornamental plants, anemones, aquilegias, begonias, campanula, dahlias, lilies and primulas being particularly susceptible.

Typical symptoms: Affected plants show irregular yellow mosaic or mottling of leaves; distorting of leaves and flowers and stunted growth.

Prevention and treatment: See page 120.

Viruses, other

Other viruses affect chrysanthemums, sweet peas (pea viruses), nicotianas and petunias (potato viruses).

Typical symptoms: Leaves are distorted and/or mottled and flowers are distorted and/or streaked.

Prevention and treatment: See page 99.

Wilt (various species)

Antirrhinums, asters, begonias, chrysanthemums, delphiniums, sweet peas and wallflowers are susceptible to wilt.

Typical symptoms: Plants wilt; at first they may recover overnight.

Prevention and treatment: See pages 116–17.

ROSES

Aphids (various species)

Aphids are common and widespread, affecting a wide range of plants as well as roses.

Typical symptoms: Green or pinkish aphids appear on plants, usually on soft shoots and buds during spring, when they can damage weak plants.

Prevention and treatment: See pages 110–11.

Blackspot (*Diplocarpon rosae*)

This is extremely common and widespread.

Typical symptoms: Dark brown or black blotches appear on leaves. Blackspot is worse in warm wet weather. (See page 99.)

Prevention and treatment: Choose less susceptible varieties (see page 92). Do not grow roses in damp, overcrowded conditions. Collect up all fallen leaves in autumn; mulch plants before new growth begins in spring. Prune affected plants severely in spring.

Caterpillars (various species)

Typical symptoms: Irregular holes appear in leaves and flower buds where the caterpillars have eaten the plants. Caterpillars may be visible.

Prevention and treatment: Examine plants regularly and crush any eggs and caterpillars found. Remove mulches over winter.

Leaf-rolling sawfly (*Blennocampa pusilla*)

Typical symptoms: Leaves of affected plants roll tightly. Damage can be unsightly but rarely harms the plant.

Prevention and treatment: Pick off affected leaves as soon as possible. If the attack is more severe, spray with insecticidal soap. Remove mulches and cultivate the soil under affected plants in winter to expose pupae to predators.

Powdery mildew (*Sphaerotheca pannosa*)

Typical symptoms: A powdery coating appears on leaves, stems, buds and, occasionally, flowers. Leaves may drop prematurely. Powdery mildew is worse in hot, dry locations.

Prevention and treatment: See page 116.

Rose cankers (various fungi)

Typical symptoms: Brown patches appear on stems; shoots die back. Sometimes a canker will girdle the stem.

Prevention and treatment: Cut out dead or damaged wood regularly and remove cankered stems. Do not leave any stumps when pruning.

Rose slugworm (*Endelomyia aethiops*)

Typical symptoms: Also known as rose skeletonizer, this pest skeletonizes leaves. Damage can be unsightly but rarely harms the plant.

Prevention and treatment: Pick off any affected leaves as soon as possible. If the attack is more severe, spray with insecticidal soap. Remove mulches and cultivate the soil under affected plants in winter to expose pupae to predators.

Rust (*Phragmidium tuberculatum*)

Typical symptoms: Bright orange pustules are visible on the underside of the leaves.

Prevention and treatment: Grow less susceptible varieties. Collect up and burn affected leaves and fruit in autumn.

BULBS, CORMS AND TUBERS

Basal rot (*Fusarium oxysporum* and others)

Affects narcissi, crocuses and lilies.

Typical symptoms: Bulbs rot in the ground, particularly after a hot summer, and leaves fail to emerge the following year. This is one of the most serious narcissus diseases.

Prevention and treatment: Grow resistant narcissus cultivars where this disease is a problem; the *Triandrus*, *Jonquil* and *Tazetta* groups are highly resistant. Lift others in early summer before the soil gets hot, when the disease is most active. Where symptoms are seen, lift all bulbs and destroy any that feel soft around the base. Check the bulbs again after a month in store. Replant healthy bulbs on a new site.

Large narcissus fly (*Merodon equestris*)

Narcissi, bluebells and snowdrops are affected.

Typical symptoms: In early to mid-summer this fly lays its eggs in the soil near the necks of bulbs. The developing large brownish larvae eat their way into bulbs which, next season, will produce narrow, yellow and distorted leaves and fail to flower. Bulbs in open sunny places are most prone to attack.

Prevention and treatment: Deter the fly from laying its eggs by raking soil or mulch over the holes left as the leaves die down. Alternatively, cover bulbs in sunny places with horticultural fleece while the leaves die down. Replant healthy bulbs in a shady spot.

Stem eelworm (*Ditylenchus dipsaci*)

Stem eelworm affects narcissi, tulips, hyacinths, scillas and snowdrops; also some herbaceous plants, vegetables and strawberries.

Typical symptoms: Infested bulbs feel soft and produce distorted leaves and flowers. Flowers may fail to appear.

Prevention and treatment: Destroy soft, discoloured bulbs and infested plant debris, as well as healthy-looking bulbs within a 1m (3½ft) radius. Do not grow susceptible plants on the site for two or three years (see page 127).

Vine weevil (*Otiorhynchus sulcatus*)

Cyclamen, begonias and many other plants are susceptible to this pest.

Typical symptoms: Plants wilt suddenly and do not recover after watering. Those in pots are particularly susceptible.

Prevention and treatment: See page 114.

White rot (*Sclerotium cepivorum*)

White rot affects ornamental alliums.

Typical symptoms: A white fluffy mould is visible on bulbs, which rot and die.

Prevention and treatment: Destroy infected bulbs; do not grow alliums in the same area again. See also pages 126–7.

Woody plants/Lawns

Soft scale on bay

Pyracantha scab

Fairy ring

WOODY PLANTS

Aphids (various species)
Aphids attack young shoots and foliage of trees and shrubs. Some, such as honeysuckle aphids, viburnum aphids and beech aphids, are restricted to one host; others are less specific.
Typical symptoms: Leaves and shoots are infested with tiny insects of varying colours. Leaves may be blistered, distorted, sticky and blackened; shoot growth may be distorted. Symptoms may persist after the pests have flown.
Prevention and treatment: Predators that seek out overwintering eggs can be particularly useful. Leave colonies where they are doing no harm; they can act as a reservoir of food for predators and parasites. (See pages 110–11.)

Brown tail moth (*Euproctis chrysorrhoea*)
Typical symptoms: Colonies of caterpillars construct protective "tents" in branches of trees. In the summer, leaves are eaten by caterpillars.
Prevention and treatment: Prune out and burn the tents. Wear gloves and avoid any contact with the caterpillars as they can irritate the skin.

Caterpillars (various species)
Typical symptoms: Many species of caterpillars eat the leaves of most trees and shrubs.
Prevention and treatment: Pick off caterpillars as they are found or spray with derris.

Coral spot (*Nectria cinnabarina*)
Coral spot affects beech, *Elaeagnus*, magnolia and *Pyracantha*; also other plants.

Typical symptoms: Pink pustules on dead twigs and branches; branches may die back.
Prevention and treatment: See page 114.

Fireblight (*Erwinia amylovora*)
Hawthorn, cotoneaster, sorbus and other related trees are susceptible to fireblight.
Typical symptoms: Leaves brown or blacken; these remain on the tree, giving it the appearance of having been scorched by fire.
Prevention and treatment: See page 134.

Honey fungus (*Armillaria mellea*)
This disease affects birch, lilac, pines, privet, and willows; also many other woody plants.
Typical symptoms: Plants die suddenly; white fungus smelling of mushrooms is found beneath bark at or just above soil level.
Prevention and treatment: See page 115.

Leaf miner (various species)
These affect many woody plants, especially lilac, privet, laburnum and holly; also other plants.
Typical symptoms: Blisters or snaking "mines" are visible in leaves.
Prevention and treatment: See page 137.

Pyracantha scab (*Spilocaea pyracanthae*)
This disease affects many woody plants, in particular pyracantha, especially in wet seasons.
Typical symptoms: Olive-brown spots appear on leaves, which may fall early; small rough lesions grow on twigs; berries are disfigured.
Prevention and treatment: Do not grow pyracantha in damp situations. Prune out and pick

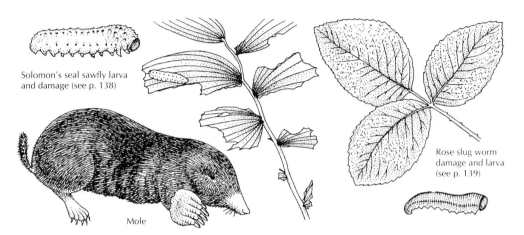

Solomon's seal sawfly larva
and damage (see p. 138)

Rose slug worm
damage and larva
(see p. 139)

Mole

off diseased leaves and twigs. Some varieties have resistance to scab.

Scale insects (various species)
Soft scale attacks greenhouse plants and woody plants in warm places, particularly bay trees, camellias and ivies.
Typical symptoms: The scales are creamy or dark brown and live on the underside of leaves, along veins. Other species attack leaves and stems of trees and shrubs; they do little harm.
Prevention and treatment: See pages 113–14.

Woolly aphid (*Eriosoma lanigerum*)
This attacks pyracantha, cotoneaster and related plants.
Typical symptoms: Tufts of fluffy white wax are found on stems.
Prevention and treatment: See pages 110–11.

LAWNS

Ants (various spp.)
Typical symptoms: Mounds of dry fine soil appear on the lawn; ants will be seen.
Prevention and treatment: see page 112.

Earthworms (*Allolobophora* spp.)
Typical symptoms: Small casts of soil appear, extruded from the soil.
Prevention and treatment: Disperse worm casts when dry, using a broom made with birch twigs.

Fairy rings
Typical symptoms: Circular rings of mushrooms

or toadstools, often with a ring of lush grass.
Prevention and treatment: These are difficult to eliminate. Keep the whole lawn growing well so the rings are less noticeable. Try replacing soil and turf to about 30cm (1ft) depth over a distance 30cm (1ft) either side of each ring.

Leatherjackets (*Tipula* spp.)
Typical symptoms: These creatures, the larvae of the crane fly (daddy-longlegs) feed on grass roots. As a result, patches of yellow or brown grass appear in dry weather. Birds often search out leatherjackets from the lawn to eat.
Prevention and treatment: See page 112.

Moles (*Talpa europaea*)
Typical symptoms: Mounds of loose fresh soil appear suddenly on the lawn.
Prevention and treatment: See page 113.

Red thread (*Corticum fuciforme*)
Typical symptoms: Reddish patches of dying grass most commonly seen in late summer, particularly in lawns on poor soils.
Prevention and treatment: Improve the fertility of the lawn.

Snow mould/*Fusarium* patch (*Micronectriella nivalis*)
Typical symptoms: Patches of yellowing or brown grass, most commonly seen over the winter, particularly after snow has melted.
Prevention and treatment: Improve drainage and aeration. Never apply nitrogen-rich material to the lawn in autumn.

Nature of weeds

Identifying all the different types of weeds in your garden and understanding their means of survival is the first step towards controlling them organically. It can pay to tolerate some weeds, but the worst offenders must be prevented from growing and spreading at the earliest opportunity.

Annual and biennial weeds
Annual weeds germinate, grow, flower, set seed and die all within one year, and may even complete several lifecycles in a single year. Biennial weeds take two years to complete their lifecycles, forming only leaves in the first year and running to seed in the second.

Annual weeds that go to seed quickly are most adapted to the frequent cultivations that take place on the vegetable plot. Common examples include shepherd's purse (*Capsella bursa-pastoris*), groundsel (*Senecio vulgaris*), chickweed (*Stellaria media*), annual meadow grass (*Poa annua*) and hairy bittercress (*Cardamine hirsuta*). Other annual weeds commonly seen in the garden include fat hen (*Chenopodium album*), sow thistle (*Sonchus oleraceus*), mayweed (*Matricaria perforata*), speedwell (*Veronica* spp.), sun spurge (*Euphorbia helioscopia*) and herb robert (*Geranium robertianum*).

Biennial weeds such as burdock (*Arctium* spp.), hogweed (*Heracleum sphondylium*), ragwort (*Senecio jacobaea*), garlic mustard (*Alliaria petiolata*) and teasel (*Dipsacus fullonum*) are more likely to be a problem among shrubs, herbaceous plants and fruit, and along paths and hedge bottoms. They usually have a deep tap root and overwinter as rosettes of leaves.

Annual and biennial weeds die quickly if pulled out, hoed off, rotavated or mulched (see page 146). However, they ensure their survival by producing large numbers of seeds and it is this that causes the problem. If you are going to make any long-term impact on their numbers you must act before they seed.

Not all the seeds that are shed germinate immediately. They become dormant and are incorporated into the soil. As a result every spadeful of topsoil in the garden can contain hundreds of weed seeds. Every time you cultivate the soil and expose the seeds to light and a difference in temperature, the dormancy of some of them will be broken and a flush of weed seedlings will result. You can therefore avoid problems by digging and turning over the soil as little as possible (see pages 38–41). Use the stale seedbed technique (see page 152) if you are sowing seeds.

Perennial weeds
These are weeds that persist for more than a year, on lawns, for example. Established plants can be very difficult to eliminate. Some have underground storage organs which enable them to survive if the top of the plant is killed by cultivation or cold. Others produce hardy rosettes of leaves which escape the mower. Many will regenerate from pieces of root or stem as well as (or instead of) seed. It is a weed's particular means of survival that determines the best method of controlling it.

With tap roots These have a large simple or branched vertical storage root. Examples are dandelion (*Taraxacum vulgaris*), dock (*Rumex* spp.), comfrey (*Symphytum officinalis*) and cow parsley (*Anthriscus sylvestris*). They will regenerate from pieces of root if these are cut up by digging, forking or rotavating, and most also produce many seeds.

Forking can bring roots out whole. However, if this is not a practical means of control, put down a light-excluding mulch for a growing season or rotavate several times. Only very regular hoeing will eliminate such weeds, but they will be most weakened if you hoe them just after they have flowered, when reserves from the tap root have been put into the blooms.

Common weeds

Broad-leaved plantain   Dandelion

With shallow spreading roots These weeds, like couch grass (*Elymus repens*), nettles (*Urtica dioica*), ground elder (*Aegopodium podagraria*) and rosebay willowherb (*Epilobium angustifolium*) spread by storage roots or rhizomes. Each bit of root or rhizome that is chopped off sends up new shoots. Most also produce seed.

The roots can be forked out if they are not too matted. Alternatively, rotavate several times or put down a light-excluding mulch for one growing season. Digging and burying the roots deeply is another possible method of control.

With deep spreading roots These have storage roots that penetrate deeply and send up new shoots if the top section is removed. Nearly all also produce some seed. Examples are coltsfoot (*Tussilago farfara*), hedge bindweed (*Calystegia sepium*), field bindweed (*Convolvulus arvensis*), horsetail (*Equisetum* spp.) and creeping thistle (*Cirsium arvense*).

These weeds are difficult to control. Hoeing or forking can be effective if you are very persistent. A light-excluding mulch will take at least two growing seasons to have any effect. In some situations, a good alternative is to grass over the area and mow it as lawn for one or two seasons.

With runners These have creeping stems above ground. Plantlets form along the stems and put down roots, finally becoming detached from the parent. Some spread by seed. Examples are creeping buttercup (*Ranunculus repens*), cinquefoil (*Potentilla reptans*), ground ivy (*Glechoma hederacea*), silverweed (*Potentilla anserina*) and selfheal (*Prunella vulgaris*).

Such weeds can be controlled effectively by digging them under or forking them out if they are not too matted. On a large area, rotavate several times or apply a light-excluding mulch for one growing season.

With corms or bulbils These have small swollen storage organs at the base of the plant which can regenerate individual plants if they are spread by cultivation. Examples are lesser celandine (*Ranunculus ficaria*) and pink oxalis (*Oxalis articulata*).

These weeds are also very difficult to control as cultivating or hoeing spreads rather than kills the bulbils. To control them, you need to dig up individual plants plus the soil around the roots, which is very time-consuming. The bulbils can survive for a long time underground without dying, but a light-excluding mulch will work if you leave it down for at least two growing seasons.

With low rosettes of leaves These are mainly lawn weeds, but they can spread to beds and borders. Examples are daisy (*Bellis perennis*), plantain (*Plantago* spp.), cat's ear (*Hypochaeris radicata*), hawkweed (*Hieracium* spp.) and yarrow (*Achillea millefolium*). They form rosettes, which often grow outwards to form a mat of plants, and spread to new sites by seed. Hoeing or forking will easily remove single specimens of these weeds, but once they have formed a mat this becomes hard work. Dig them under if practical or, on a larger area, rotavate several times. Alternatively, apply a light-excluding mulch for a growing season.

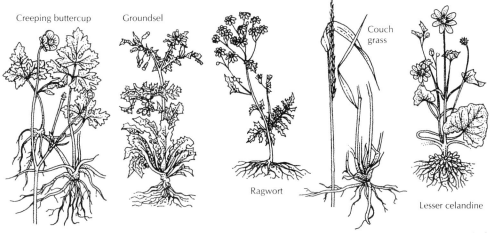

Creeping buttercup   Groundsel   Couch grass   Ragwort   Lesser celandine

143

Problems and benefits

After identifying the weeds in your garden, you need to decide when and why they are a problem – or indeed whether they are a problem at all. Not all weeds are bad all of the time, and it makes sense to concentrate your efforts where they are most needed.

Problems

Weeds have an adverse effect on garden plants when they start to compete for water, nutrients and light. This can stunt plant growth and cause loss of yield in fruit and vegetables. Slow-growing, slender-leaved crops such as onions are more susceptible to competition than vigorous crops with broad leaves, so give them priority when weeding.

Competition is not the only problem, for weeds can also harbour pests and diseases. Some shelter insect pests at times when there are no other hosts. For example, greenhouse whitefly can overwinter on chickweed, ready to infect tomatoes and cucumbers next year, so ensure that you remove this weed from the greenhouse and sheltered places nearby. Similarly, weeds in the brassica family such as shepherd's purse can carry clubroot disease. Remove them promptly from the vegetable plot or they will reduce the value of crop rotation (see pages 46–9). Several virus diseases are also carried by weeds; one of the most troublesome is cucumber mosaic virus (see page 120), which can affect groundsel and chickweed.

The presence of any weeds may also encourage fungal diseases by restricting the airflow round crops.

Another problem with weeds among fruit and vegetables is that they can cause difficulties in harvesting the crops. Something like a small annual nettle can make picking low-growing crops like strawberries slow and uncomfortable. Weed seedlings mixed with cut-and-come-again salads are not always easy to spot after they have been picked; whereas chickweed and bittercress are edible, groundsel and foxglove are poisonous.

Finally, weeds can look unsightly. In formal gardens, any weeds in beds, borders, paths, and even the vegetable plot are out of place.

Benefits

In most gardens, however, weeds can have a place. If they are not threatening to compete with your plants or causing other problems, you do not have to get rid of them. Although you are not likely to tolerate any among your bedding plants, for example, there is no reason why they are not welcome along a hedge or next to the compost heap.

All weeds add diversity to the garden and some are positively beneficial, providing food for useful insects and even making attractive plants. A few are edible, adding flavour and interest to dishes in a similar way to garden herbs. At the very least, when you do remove them, they make good compost material. Weeds can also help prevent soil erosion because their roots penetrate the soil strata and knit the layers together.

Weeds that encourage wildlife (see pages 24–7) Weeds of the Labiatae family such as red dead nettle (*Lamium purpureum* z 4) and ground ivy (*Glechoma hederacea* z 3) are good bee plants and small patches can look attractive among fruit bushes or along a hedge bottom. Bees also love the flowers of clover (*Trifolium* spp. z 3–7), and this plant has the added advantage that the bacteria associated with its roots add nitrogen to the soil so it actually feeds your lawn or fruit bushes. Hoverflies are attracted to

Beneficial weeds

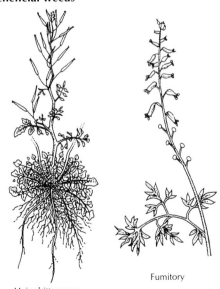

Fumitory

Hairy bittercress

Umbellifers such as cow parsley (*Anthriscus sylvestris* z 7). Cow parsley can be left to flower in patches of long grass, along with daffodils, for example. Cut the grass down in mid-summer.

Ivy (*Hedera helix* z 5) is one of the best plants for wildlife. It provides dense cover and nectar, pollen and berries late in the season when other food is scarce. It can be left to climb up an old tree stump. The common nettle (*Urtica dioica* z 3) is valuable as a nursery plant for aphids, hence boosting the ladybird population (see pages 18 and 26). Nettles also make a good liquid feed (see page 87). A nettle patch in the sun may attract red admiral and small tortoiseshell butterflies to lay their eggs.

Attractive weeds

Delicate annuals such as field poppies (*Papaver rhoeas* z 5), fumitory (*Fumaria muralis* z 5) and wild pansies (*Viola tricolor* z 4) can be very attractive. Leave a few seedlings in an informal border or vegetable plot. Ivy-leaved toadflax (*Cymbalaria muralis* z 3) grows in wall crevices, with drapes of small green leaves and pretty yellow and purple flowers. Leave it to colonize some areas of wall – it does no harm and is easy to pull out if necessary.

Edible weeds

The leaves of the biennial weed garlic mustard (*Alliaria petiolata* z 3) add a mild garlic flavour to salads – leave a patch to reseed – and the leaves of short-lived annuals like chickweed (*Stellaria media* z 3), shepherd's purse (*Capsella bursa-pastoris* z 7) and hairy bittercress (*Cardamine hirsuta* z 3) can also be used in salads. Young nettle leaves can be used in soup.

GROUND COVER FOR WILDLIFE

Convallaria majalis (lily-of-the-valley) z 3 (flowers for bees)
Cotoneaster microphyllus z 5 (flowers for bees; berries)
Erica spp. (heathers) z 5–10 (flowers for bees)
Galium odoratum (sweet woodruff) z 5 (native)
Lamium maculatum (deadnettle) z 4 (flowers for bees)
Lysimachia nummularia (creeping Jenny) z 4 (native)
Pulmonaria spp. (lungwort) z 4–6 (early flowers for bees)

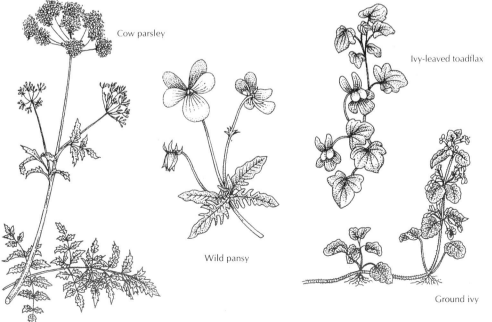

Cow parsley

Ivy-leaved toadflax

Wild pansy

Ground ivy

Clearing the ground

Forking and removing weeds
Forking out the roots of weeds is most success-ful on a small plot containing annuals and tap-rooted perennials. It enables the area to be cleared for immediate planting. Creeping weeds and shallow-rooted perennials can also be cleared fairly easily in this way. Forking is much easier if the soil is light; never attempt it when the soil is wet and sticky or baked hard.

Digging and burying weeds
Turning over the soil with a spade and burying weeds and their roots is a good method for clear-ing a small plot containing annuals or creeping and shallow-rooted perennials. You can clear old pastures or lawns in this way, even if they contains couch grass. It is hard work, but it means you can plant immediately and the turf will decay to provide nutrients.

The deeper the turf is buried the better – it should be dug down at least 15cm (6in), so this is not a suitable method if you have a thin top-soil. Subsoil and topsoil should not be mixed.

Rotavating
A rotavator has tines which chop up the surface layer of the soil. Rotavating can successfully clear annual and most perennial weeds, except those that are very deep-rooted. However, a sin-gle rotavation can make the weed problem worse, as individual pieces of chopped-up root and stem will regrow and thus multiply. To kill them, the ground must be rotavated sever-al times during the growing season. After the initial pass, wait two or three weeks for the root fragments to sprout, then rotavate again. Repeat until the roots eventually become weak and exhausted.

Pulling a tap root

To avoid breaking the root, put a garden fork underneath it to loosen the soil and do not pull too hard.

Rotavating for weed control is most effective in dry weather and on light soils. Adjust the rota-vator and tine speed so that the weed roots are chopped up as finely as possible. One disad-vantage is that rotavating damages the soil struc-ture and can cause a pan. If possible, sow an extensive rooting green manure such as graz-ing rye (see page 85) after the last rotavation to help restore the soil structure.

Mulching
One of the best methods of clearing weedy ground is to use a mulch to exclude the light. If weeds are kept in the dark when growing the roots will eventually become exhausted and die. Suitable mulches include carpet, cardboard, newspaper and black plastic.

To be effective, the mulches must be in place when the weeds are trying to grow. Lay them in spring, just as growth is beginning. Prepare the area by cutting down all the tall weeds and grass with a strimmer, mower, sickle or shears. Small amounts of debris can be left on the surface of the ground. Remove very bulky mate-rial to the compost heap and put down the mulch.

Black polythene Use 400–500 gauge (100–125 micron) polythene. This will last up to three years and can be reused. Bury the edges 7.5–10cm (3–4in) in the soil with a spade. On a large area, use a few bricks, logs or sandbags to keep the plastic flat and cover any joins.

Cardboard Use the largest sheets that you can find. Overlap them 10–15cm (4–6in) where they join. Use bricks, pieces of wood or thick wads of straw to hold them in place. This mulch should last several months.

Carpet Use hessian-backed wool carpet held down with wire pegs made by bending 25cm (10in) lengths of stout wire. If necessary, use a stout nail and hammer to make holes in the car-pet. Most carpets will start to let weeds through after one growing season, but good-quality ones can last longer. Remove the carpet before it decays as dyes and persistent pesticides are often used in the manufacture of carpets.

Newspaper Use a minimum thickness of one whole newspaper opened out and overlap the sheets well. Cover with a 5–10cm (2–4in) layer of hay, straw or grass mowings to hold the paper down. This will suppress most weeds for a month or two.

CLEARING THE GROUND

Method	Time to planting	Size of area	Weeds cleared	Comment
Light-excluding mulch	From two months in the growing season up to two years, depending on weeds	Large or small	Any weeds	Can be difficult to find materials
Forking and removing weeds	Immediately or up to several months in the growing season	Small	Annuals, tap-rooted weeds, small numbers of creeping and shallow-rooted perennials	Easiest on light soils
Digging and burying weeds	Immediately	Small	As above	Not suitable on shallow soils
Rotavating	Two to three months in the growing season	Large	All except very deep-rooted weeds	Can harm soil structure

Period of mulching

The period of mulching depends on the weeds. Annual weeds need to be mulched for only one or two months, creeping weeds, turf weeds and shallow-rooted perennials such as couch will be killed or considerably weakened after one growing season, while deep-rooted perennials and weeds with bulbils will need more than one growing season and will be killed or weakened in two. To finish clearing a patch of weakened weeds, simply fork it over.

It is often possible to use the ground even while it is being cleared because widely spaced, vigorous vegetables such as Brussels sprouts will push up through a light-excluding mulch, as can fruit bushes and shrubs. This practice is most likely to be successful where weeds are not rampant – in old pastures or lawns, for instance – or where the weeds have already been partly eliminated by forking or digging.

However, it is not a good idea to grow crops on very weedy ground as plant growth can be affected by the decomposition of the weeds. Also, vigorous weeds such as bindweed grow up to the light and may poke through the planting holes.

Laying a cardboard mulch

1 Cut down tall weeds and grass, then lay large sheets of cardboard on top of the ground, overlapping the edges generously.

2 Put wads of straw, bricks or pieces of wood at the edges and over the joins to hold the sheets in place.

Controlling weeds 1

Even if you start with a clean plot, weeds will continually try to invade. As well as ways of discouraging them from taking hold, there are ways of removing them easily when they appear.

Weed barriers

Sinking barriers that are impervious to weed roots can help to stop troublesome weeds coming in from your neighbour's garden. Seedlings will always be blown in by the wind, although growing a tall hedge will help. Creeping weeds can be kept out by digging a 15cm (6in) deep trench, lining it with heavy-duty polythene and filling it with soil. The roots of couch grass and ground elder, however, can pierce polythene, so to discourage these weeds line the trench with gravel boards or breeze blocks instead; sink them to a depth of 30cm (1ft) and fill the trench with soil. Very deep-rooted weeds like bindweed are difficult to keep out; they tend to push under most barriers eventually.

Mulching

Loose biodegradable mulches such as straw, leafmould, bark and shreddings put down on clean ground between plants can stop weed seeds germinating and can smother small annual weeds. However, they will not prevent established perennials from pushing through.

A 10cm (4in) layer is usually recommended for the best control as this will prevent light reaching the soil surface, but even a thin layer helps because it makes the soil surface more friable and so the weeds are easier to pull out. Top up the mulch annually as it will gradually decay into the soil. For properties and application of these mulches see pages 36–7. Their effectiveness for weed control can be increased by putting a layer of newspaper or cardboard underneath as for clearing the ground.

Non-degradable mulches made from plastic and polypropylene sheeting are durable and can be very effective at long-term weed control – on paths, for example. A sheet mulch such as this can also be put down around widely spaced shrubs. Disguise it with bark or shreddings.

For small, closely spaced plants the sheet must be put down before planting. Anchor it by pushing the edges into the soil or weighting them with bricks. The soil must always be moist before this type of mulch is put down. Cut a small cross into the sheet so that you can make a hole with a trowel to plant in the normal way. Remove plastic mulches on annual crops carefully at the end of the season so that they can be reused; throw-away plastic mulches are not acceptable in an organic garden.

Apart from black plastic sheeting, most of the materials sold for mulching are porous – that is to say, they allow air and water through to the soil. This makes them suitable for permanent use on large areas. Black plastic is good for tree mats (see page 150) and on narrow beds because moisture can seep sideways enough to benefit mature plants and soil life. Initially water by hand through the planting holes or through seep hose laid beneath the sheet.

Liquid feeds can be applied through a non-degradeable mulch, but there is no way of adding organic matter. Before the mulch is laid the soil must be moist and prepared with sufficient organic matter to last the whole time the mulch is down. This restricts the use of non-degradeable mulches in an organic garden.

Sheet mulches

Cardboard (covered with old straw or hay)

Biodegradeable. Lasts a growing season. Cheap. Can be put down on weedy ground.
Examples of use: round fruit bushes and trees; between rows of raspberries; as tree mats.

Paper

Biodegradeable. Lasts two to three months. Newspaper is available free. Rolls of recycled paper mulch are relatively cheap. Can be put down on weedy ground.
Examples of use: between widely spaced vegetables (cover with grass mowings); on paths between vegetable beds (cover with shreddings or straw).

Wool matting (brown felted)

Biodegradeable. Lasts one growing season in a damp place, longer if dry. Expensive. Do not put down on ground containing perennial weeds, especially couch. Easy to plant through. Not unattractive.
Examples of use: tree mats; shrubs; strawberries; other fruit.

Black plastic (300 gauge or thicker)

Non-degradeable, non-porous. Lasts two to five years; lifetime improved if covered with loose

material to prevent damage by wind and sun. Relatively cheap. Can be put down on weedy ground. Easy to plant through. Warms the soil, and keeps air above it warm at night.
Examples of use: tree mats; hedges (cover with shreddings or hay to disguise and protect plastic); vegetable beds (widely spaced crops can be planted through the mulch; take care to clear the crop very carefully so the plastic can be used another time).

Black/white polythene (black underneath, topside white)
As for black polythene except that the white surface reflects light and heat. This keeps the soil cooler and helps fruit to ripen.
Examples of use: round summer fruiting crops such as tomatoes, melons, peppers.

Woven black plastic (sometimes sold as ground cover)
Non-degradeable. Porous. Usually lasts for at least five years. "Stabilized" to stop it degrading in sunlight. More expensive than ordinary plastic. Cut edges will fray unless they are heat-sealed and strands can tangle round plants and wildlife. Keeps down some perennial weeds but is pierced by couch grass.
Examples of use: to stand pots of plants on outside the greenhouse – cover with gravel to disguise mulch and help keep surface even. It can also be used underneath gravel, bark or woodchips on paths.

LAWN WEEDS

LAWN WEEDS
The following lawn weeds are encouraged by poor conditions:
Daisy (*Bellis perennis*) – compact soil, lawn mown too short
Yarrow (*Achillea millefolium*) – soil poor, low in nitrogen and organic matter
Black medick (*Medicago lupulina*) – soil poor, low in nitrogen
Annual meadow grass (*Poa annua*) – soil compact, area shaded
Sheep's sorrel (*Rumex acetosella*) – soil acid
Moss – poor and/or compacted soil, drainage poor, shade, lawn mown too short.

Black polypropylene (sometimes sold as black fleece)
Non-degradeable. Lasts about four years. More expensive than plastic. Porous. Do not put down on weedy ground, especially if couch grass is present. Easy to plant through. Warms the soil.
Examples of use: strawberries planted through the mulch; round shrubs (cover with shreddings or bark to disguise); shrubby herbs or alpines (planted through mulch, disguised with gravel or stone chippings); under the gravel or hardcore on paths to stop soil mixing with the surfacing materials and weeds rooting through. Grey polypropylene can be used similarly where it can be covered to exclude light.

Using a sheet mulch

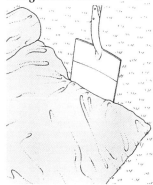  

1 Hold the sheet in place by sinking the edges in the ground using a spade.

2 Cut a cross in the sheet and make a small planting hole in the soil beneath.

3 Put the plant through the sheet into the hole and firm the soil around it.

Controlling weeds 2

TREE MATS

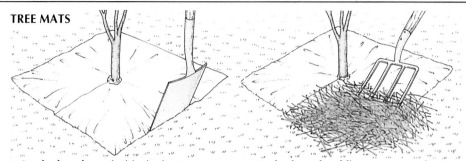

1 Spade the edges of a black plastic or polypropylene mat down into the soil.

2 Put bark or shreddings on top to disguise it, keeping the material clear of the trunk.

If you are planting a tree or shrub into grassland, use a mat to keep clear an area at least 1m (3¼ft) square at its base. This stops competition from weeds and keeps the ground moist so the tree will establish and grow much more quickly.

Black plastic works well, even where the ground is very weedy. You could also use cardboard or newspaper. Wool matting or black polypropylene (see pages 148–9)

would be suitable where the ground is reasonably weed-free to start with. In ornamental areas, the mat can be disguised with bark or shreddings, but keep loose material away from the trunk.

Leave the mat on for at least two growing seasons until the tree is well established. Trees on dwarfing rootstocks and shrubs which are not vigorous growers may need permanent mats.

Close spacing
If vegetables are planted close together in blocks rather in than rows (see pages 42–5), they can smother small weeds and will prevent other weed seeds from germinating. Some crops are more effective at this than others, for instance, onions, with their slender, slow-growing leaves, have little effect whereas quick-growing crops with broad leaves such as spinach soon form a close canopy. Vegetables that need a wide spacing but grow slowly can be intercropped with a quick-maturing crop to cover the ground:

Intercropping for weed control

1 Plant lettuces between a widely spaced row of Brussels sprouts to cover the ground.

2 The lettuces will be ready to harvest just before the Brussels sprout leaves cover them.

WEED CONTROL IN LAWNS
(see pages 182–3)

Organic weed control in lawns concentrates on encouraging the grass to grow well, as a vigorous dense sward will overcome the weeds.

However, a lawn does not have to consist entirely of grass. Unless you are trying to reproduce a cricket wicket or a putting green, some weeds can even be desirable as they can help the lawn resist wear and stay green. Clover, for example, feeds the lawn with nitrogen produced by its root bacteria, and yarrow keeps green under dry conditions. The varied leaf shapes and textures and a few flowers from daisies, bird's-foot trefoil and selfheal can add to rather than detract from a lawn's appearance. Nevertheless, weeds must be prevented from getting out of hand.

The first principle of lawn weed control is therefore to make sure that conditions are suitable for grass to grow. There are many weeds that do better than grass in very shady situations or wet places, or where the soil is compact. If you cannot correct the conditions, grow another ground cover plant that will tolerate them. However, be wary of using invasive species as these can become weeds themselves. Alternatively, where appropriate, lay a hard path, paving or gravel instead of grass.

On an established lawn, encourage the grass to grow strongly and healthily by cutting it regularly but not too closely, and liming if necessary. Leave the mowings on the lawn except in cold, wet conditions, as the mowings will feed the lawn and encourage worm activity.

Remove weeds such as dandelions and plantain which have large, flat leaves. This is because the foliage tends to smother the grass. In an organic garden this has to be done by hand: loosen them with a garden fork and pull them out, or cut them out with an old kitchen knife. Special lawn-weeding tools are also available, however. They are particularly useful because they enable you to remove weeds along with a plug of soil without getting down on your hands and knees.

two rows of Brussels sprouts planted approximately 60cm (2ft) apart could be intercropped with a row of lettuce down the middle, for example.

The same principle applies to planting annual flowers, and even perennials if sufficient plants are available – perhaps if you have propagated them yourself from seed or cuttings. For example, plant five small sage plants in a group approximately 23cm (9in) apart; they will grow up to look like a single bush, but will cover the ground more quickly than just one plant.

Ground cover plants
Bare areas of soil can sometimes be kept weed-free using ground cover plants – low, spreading, vigorous plants that are able to suppress weed growth.

Grass is one of the commonest ground cover plants and it can be used effectively between trees and specimen shrubs. The disadvantage of grass, however, is that it needs regular mowing, although some areas can be turned into wild-flower meadows. Other effective ground cover plants are low evergreen shrubs or herbaceous plants which keep a covering of foliage over winter. As well as suppressing weeds, they provide food and shelter for wildlife.

One disadvantage of using ground cover is that if weeds do become established between the plants they are very hard to get rid of. It is essential to clear the ground thoroughly before planting and to keep it weed-free between the plants until a tight canopy has formed. Hoe or mulch the plants, or plant them through wool matting or another biodegradeable sheet mulch that will eventually disappear.

On bare areas for future cultivation, use a suitable type of green manures as ground cover (see pages 80–5).

Controlling weeds 3

Stale seedbed

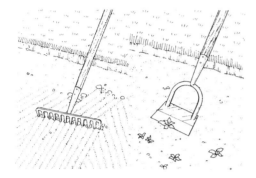

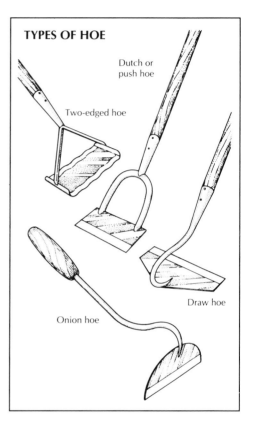

TYPES OF HOE

Dutch or push hoe

Two-edged hoe

Draw hoe

Onion hoe

Stale seedbed

This is a traditional technique that is particularly useful when you are scattering seed over an area (broadcasting) because it is difficult to weed. It is also useful when you are sowing seed that is slow to germinate because otherwise weed seedlings get a head start.

Make the seedbed by forking and raking in the usual way, but do it a couple of weeks before you need to sow. If the weather is cold, cover the bed with clear polythene or horticultural fleece. There will be an initial flush of weed seedlings, stimulated by the light and warmth. Hoe shallowly to kill them, disturbing the soil as little as possible, or go over the bed with a flame weeder. Sow as normal; the seedlings should get little competition from weeds.

Growing in modules

Plants that are started off in pots, trays or modules can compete far better against weed seedlings than those that are sown directly into the soil. This is particularly advantageous early in the year, as many common annual weeds germinate and grow at low temperatures better than crops.

Covering seed drills

Prepare the seedbed well in advance, then wait and hoe off the initial weed growth. In some situations it is difficult to remove weeds from within a row of seedlings, from a wide drill of spring onions or a row of staked peas, for example. After sowing the seeds in the drill in the normal way, try filling it with leafmould, seed compost, old potting compost or similar weed-free material instead of soil.

Hoeing

Hoeing cuts off weeds from their roots just below the soil surface. You can use a hoe to weed between plants or rows of plants, or to clear an area for planting. It is one of the quickest ways of dealing with weed seedlings and even large annual weeds, as the roots of these do not regenerate. Only persistent hoeing over a long period can kill perennial weeds with deep or spreading storage roots.

For hoeing to be most effective, keep the blade sharp. Hoe when it is dry and sunny so that weeds die quickly; some may re-root if the soil is wet. Hoe shallowly, keeping the blade parallel to, but just below, the surface; this keeps moisture loss to a minimum and brings few weed seeds to the surface. Hoe regularly when the weeds are small, but do not over do it as this can dry out moist soils and damage the surface structure. Try not to harm the roots of shallow-rooted plants.

Flame weeder

A traditional **Dutch or push hoe** is moved back and forth parallel to the soil surface. It clears weeds between rows and widely spaced plants. A **two-edged hoe** is used in the same manner: the serrated blade cuts on both edges. A **reciprocating hoe** has a similar blade but is pivoted, and a **draw hoe** is used to chop off larger weeds. An **onion hoe** is useful for close work and in confined spaces.

Handweeding
Most small weeds and many large annuals can be pulled out easily by hand. For those that break off just above the ground, such as herb robert, and those that bring up a mass of soil, disturbing the roots of your plants, easing the roots with a fork can help. Handweeding is easier when the soil is not compacted, as on a bed system and where mulches have left the surface friable.

Flame weeding
Flame weeding is good for controlling weeds in areas where hoeing or mulching are inappropriate, as on hard gravel paths. The weeds do not have to be burnt: pass the flame over them for a second or two until they change colour – usually to a brighter green. This indicates that the heat has caused the cell walls to burst. Seedlings and annuals are easily killed in this way, but perennials will need treating at intervals until the roots are exhausted.

A flame weeder is a good way to kill weed seedlings on a prepared seed bed as it does not disturb the soil and bring fresh weed seeds to the surface. It can also be passed over a bed sown with a slow-germinating crop after the seed has been sown but before it comes up.

WEED CONTROL IN PATHS

Weedy paths are a common problem, but instead of using weedkillers the problem can be tackled without chemicals or, even better, avoided in the first place.

Is a path necessary? A weedy path could indicate that it is rarely used. Individual stepping stones through a bed of plants or mown grass can be easier to maintain.

Would another surface do? Concrete and well-laid paving slabs give the least weed problems. In an informal situation such as a vegetable plot, paths of old carpet covered in shreddings or newspapers covered with straw are easier to replace when they become weedy than makeshift paths of old bricks.

Does the path need relaying? Give all permanent paths firm, deep foundations to stop weeds and soil coming up, and lessen the chance of weed seedlings getting established. A porous polypropylene membrane laid between the foundations and the surface gives extra protection.

Retaining edges are essential for paths with a loose surface such as gravel to prevent soil spilling onto the path. Paving slabs, bricks and pavers must fit together closely; brush a mixture of dry sand and cement into the cracks where they join to prevent them silting up with soil.

How can weeds be eliminated? Tackle weeds that seed into paths as soon as possible, before they put down a good root system. A gravel path can be hoed and weeds in between paving slabs removed with an old kitchen knife or special tools. Alternatively, use a flame weeder.

Timing is critical: the longer you wait the more the weeds will germinate and be killed, but the greater the risk of damaging the crop. As a guide, place a small piece of glass over one part of a row: the crop seedlings under it will emerge two or three days ahead of the rest; this is the last chance to flame weed.

Flame weeders are powered by paraffin or propane gas. Never use one unless absolutely necessary: it is a waste of valuable resources.

Seeds 1

The technique of raising plants from seed rather than buying ready-grown subjects is particularly important to organic gardeners because the plants will be organic right from the outset. Growing from seed is also important because it gives much more choice in what you can cultivate: you can pick types and varieties that are well suited to a particular soil or situation, along with those that are resistant to disease. Unlike plants, seeds rarely carry diseases, so there is much less risk of introducing problems into the garden. However, germinating seeds and young seedlings are very vulnerable to pests and diseases as they do not have the resources to recover from an attack. The faster and stronger they grow, the more likely they are to survive and be healthy.

Sources of seed

Some catalogues have a limited range of organically grown seed, and more is likely to be available in the future. You can also save the seed of some crops and flowers from your own garden if you have time and space.

Otherwise use conventionally grown seed, but try to check that it has not been chemically dressed with fungicide between the time that it was harvested and when it was packeted. If it has, a warning should be given on the packet. Some seed catalogues state that none of the seeds they sell have been chemically treated.

Getting a good start

If seeds are to germinate quickly and seedlings grow vigorously they must be grown in the correct way and have the right conditions. See pages 184–5 for information on greenhouses.

Good seed Make sure you get good-quality seed. Seed deteriorates in storage, not only affecting the percentage of seed which germinates but also the germination time and the vigour of the resultant seedlings. Always store seed in a sealed packet in a cool dry place.

The lifetime of different seeds varies, but many will still germinate after three or four years if stored well. If you are doubtful about any of your seed stocks, put a few on moist kitchen towel in a warm place so that you can see how many germinate.

Seed treatments

Store seed in an airtight container and include a packet of silica gel to absorb moisture; keep it in a cool place.

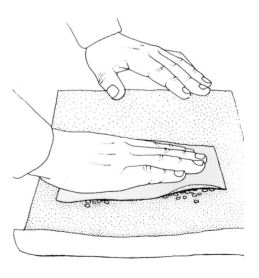

Rub hard seeds gently between two sheets of sandpaper to weaken the seed coat and allow moisture through more easily.

Correct temperature In general, plants that need a warm climate in which to grow need higher temperatures to germinate. Consequently, broad beans, which are cool season crops, will germinate at a temperature of about 5°C (41°F), whereas courgettes need a minimum temperature of 12 or 13°C (54 or 56°F), and lobelia needs at least 15°C (59°F). It is best to aim for temperatures a few degrees above these minimum figures.

Up to a point, the higher the temperature the quicker the seeds will germinate and the more rapidly the seedlings will grow. However, too high a temperature can be detrimental, and for some seeds this threshold is easily reached. Butterhead lettuce, for example, does not germinate well above about 25°C (77°F) – a temperature often exceeded on a hot summer's day.

It is easier to reach higher temperatures in spring if seeds are sown in pots and trays placed in a greenhouse and transplanted later. In summer, seeds that are temperature-sensitive can be sown in containers and put in a cool place until they germinate. However, there are also ways of raising or lowering the

TEMPERATURES FOR GERMINATION

Lettuces (non-crisp) 0–25°C (32–77°F)
Lettuces (crisp) 0–29°C (22–84°F)
Brassicas/peas/broad beans 5–32°C (41–90°F)
Leeks/onions 7–24°C (45–75°F)
Carrots/parsnips/beetroot over 7°C (45°F)
Cucumbers/marrows/courgettes over 13°C (56°F)
French and runner beans/tomatoes over 12°C (55°F)

temperature of seedbeds outside to accommodate different needs (see page 158).

Moisture and air Seeds need moisture and air to germinate, but too much moisture will lower the temperature, drive out air and encourage fungal diseases. Emerging seedlings need to be moist but not waterlogged. Getting the right balance is easier if you start your plants off in a greenhouse.

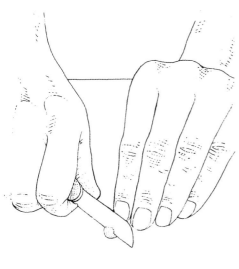

Treat large hard-coated seeds individually, making a small nick in each one with a sharp knife or a nail-file.

Soften the coat of some hard seeds by leaving them in a thermos flask of warm water for several hours.

Seeds 2

Germinating wild-flower seed

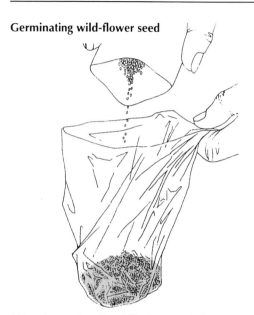

1 Put the seeds to be chilled in a polythene bag with about half a cupful of moist sand, and mix thoroughly.

2 Seal the bag, mark it with the species name and the date, and leave it in the refrigerator for 6–8 weeks.

Seeds with hard coats can take a long time to germinate because moisture cannot easily enter the seed, and sometimes you can speed up the process by scarifying them. To do this, rub hard-coated seed gently between two sheets of sandpaper. Once the seed coat has been weakened moisture can penetrate easily and hence speed up the germination process. Examples of commonly grown seeds which need this treatment include cranesbills (*Geranium* spp.), rock roses (*Cistus* spp.) and vetches (*Vicia* spp.)

Alternatively, some hard-coated seeds can be softened in water first prior to sowing. To do this, soak them in warm water for several hours; if you put them in a thermos then this will keep the water warm. Examples of seeds which benefit from being soaked like this include morning glory (*Ipomoea*) and New Zealand spinach (*Tetragonia expansa*).

For large, hard seeds like sweet pea seeds, it is possible to nick them carefully with a knife.

Light

Most seeds germinate well in both light and dark. However, some germinate much better if they are exposed to the light – a number of wild flowers, herbs and half-hardy annuals, for example. Look for instructions on seed packets for this information.

The seeds must be sown on the surface of the soil or compost and kept moist by a covering of clear polythene or glass if necessary. There are only a few common seeds which do better in the dark: pansies (*Viola*) and nemesias (*Nemesia*) are two examples.

However, all seedlings need good all-round light otherwise they will become weak, spindly and generally sickly-looking.

Pre-chilling

Some seeds, particularly those of wild flowers, require a period of cold before they will germinate. Seeds which are likely to need this treatment include angelica (*Angelica archangelica*), sweet cicely (*Myrrhis odorata*), bluebell (*Endymion non-scriptus*), ramsons (*Allium ursinum*), some types of poppy (*Papaver*), cowslip (*Primula veris*) and primrose (*Primula vulgaris*). The seed should be put in the fridge for six or eight weeks, after which they should be sown.

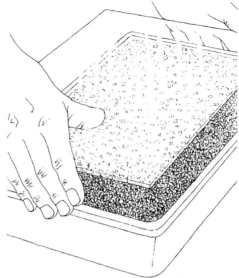

3 Take the bag out of the refrigerator, spread the sand evenly on a tray of seed compost and water it with a fine spray.

4 Cover the seed tray with either a sheet of glass or clear polythene and leave it in a fairly warm light place.

WILD FLOWERS FROM SEED

Most seeds of vegetables and cultivated flowers come up quickly and evenly. However, this is largely the result of plant breeding, and wild flowers are much more erratic. It is not after all in the plant's interest to have all its seed germinate at once, since in a wild environment bad weather or disease could destroy them all.

Some seeds take a month or two to germinate and sometimes come up in two or more flushes. Always keep a seed tray for up to a year if only a few seedlings have emerged – the seeds are not necessarily dead. Some seeds need special conditions for germination, the most common being a period of very low temperatures or fluctuating warm and cold. To do this, sow them in a seed tray in autumn and leave them outside over winter, covered with a piece of glass or plastic to keep out pests and excess wet. Most seed should germinate in spring. If you need to sow in spring, sometimes you can trick the seeds into germinating by giving them an artificial winter in the fridge. The exact conditions necessary will depend on the species, so look for instructions on the seed packet. If none is given, or if you have collected your own seed, try the following method.

Chilling seeds

Mix the content of the seed packet with about half a cupful of moist sand in a polythene bag. Tie the top of the bag, label it with the species and date and put it in your fridge (not freezer) and leave for 6–8 weeks.

After this time, remove the bag and spread the sand out on a seed tray of moist compost. Water the tray using a fine rose attachment, cover it with glass or clear polythene, and leave it in a fairly warm place where the temperature is approximately 15°C (59°F). Make sure there is enough light but avoid direct sunlight.

Seeds 3

Sowing outdoors

There is much you can do to aid germination outdoors, despite the weather.

Do not sow seed until the soil has warmed up in spring. To speed up the process, cover the seedbed with clear polythene or cloches for a week or two before sowing. A well-drained soil warms up more quickly. On heavy soils, raised beds (see page 42) can help to improve drainage. To cool down the soil for summer sowings of temperature-sensitive seeds, water it well and cover with newspaper, white plastic or other reflective material.

If necessary, water the seedbed the day before sowing – the soil should be just moist. The seeds must make good contact with the soil particles, so rake the bed to give a good tilth: the smaller the seed the finer the tilth should be. There will be adequate supplies of air if the seedbed is well drained. Soils that have previously been mulched with organic matter have a good crumbly surface structure and stay moist without becoming waterlogged.

To sow, draw the end of a trowel blade or the corner of a hoe along a line to make a shallow drill. Small seeds run out of resources if they do not reach the light quickly, so sow them nearer the surface than large seeds. Sow the seeds thinly: space small seeds about 2.5cm (1in) apart and large seeds, such as peas or beans, at the recommended spacing. Overcrowded seedlings become weak and spindly as they compete for moisture, air and light, and are more at risk from fungal diseases.

Cover the drill with soil or, if the soil is cloddy, use seed compost, leafmould or old potting compost. If the seeds are in danger of drying out, cover the seedbed with plastic film, newspaper or a piece of old carpet to keep moisture in. This is preferable to watering after sowing, which can cause a hard crust or "cap" to form, so hindering the emergence of seedlings. Remove the covering as soon as there are signs of growth.

Sowing inside

You can sow seeds into a single pot or tray and prick out individual seedlings later or sow directly into modules (multi-celled or divided trays). Either way, it is important to use clean containers and a good mixture for sowing into (see pages 160–1).

Using pots and trays

Fill a shallow pot or small tray with moist seed mixture and sow the seeds thinly on the surface. Cover them with a thin layer of seed mixture, except for very fine seeds, which should be left on the surface. Put a piece of glass or clingfilm or a clear plastic bag over the pot to retain moisture and keep it out of direct sunlight. Prick out the seedlings into trays as soon as they are large enough.

The advantage of this method is that the pot takes up little room in a heated propagator where space may be limited. The disadvantages are that this is a time-consuming process and that the growth of seedlings can be upset by pricking out.

Sowing outdoors

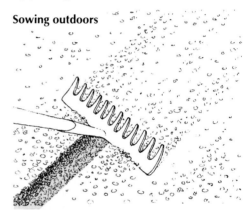

1 Cover seed drills with fine soil, then lay down newspaper to keep in moisture.

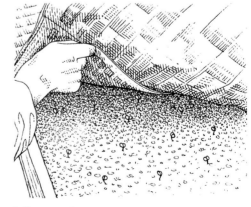

2 Remove the newspaper as soon as you see the first sign of seeds germinating.

Sowing in pots

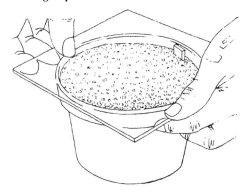

1 Cover the seeds with a thin layer of seed compost and cover the pot with glass.

2 Prick out the seedlings into seed trays, handling each gently by a leaf.

Using modules

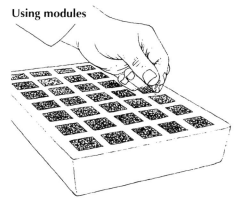

1 Sow two or three seeds into each cell. After germination, reduce to one seedling per cell.

2 Remove young plants for transplanting by pushing them out gently from below.

Using modules

The advantages of modules is that there is no pricking out and no root disturbance when transplanting. It also allows plants that would normally be sown directly *in situ* to be started off inside. However, modules do take up a lot of space in a propagator or greenhouse.

Use a sowing mixture which will sustain the growth of the seedlings. Sow seeds as above but directly into the modules, two or three per cell, and take out the extra seedlings as soon as it is practical, leaving one strong seedling to grow on. When the roots fill the module, take out the young plants by pushing them from below and transplant them.

Some vegetable crops can be "multi-sown". Sow several seeds in each cell and leave them to grow on. Plant each group out as one plant, but spaced wider than normal. This works well for onions and leeks (use six seeds) and beetroot (use two or three), for example. It saves space and time spent on planting out.

Hardening off

Plants sown inside must be acclimatized to the harsher garden conditions. For about a week before planting, stand the trays or modules outside during the day; bring them inside at night or in bad weather until they have hardened off enough to stay outside.

Growing media 1

Choosing the mixture

In an organic garden, plants growing in containers should ideally be fed by the action of micro-organisms releasing nutrients from organic matter rather than directly by chemical fertilizers. This gives a gradual supply of a whole range of nutrients, and should result in healthy, balanced plant growth.

It is therefore important to buy suitable organic mixtures for sowing seeds and potting on plants. These are often called "compost" but are not to be confused with garden compost.

Alternatively, you can make up your own growing media. These mixtures require certain properties appropriate to their intended use.

Seed mixtures

These need to drain freely to allow air into the mixture and enable it to warm up quickly, but they must also retain some moisture. They need to have a fine texture so that they make good contact with the seeds, and they need to be free from weed seeds, pests and disease organisms.

Mixtures that are used for seed sowing when the seedlings are to be pricked out do not need many nutrients as the seed has its own reserves. In fact, a high concentration of nutrients can inhibit the germination of some seeds and damage seedlings. However, if you are sowing into modules, the mixture needs to contain enough nutrients to sustain the growing plants for a short time.

Potting mixtures

These are used for potting on plants that are eventually to be transplanted, and also for plants that are growing permanently in pots and other containers: houseplants, patio plants and cropping fruits and vegetables such as tomatoes and strawberries, for example.

Potting mixtures need to retain moisture, yet also allow sufficient drainage for air to get to the plant roots. However, there is less risk of waterlogging with strongly growing plants as these will be taking up a lot of water.

Potting mixtures do not need to be as fine as seed compost, but the texture will depend upon their use: you could use a coarser mixture for tomatoes in large pots than you would for pot plants, for example.

All potting mixtures need to contain both short-term and long-term food supplies, in greater concentrations for the more vigorous plants. However, too many readily available nutrients can cause toxicities and imbalances. The mixtures should also be free of pests and disease organisms, and generally from weed seeds, although a few weed seedlings are not such a problem in large containers.

Multi-purpose mixtures

Many manufacturers sell "multi-purpose" mixtures, to be used both for sowing seeds and for growing on young plants. These should contain some nutrients, but not such a high concentration that seed germination is affected. They can be useful when you are sowing in modules, but plants potted up into these mixtures are likely to need feeding at an early stage.

Choosing ingredients

The required properties of seed and potting mixtures are obtained by mixing the right ingredients together in the right proportions.

The balance between retaining moisture yet draining freely is determined by the size of the particles that make up the mixture. If the particles are large or fibrous, the spaces between them will be large and the mixture will drain easily. This allows air in but means that the mixture will dry out quickly. Conversely, if the particles are small, the spaces between them will be small and will hold water, meaning the mixture will not dry out so rapidly but there is a risk of waterlogging.

The ideal basic ingredients for a potting mixture should therefore include a range of particle sizes, and hence space or "pore" sizes (see page 32). The mixture must also be stable enough to maintain this structure when packed into pots and continually watered from above. This is one of the main reasons why soil on its own is not suitable for putting into pots: it becomes solid and airless. Processed peat has an ideal structure, which partly accounts for its popularity in growing media. However, other materials such as bark and coir (see page 163) can also work well, although leafmould (see page 164) is one of the best basic ingredients to use in homemade potting mixtures.

Many of the most suitable base materials such as peat and leafmould contain very few plant nutrients. However, these can be added in the form of organic fertilizers such as blood, fish and bone and/or composted nutrient-rich organic matter like manures or vegetable waste. Proprietary potting mixes are increasingly using what were previously "waste" materials, and in home-made mixtures you can use your own garden or worm compost.

Mixtures containing only organic fertilizers are probably the safest to use for sensitive seeds because composted organic matter can sometimes contain a high concentration of nutrients. However, composted organic matter is a very desirable component of other mixtures, for it provides a long-lasting source of a range of plant foods and there is also evidence to suggest that it can suppress soil-borne diseases. It can also help to improve the structure of the mixture.

The right pH
The pH of most seed and potting mixtures is 5.0–5.5, suitable for most plants. However, in practice, a higher pH (up to 7.0) causes few problems. Acid-loving plants like azaleas grown in pots require a low pH compost. For your own mixtures, measure the pH using a testing kit (see pages 34–5). Peat is very acid, so any mixtures containing peat usually require the addition of lime. Other base materials are less acid, so a correction may not be needed.

Making your own mixtures
You can vary the ingredients of home-made seed and potting mixtures according to the materials available and the plants you are growing, as long as the mixtures meet the same basic requirements. The ingredients must be mixed well in order to obtain a uniform end product.

First, weigh out any fertilizers or limestone required into individual plastic cartons. Mark the levels they reach and label each carton, to save weighing in future. Mix them all together in a larger container. Find an appropriate measure for the bulky materials – a clean 10l (2gal) bucket for example – and put in sufficient bulky material to fill it without any compaction. Riddle coarse materials through a 6mm (¼in) sieve if a fine mixture is required.

Fill the bucket with the first of the materials, then spread the contents out on a clean hard surface – a concrete floor or piece of board, for example – and sprinkle over some of the lime/fertilizer mixture. Repeat with further bulky ingredients until they have all been added.

Mix the ingredients thoroughly with a clean spade or shovel by piling them in a heap, then into another heap, and then a third, by which time the mixture should be thoroughly mixed and of a uniform colour.

Making your own potting mixture

1 Tip several bucketfuls of bulky ingredients onto a clean hard surface and sprinkle over a little fertilizer and lime as required.

2 Repeat this until all the ingredients have been used up, then mix them thoroughly with a clean shovel or spade.

Growing media 2

Soil

This should be good loam. For home-made mixes, soil from an old turf stack is ideal. It is well structured and provides a source of nutrients over a long period. It also has a controlling influence over the supply of water and nutrients to plants. However, it may contain pests and disease organisms, and is likely to contain weed seeds. These can be killed by sterilizing the soil with heat, although this may also harm some beneficial organisms.

If you are going to heat-treat soil, it is wise to use one of the small steam sterilizers available as the temperature and time of heating are critical. There are various methods of sterilizing small amounts of soil in the kitchen using an ordinary stove or microwave oven, but the soil is easily "overcooked". Whichever method you use, spread out the soil in a thin layer to cool before adding other ingredients.

It is not always necessary to sterilize soil for a potting mixture for large plants, as weed seedlings can be easily dealt with and the risk of troublesome pests or diseases is small.

Garden compost

Well-matured compost that is a dark colour and crumbly in texture is a good source of long-term nutrients. It will also help to hold moisture. It can contain weed seeds and disease organisms, although the risk is less if your compost heap has heated up well (see page 61). Mixtures should not contain more than approximately 50 per cent compost by volume.

Worm compost

Worm compost (see page 74) is mostly a more concentrated source of nutrients than garden compost, so you need to use less. It also has a fine texture. This makes it a very useful material for home-made mixtures. If you feed your worms only on kitchen scraps and vegetable peelings, the compost should be free of weed seeds. Worm-worked materials of various kinds are included in some commercial mixtures.

Manures

As long as they are very well rotted, farmyard or stable manures (see page 54) can be chopped up and included in rough home-made mixtures, but the concentration of nutrients is likely to

---

MAKING A TURF STACK

The best soil for potting mixtures comes from a turf stack, which you can make with turf taken from a lawn or pasture when you creating a path or wild-flower meadow. It is a very valuable product because the grass roots improve the structure and stability of the soil and also increase its organic matter content.

Cut turves 10cm (4in) deep and stack them grass-side down. Stack with a base 1–2m (3¼–6½ft) square and 1.2m (4ft) high. Water the layers if the turf is dry, and add a 5cm (2in) layer of straw manure between every two or three layers.

Cover the stack with a sheet of thick black polythene well secured with string or bricks, and leave it for at least six months until the turves have rotted.

When potting soil is needed, remove the cover and cut through the stack using a sharp spade. It may be necessary to put the soil through a coarse sieve to break up the clods.

Making a turf stack

1 Using a sharp spade, cut turves 10cm (4in) deep and stack them grass-side down.

be high. Manures are included in many proprietary mixtures but they are composted in some
way: anaerobically in a "digestor", for example, or worked by worms. Manures from intensive livestock systems are not acceptable in an
organic garden.

Shredded bark

Some proprietary mixtures contain up to 25 per
cent bark, and you can also buy bags of fine-
grade bark suitable for home-made mixtures.
This should have been composted or weathered
to remove naturally occurring toxins that can
harm plants. Avoid coarse grades intended for
mulching. Some bark may have been composted with chemical nitrogen, but this is difficult to determine – ask the manufacturers or
look for a brand with a recognized organic symbol. Bark tends to make mixtures more open,
reducing waterlogging, and there is also evidence that it can suppress diseases such as
damping off (see pages 116–17). It has little
nutrient value and can deplete the mixture of
nitrogen as it breaks down; mixtures containing bark tend to need extra fertilizers or composted manure to allow for this.

Peat

Peat has an ideal structure for seed and potting
mixtures and it is also a stable and sterile material. It has a very low pH. However, peat is not
a quickly renewable resource and its extraction
is destroying valuable wildlife habitats. It is
therefore best to use a substitute such as coir
wherever possible.

Coir

This is waste from coconut husks after the long
fibres have been used to make matting and
ropes. Coarse and finely milled grades are available. It is substituted partly or wholly for peat
in proprietary mixtures and can be bought for
using in home-made mixes, either in bags or in
compressed bricks which have to be soaked in
water before use.

Coir has a good structure and low nutrient
value. Its pH is generally higher than that of
peat. Some coir is chemically sterilized, so look
for a brand with a recognized organic symbol.
One disadvantage of this material is that it has
to be shipped from countries such as India and
Sri Lanka; local materials are more acceptable
and likely to be cheaper.

2 Water the turf if it is dry and put straw
manure between every few layers.

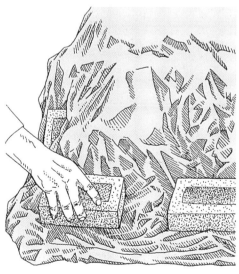

3 Cover the stack with a sheet of thick black
polythene and secure it with bricks.

Growing media 3

Coarse sand or grit
This can help drainage and make the compost heavier, which is useful if you have pots outside exposed to wind. Use a material with a particle size of 3.0–1.5mm (⅛–¹⁄₁₆in). If it is too fine it will fill up air spaces and impede drainage. It is best to buy "horticultural" sand and grit from a garden centre, as materials from builder's merchants may have a high lime content.

Composted crop wastes
Products such as brewer's waste and milled straw are sometimes used in proprietary composts.

Composted municipal waste
This is an ingredient of some proprietary composts. Problems of using general waste include the possibility of contamination by heavy metals, glass and plastic fragments and disease organisms, and the fact that it is mixed makes it a very variable commodity. Separate collection of green waste is much to be preferred. A few local authorities may sell bags of composted waste to gardeners.

Leafmould
Two- or three-year-old leafmould (see pages 56–7) is one of the best basic ingredients for homemade mixtures. It is stable and holds air and water well, although it tends to drain more quickly than peat. The older it is, the better it holds water. It generally contains few weed seeds or pests and disease organisms, and contains very few nutrients. For fine-textured composts, use leafmould that has passed through a 6mm (¼in) sieve.

Comfrey leafmould
A mixture of chopped comfrey and leafmould left to break down (see pages 88–9) is a very useful ingredient for home-made mixtures. The comfrey supplies a good range of nutrients and the leafmould gives the mixture the required physical properties. The concentration of nutrients can be increased by adding organic fertilizers or it can be decreased by adding extra leafmould.

Perlite and vermiculite
These are sometimes used like sand to aid drainage but they are much lighter. They are avoided in organic mixtures because their manufacture requires a lot of energy.

Wood fibre
This is a waste product successfully used in some proprietary mixtures and available for homemade mixes. It can give the same problems of nitrogen depletion as bark.

Organic fertilizers
Mixtures of organic fertilizers (see pages 50–5) can be used to boost the nutrient content of growing media. They generally release nutrients slowly enough to be used safely in mixes without jeopardizing seed germination or growth of seedlings.

Limestone/dolomite lime/calcified seaweed
Any of these materials (see page 35) can be used to raise the pH of mixtures if necessary.

Using new mixtures
Try to find out the ingredients of any product you buy before using it. If possible, choose a brand of growing media which displays a recognized organic symbol, and check that mixtures from garden centres are new stock and

Potting up plants

Hold the plant central in the pot and fill the space around it with potting mixture.

have not been stored outdoors in the sun and rain. Do not sow or plant everything into an unfamiliar mixture at once – try a few sample seeds and plants first in case it is unsuitable. You may have to adjust your watering: water little and often at first, as it is easier to correct underwatering than overwatering. If the mixture is dry on the surface, poke your finger or a plant label in it to see if it is wet underneath.

Small black sciarid or mushroom flies are sometimes attracted to mixtures that contain organic matter, particularly if they are over-watered. The larvae of some species feed on young roots, weakening plants and sometimes killing seedlings. Repot affected plants into new compost, destroying any maggots that you see. A biological control similar to that used against vine weevil (page 105) is also effective.

Storing mixtures
All seed and potting mixtures are best used fresh, particularly with those containing organic matter and organic fertilizers. Micro-organisms continue to work when the mixtures are stored, and in airless conditions this can cause the build-up of substances harmful to plants.

It is best to make up your own mixtures as you need them – ideally not more than two or three weeks in advance. Put them in clean plastic bags or covered bins which have some air holes. Store all mixtures in a cool, dry place.

If you have old mixtures, tip them out into a thin layer for a day or two before using them.

Potting up plants
Before potting up, water plants thoroughly. Loosen them by gently knocking the side of the pot on a firm surface or with a hammer.

The new pot should be large enough to allow about a 2.5cm (1in) gap all round the rootball of the plant. It should also be tall enough to allow a space between the top of the potting mixture and the rim of the pot so that you can water without spillage.

Place the plant in the new pot and fill the space around it with moist potting mixture, tapping the pot gently and lightly firming the mixture with your fingers. Water to settle it in.

Plants newly transplanted into a nutrient-rich mixture may have difficulty in taking up water at first, so give them shade in sunny weather and make sure they do not dry out.

SOIL CONDITIONERS

"Soil conditioners" or "planting mixtures" are often sold in similar bags to seed and potting mixtures and contain similar ingredients: a bulky low-nutrient material such as peat or coir, plus composted organic matter to supply nutrients. They are useful for improving the structure and fertility of poor soils, particularly if sources of leafmould or compost are limited. Do not used them for sowing or potting, as results are likely to be poor.

RECIPES

These recipes are given in parts by volume. Test the pH of all mixtures when you use a recipe for the first time and add lime or calcified seaweed as necessary.

Seed mixtures

Recipe 1 For plants which require very low nutrients: sieved leafmould on its own.
Recipe 2 For sowing in modules and small pots and pricking out seedlings: 1 part-sterilized loam, 1 part sieved leafmould or coir, 1 part sharp sand.
Recipe 3 For sowing in modules and small pots and pricking out seedlings: 2 parts sieved comfrey leafmould, 3 parts sieved leaf mould.

Potting mixtures
Recipe 1 2 parts matured garden compost, 1 part loam, 1 part bark.
Recipe 2 Comfrey leafmould on its own.
Recipe 3 3 parts comfrey leafmould, 2 parts 3-year-old leafmould. To every 10l (2gal), add 33g (1oz) hoof and horn, 33g (1oz) seaweed meal, 20g (³⁄₅oz) bonemeal.
Recipe 4 4 parts loam, 2 parts leafmould or coir. To every 10l (2gal), add 40g (1¼oz) seaweed meal, 20g (³⁄₅oz) bonemeal.
Recipe 5 3 parts leafmould, 1 part worm compost.

Planting

Transplanting checks plant growth and makes plants vulnerable to pests and diseases. It is therefore important to minimize the shock and help the plants to establish quickly.

Bedding and vegetable plants

Prepare the planting site at least a week or two in advance and transplant on dull days or wait until evening if it is hot. A warm, moist soil is ideal – never plant in very cold or waterlogged conditions. Do not let plants in pots or modules become root-bound or starved, or allow plants in seedbeds to grow too big – brassicas, for example, should be about 10cm (4in) high. Water them thoroughly before transplanting.

Make a hole large enough to accommodate the roots easily. Put in the plant, fill with soil around the roots, firm the surface and water well around the base of the plant. If it is sunny it is important to shade the plants with newspaper or horticultural fleece for the first few days. Water regularly in dry spells until the plants become established. Give approximately 150ml (¼pt) to each individual plant every time you water.

Trees, shrubs and fruit

When to plant depends on the type of plant you have chosen as well as weather and soil conditions. For example, the best time to plant evergreens is in mid- to late spring, although they can be planted from early to mid-autumn in mild areas. The best time for planting deciduous plants is late autumn, or late winter or early spring if the soil is not frozen or waterlogged. Containerized plants can be planted in summer if you water them in dry spells.

If you are planting into a well-cared-for bed or border, little preparation is necessary, especially if your plants are bare-rooted. Make a hole wide enough to take the spread of roots of bare-rooted plants; in the case of container-grown plants, allow at least 10cm (4in) on each side of the rootball. The depth of the hole must allow the plant to sit at the same level as it was in the nursery bed or pot.

Fill up the hole gradually, shaking bare-rooted plants lightly to ensure that the soil filters through the roots. Gently firm the soil as you go, but do not tread down too heavily.
On a new or neglected planting site, prepare an area of at least 1m (3½ft) square. If it is a lawn or meadow, strip off the turf and keep it aside. Dig out the topsoil and fork the subsoil to remove any compaction. Put the turf back in the bottom of the hole and chop it up with a spade. Add compost, leafmould or a proprietary planting mixture (see pages 162–3) to

Small transplants

1 **Make a hole** with a trowel that is easily large enough to accommodate the plant roots.

2 **After planting, water each transplant** gently round the base of its stem using a watering can.

WATERING

Lack of water puts stress on plants, reducing their growth and making them prone to pests and diseases. This happens long before they wilt. Powdery mildew and powdery scab (see pages 116 and 128), for example, are particularly exacerbated by dry conditions.

Although you should try to conserve moisture in the soil by adding organic matter and mulching, watering is usually necessary. Apart from new transplants, some fruit and vegetables need watering to give the best yields. Watering is also critical for plants in containers and greenhouses (see pages 184–5).

How much to water

Watering heavily every so often is more effective than a daily light sprinkling, which will evaporate without penetrating to the deeper roots. Generally, apply at least 11 litres/sq m (2½gal/sq yd) at one time, although some vegetables benefit from more (see pages 170–1). Do not overwater as this can cause lush leafy growth at the expense of flowers, roots or fruit, leaching of nutrients and loss of flavour. It also discourages plants from making deep roots.

When to water

Dry soil 23cm (9in) down is a good indication that water is needed. Sandy soils need watering more often than clay soils. There are certain times when some fruit and vegetables need extra water; if time and/or water are limited, water the crops during this period. You can also save on watering by choosing ornamentals that are able to tolerate dry conditions.

Watering systems

Apart from watering cans and hoses, the most efficient means of watering plants is with lengths of perforated or porous "seep hose". These are laid on the soil surface or under a mulch and deliver water to the plant roots without wastage to paths or evaporation. This method also causes less damage to the soil surface and, because the foliage of the plant stays dry, does not lead to fungal diseases.

the topsoil as you put the plant in and refill the hole as before.

When the hole is filled to surface level, water to help the soil settle round the roots and put on a mulch or tree mat (see page 150). The plants will need regular watering in dry spells until they become established. The amount will depend on the size of the root system, but be prepared to give large trees and shrubs up to 11 litre (2½gal) every one or two weeks.

Planting trees

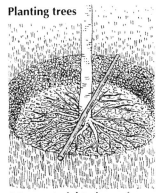

1 Lay a straight piece of wood across the hole to help measure the planting depth.

2 Fill in the soil around the tree roots gradually, gently firming it as you go.

3 When the hole is full, water round the base of the tree and apply a mulch.

Pruning

Pruning shrubs

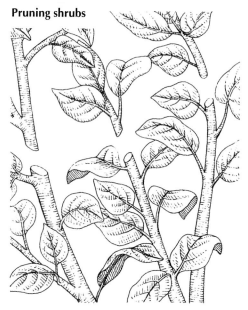

Make pruning cuts to shrubs or fruit just above a bud or pair of buds, and slope the cut away from the buds.

Why prune?

There are three basic reasons for pruning trees, shrubs and fruit: it improves their shape; it encourages flowering and fruiting; and it keeps them vigorous and healthy. It is this last reason which makes attention to pruning particularly important in an organic garden.

Pruning cuts

Cuts to shrubs or fruit should always be made just above a healthy bud or pair of buds, and should slope away from the buds so that rainwater does not collect in the cut and cause rotting. When removing small branches from trees, cut close to a healthy branch or the trunk, cutting from above and angling the cut slightly away from the trunk or main branch to avoid creating a large wound. With bigger branches, reduce the weight of the branch by cutting it back in stages until you are left with a stub about 30–45cm (12–18in) long. Then make a small cut underneath this stub, close to the trunk of the tree. This will prevent the bark from being torn as you cut from above and the stub falls away.

Pruning trees

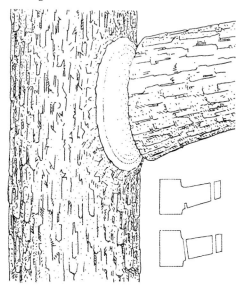

Cut heavy tree branches in stages to reduce their weight, then make a final slightly sloping cut close to the trunk.

Always keep pruning tools sharp so that cuts are made cleanly. Never leave a stub or snag as this will almost certainly die back and form an entry point for disease.

Provided the cuts are made properly and in the right place, woody plants have a remarkable power to heal themselves and wounds do not generally need painting. If you do paint a wound, you must do so immediately after cutting as it only takes seconds for infection to occur. The wound paint acceptable to organic gardeners is a solution of the fungus *Trichoderma viride* (see page 109), which is sold as a wettable powder by specialist suppliers. This fungus is able to overcome decay and disease fungi on the surface of the wound.

If your only reason for using a paint is to disguise the wound, rub the cut surface with earth or manure instead.

Pruning for shape

Pruning can sometimes put plants under stress: they have to grow new wood and leaves, and every pruning cut is a site where disease might enter. It therefore makes sense to keep this

Pruning for plant health

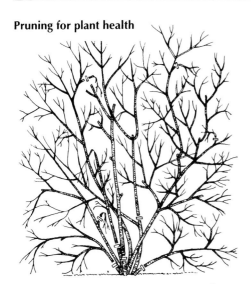

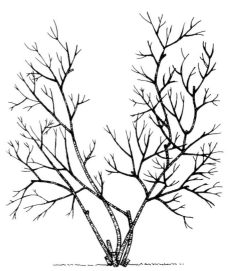

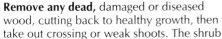

Remove any dead, damaged or diseased wood, cutting back to healthy growth, then take out crossing or weak shoots. The shrub should contain only healthy wood and have an open structure, allowing good air circulation and helping to prevent disease.

type of pruning to a minimum where possible, with the aim of simply helping the plant to achieve its natural shape. If you find yourself pruning a shrub vigorously each year just so that it does not outgrow its space, think of replacing it with one that is more suitable. However, most ornamental trees and shrubs benefit from pruning to train them into shape whilst young, and this is particularly the case with fruit trees and bushes (see pages 174–7).

Pruning for flowers and fruit
In order to prune at the right time it is essential to know the plant's growth habits, the time it flowers, and whether it is the current year's shoots or older growth that produces blooms.

Most formative pruning of deciduous trees and shrubs is carried out during winter. However, there are exceptions. Plums and cherries should not be pruned in winter because of the risk of silver leaf disease (see page 136). Early-flowering shrubs such as *Ribes sanguineum* should be pruned immediately after flowering so as not to reduce the number of blooms it will produce the following year. Late-flowering shrubs that flower on the current year's growth such as *Buddleja davidii* should be pruned in mid-spring.

Pruning to encourage fruiting of gooseberries, redcurrants, whitecurrants and trained forms of apples, pears and plums is carried out in summer. The leading shoots are left unpruned, but unwanted lateral shoots are cut back to five leaves in the case of gooseberries and currants, three leaves in apples and six or seven in plums. Removing shoots at this time of year reduces the vigour of the plants and stimulates the formation of fruit buds for next year. It also gives the ripening fruit more air and light, improving its quality and making picking easier. Sometimes summer pruning can directly remove the source of pests or diseases – currant blister aphid on redcurrants and mildew on gooseberries, for example (see page 130).

Pruning for plant health
This type of pruning can be done at any time of year: act as soon as you spot any problems. First remove dead and damaged wood as this can be a point of entry for disease. Similarly, remove diseased wood, cutting right back into healthy wood. Finally, remove any crossing or weak shoots, especially in the centre of a bush or shrub. This allows in air and helps to prevent fungal diseases.

Vegetables

Most crops do best in a well-sited, well-prepared vegetable plot planted in rotation. Growing on a bed system has many advantages, especially in a small garden (see pages 42–5). However, perennial vegetables like globe artichokes and rhubarb fit well among ornamentals, and crops such as red- and green-leaf lettuces can be used to fill in gaps. Bush tomatoes will grow well in pots or hanging baskets.

• **The ideal site** is sunny, well-drained and sheltered, although some vegetables like Jerusalem artichokes and summer salads tolerate partial shade. Avoid frost pockets and sites with overhanging trees. The soil should be deep, fertile and slightly acid, with a pH of about 6.5 (see pages 33–5), but you can grow crops while clearing the ground using a light-excluding mulch and while improving the soil.

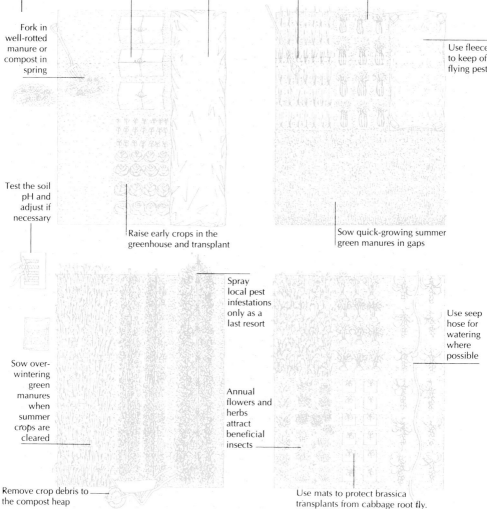

N

Warm the soil with cloches or plastic before sowing early crops

Hoe or hand weed when plants are young

Mulch established plants

Fork in well-rotted manure or compost in spring

Use fleece to keep off flying pests

Test the soil pH and adjust if necessary

Raise early crops in the greenhouse and transplant

Sow quick-growing summer green manures in gaps

Spray local pest infestations only as a last resort

Use seep hose for watering where possible

Sow over-wintering green manures when summer crops are cleared

Annual flowers and herbs attract beneficial insects

Remove crop debris to the compost heap

Use mats to protect brassica transplants from cabbage root fly.

An organic vegetable plot throughout the year

• **Grow a range of crops and varieties** to increase diversity and help to lessen the effects of pests and diseases. Plan for year-round produce but, in limited space, select crops that are better fresh rather than bought, and those that are not easy to find. Choose pest- and disease-resistant varieties if necessary (see page 92).

• **Raise plants** like half-hardy tomatoes and courgettes and slow growers like celery inside. Sowing inside or under cloches also gives some other crops a good start. Outside, sow either directly in the growing position or into a seedbed for transplanting (see pages 156–9).

• **Dig the soil** only if necessary. Manure, compost and other organic matter is essential (see pages 50–89). Use as a surface mulch or fork into the topsoil. Rotate crops for the best results (see pages 46–9).

• **Hoeing and hand-weeding** are the main methods of weed control (see page 152–3). In some cases short-term mulches and green manures can be used. A flame weeder is appropriate for a stale seedbed or to destroy weed seeds in a bed of a slow-germinating crop.

• **Regular feeding** of crops in the soil is not necessary – they get all they need from the soil. Feed vegetables grown in pots with a liquid feed (see pages 86–7) or by top-dressing with organic fertilizers or worm compost (see pages 50 and 74–7). Organic fertilizers or comfrey leaves can be used in poor soils while the fertility is built up. Crops which overwinter in the ground and crop in spring may need extra feeding in spring with a nutrient-rich mulch or by top-dressing with a quick-acting organic fertilizer.

• **Water** your crops if necessary. Leafy crops require regular watering in dry spells at a rate of 11–16 litres per sq m (2–3½gal per sq yd) per week. For root crops, apply 5–10 litres per metre (1–2gal per yd) of row as necessary. Fruiting vegetables such as tomatoes, courgettes, peas and beans need water most when flowering and when fruit is setting: apply 22 litres per sq m (4gal per sq yd) per week. Potatoes need water most when the tubers start to form, which often coincides with flowering; give a single watering of 22 litres per sq m (4gal per sq yd).

• **Pests and diseases** are less likely to attack strong, well-grown plants. Good soil preparation and a well-planned rotation are the best lines of defence. Grow some annual attractant flowers (see pages 24–7).

Soil treatments
The following gives advice on the best soil treatment for individual crops.

Artichokes, Jerusalem (z 4) Little feeding; add compost or leafmould on heavy soils.

Beetroot (z 5) Grow in ground manured or composted for previous crop.

Brassicas (Brussels sprouts, broccoli, cabbage, kale, cauliflower) (z 8) Grow after nitrogen-fixing crop and overwintering grazing rye, or add manure or compost in spring.

Beans, broad (z 8) These add nitrogen to soil; grow after overwintering grazing rye or add compost.

Beans, French (z 10) Grow in ground manured for previous crop or add compost.

Beans, runner (z 10) These add nitrogen to soil. Add organic matter for moisture retention.

Calabrese (z 8) Grow in ground manured for previous crop or add compost.

Carrots (z 6) Grow in ground composted or manured for previous crop; extra leafmould on heavy soils.

Celery, celeriac (z 8) Manure ground in spring before planting.

Cucurbits (cucumbers, squashes, courgettes) (z 9–10) Add compost to planting holes.

Fennel, Florence (z 5) Grow in ground manured in spring for previous crop or compost ground before planting.

Leeks (z 6) Grow in ground manured in spring.

Lettuce (z 6) Grow in ground manured for previous crop or add compost.

Onions, shallots, garlic (z 5) Plant in ground manured for previous crop or add compost.

Parsnips (z 6) Grow in ground composted or manured for previous crop; add extra leafmould on heavy soils.

Peas (z 7) They add nitrogen to soil; add organic matter on poor soils for moisture retention.

Potato (z 7–8) Give this crop priority for manure in spring.

Salsify, scorzonera (z 5) Grow in ground composted or manured for previous crop; add extra leafmould on light soils.

Spinach, chard (z 5) Add compost or manure in spring.

Swede, turnip (z 7) Grow in ground manured for previous crop or add compost.

Sweetcorn (z 7) Grow in spring-composted soil.

Tomato (z 9) Add manure or compost before planting.

Herbs

Herbs are grown for their flavour, scent or medicinal properties, although many are also attractive plants. They are suitable for an organic garden because many attract bees and predatory insects (see pages 18–23) and are reputed to be good companion plants (see page 95), deterring pests and helping plant growth.

The efficacy of herbs results from the action of powerful natural substances, which are only produced in high concentrations if the plants are grown in the right conditions. The aromatic oils contained in shrubby herbs like thyme lose their strength if the plants are grown in wet or shady conditions or in rich soil.

Herbs do not have to be grown in a special herb bed. They comprise a wide range of plants: annual and perennial; herbaceous and shrubby; hardy and half-hardy. There are vigorous, invasive herbs and weak, low-growing ones. It can sometimes be easier to give each a suitable position if they are spread throughout the garden.

Although it is mostly the leaves that are used, some herbs are grown for their flowers, seeds, stems or even roots. To some extent this influences where they are planted: you must be able to harvest them easily without disturbing other plants or the look of your garden.

Obtaining plants

It is easy to grow most hardy annual and biennial herbs from seed, sowing them outside directly in their growing position (see pages 154–9). Many will self-seed in future. You can grow some perennials from seed, although herbs such as French tarragon do not set seed and others such as variegated herbs and named varieties do not come true. Alternatively, buy them from a garden centre or specialist nursery: it is often possible to obtain organically grown plants.

It is important to keep herb plants young and vigorous, and most perennials should be replaced every three or four years. Dig up and divide herbaceous herbs. Enrich the soil with compost before replanting young clumps from the outside of the old plants. Propagate shrubby herbs from seed or cuttings or buy new plants.

Growing conditions

• **Hardy annual and biennial herbs:** parsley *Petroselinum crispum*) z 5; coriander (*Coriandrum sativum*) z 8; dill (*Anethum graveolens*) z 8; summer savory (*Satureja hortensis*) z 8

These need a sunny position and fairly fertile soil. Grow them on ground manured for a previous crop or fork in compost before sowing. They are often easiest to grow in the vegetable garden, where sowing is easy and they can be part of the rotation. Parsley, for example, is more likely to suffer from virus diseases and carrot root fly if it is always grown in the same spot.

• **Shrubby evergreen herbs:** lavender (*Lavandula* spp. z 5; sage (*Salvia* spp.) z 3–10; hyssop (*Hyssopus officinalis*) z 3; thyme (*Thymus* spp.) z 5–9; rosemary (*Rosmarinus officinalis*) z 6

Most shrubby evergreen herbs need a very sunny, well-drained site and light soil. Add leafmould to heavy soils. Mulch with bark, shreddings or gravel to help keep the foliage clean and dry. If possible plant near the house or patio, where they will benefit from the reflected heat. On heavy or poorly drained soils, grow on raised beds. Most will grow in containers.

• **Herbaceous perennial herbs:** lovage (*Levisticum officinale*) z 4; fennel (*Foeniculum vulgare*) z 5; tarragon (*Artemisia dracunculus*) z 3; lemon balm (*Melissa officinalis*) z 4; chives (*Allium schoenoprasum*) z 5

These are best grown in a sunny spot with fertile, well-drained soil. Fork in compost before planting and use it to mulch established plants. Put tall herbs at the back of a herb bed and short ones at the front. Some are attractive enough to grow in a flower border, but make sure that they are accessible for picking.

• **Herbs with invasive roots:** mint (*Mentha* spp.) z 3–7

Mints do well in a partially shaded position in rich, moist soil, although they will tolerate other conditions. Grow them in an old bucket, thick plastic sack or other container about 30cm (12in) deep to prevent the roots spreading. Make drainage holes in the base. Sink it into the ground up to its rim and fill it with a mixture of soil and well-rotted manure. Plant a small clump of mint in the centre. Water regularly in dry weather. Dig up the container every year, renew the soil and divide and replant a small clump.

• **Herbs grown for their roots:** horseradish (*Armoracia rusticana*) z 5

Horseradish will grow in sun or partial shade. It needs a fertile soil; dig in compost or well-rotted manure before planting. A clump can be grown in the herb garden only if occasional roots are needed, but even then, harvesting can be destructive. Alternatively, grow in a separate bed in the vegetable garden. Every year or two, dig up all roots, enrich the soil and replant.

• **Half-hardy annual herbs:** basil (*Ocimum basilicum*) z 10; sweet marjoram (*Origanum majorana*) z 7

These need a warm, sunny spot and fairly fertile soil. In pots, use a nutrient-rich potting compost. Choose a sunny, sheltered, frost-free spot in a herb bed or flowerbed or grow them in pots on the patio.

• **Tender perennials:** bay (*Laurus nobilis*) z 8; lemon verbena (*Aloysia triphylla*) z 8

These also need a sunny, frost-free site and nutrient-rich potting mixture. Grow them in pots and move to a frost-free greenhouse or conservatory in winter. Bay is fairly hardy – in Britain it will survive most winters outdoors.

A herb bed

If you have room for a special herb bed, choose a sunny, well-drained spot as this will suit most herbs. Make sure you can picking them easily and design the bed so that you can reach all the herbs without stepping on the soil – put in paths or stepping stones, for example.

Cutting and harvesting

Herbaceous herbs need picking and trimming regularly so that there is a constant supply of young foliage for use. Leave some shoots in the middle of the clump to flower and set seed and cut them back in late autumn or spring.

The leaves of shrubby herbs can be picked any time during the growing season. They generally peak in flavour just before the plant flowers, so this is when they should be harvested for drying. Let the flowers set seed for the benefit of the birds and trim them back in early autumn.

Put any herb clippings on the compost heap; the wide range of minerals that they contain are valuable to the soil.

Pests and diseases

In the past, but now illegal, home-made infusions were used as sprays against pests and diseases. It is therefore hardly surprising that herbs themselves are relatively trouble-free. However, aphids can be a problem on young shoots; Umbellifers may suffer from carrot root fly; and mint may be attacked by rust (see pages 110, 123 and 137).

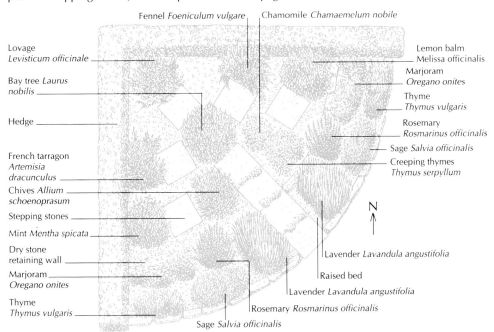

Lovage *Levisticum officinale*

Bay tree *Laurus nobilis*

Hedge

French tarragon *Artemisia dracunculus*

Chives *Allium schoenoprasum*

Stepping stones

Mint *Mentha spicata*

Dry stone retaining wall

Marjoram *Oregano onites*

Thyme *Thymus vulgaris*

Fennel *Foeniculum vulgare*

Chamomile *Chamaemelum nobile*

Lemon balm *Melissa officinalis*

Marjoram *Oregano onites*

Thyme *Thymus vulgaris*

Rosemary *Rosmarinus officinalis*

Sage *Salvia officinalis*

Creeping thymes *Thymus serpyllum*

N

Lavender *Lavandula angustifolia*

Raised bed

Lavender *Lavandula angustifolia*

Rosemary *Rosmarinus officinalis*

Sage *Salvia officinalis*

This small herb garden containing mainly culinary herbs is designed to be attractive and useful. It is set in a sunny sheltered corner, with a raised bed to provide extra drainage.

Top fruit

In a large garden you can grow fruit trees such as apples (z 4), pears (z 4), plums (z 5) and cherries (z 3) together in a mini-orchard. Where space is limited, train them against walls or fences or along a framework of posts and wires. Alternatively, plant them as specimen trees in a lawn or border; dwarfing rootstocks will keep them small, but make sure pollination requirements are satisfied.

Site and soil
• **Growing conditions** Most fruit trees do best in a sunny, sheltered spot. This is particularly the case with dessert varieties because sunshine affects the flavour and colour. Cooking varieties of apples and plums are the most tolerant of some shade. Wind causes fruit to fall, damages growth and deters pollinating insects. Avoid frost pockets as the blossom of most tree fruits is very sensitive to frost. In cold areas, train trees against walls to give them extra warmth and shelter.
• **Soil** A deep well-drained soil is essential, and ideally the pH should be about 6.5 (see pages 32–5). Break up any hard pans and improve poor or heavy soils with compost or leafmould. Correct any mineral deficiencies (see pages 102–3) and dig in well-rotted manure before planting.
• **Clearing ground** It is not always necessary to clear ground completely before planting. Surround trees with a light-excluding mulch – cardboard or newspaper under hay or straw, for example (see page 150).

Choosing plants
• **Rootstocks** Dwarfing rootstocks are available for most types of fruit trees. They reduce their vigour and also bring them into cropping earlier. For example, an apple tree on an M27 rootstock has a spread of only 2.5–3m (8½–10ft) and can bear fruit within three years of planting. The size of the tree will also depend on the variety you choose and your soil. For example, an apple variety such as Bramley is very vigorous and can be grown on a more dwarfing rootstock than a weak variety. On poor soils choose less dwarfing rootstocks as trees will naturally have less vigour.
• **Pollination** To get good crops, many types of fruit tree must be grown with another variety of the same fruit that flowers at the same time.

The transfer of pollen can then occur between the two varieties. This cross-pollination is necessary for most apples, pears, sweet cherries, and some plums and gages. It can also improve the cropping of other fruits.

Nursery catalogues should give the "pollination group" of each variety, determined by when it flowers. In general, varieties that are either in the same or adjacent groups will cross-pollinate.
• **Choosing varieties** Different varieties of apples, plums and pears can have very different properties and it is important to choose one to suit your site – for example, grow late-flowering or frost–tolerant varieties in areas prone to late frosts. Look for varieties particular to your locality as these are likely to do well, and also those less susceptible to prevalent pests and diseases (see page 92). Specialist nurseries are most likely to have a range of varieties and stock certified as virus-free.

Maintenance
• **Mulching** Mulch around young trees to keep at least 1sq m (1sq yd) clear of weeds and grass. Maintain these clear areas around trees on dwarfing rootstocks throughout their life. Hay makes a good mulch as it also feeds the trees. Do not apply it until late spring as its light colour increases the risk of frost damage. Remove any remains of the previous year's mulch in late autumn, along with fallen leaves and fruit. If the trees need supplementary feeding, mulch with compost in spring. It is important to note that feeding with nitrogen-rich manures or fertilizers can cause growth of leafy shoots at the expense of fruit and increase the risk of some diseases.
• **Pruning** Prune apples and pears in winter to remove any diseased or damaged wood and shape the trees (see pages 168–9). Trained forms such as cordons and espaliers should be pruned from mid- to late summer to keep them in check and to encourage fruiting. Never prune plums and cherries in winter because this increases the risk of infection by silver leaf disease (see page 136).
• **Watering** Water regularly in dry spells when fruit is forming, applying up to 22l (4¾gal) per week to mature trees in mid- to late summer. This helps to avoid fruit splitting, premature leaf fall and disorders.

• Pests and diseases

Many predators of fruit pests become established in and around fruit trees that are not sprayed. Encourage beneficial insects into an orchard by underplanting some areas with attractant plants (see pages 25–7).

Good hygiene is very important. Remove fallen fruit and leaves if possible, or mow to chop them up and hasten their decay. Pick all mummified fruit off trees to help prevent the carry over of disease to the next year. See pages 132–5 for details of pests and diseases.

Fruit tree care (dwarf apple)

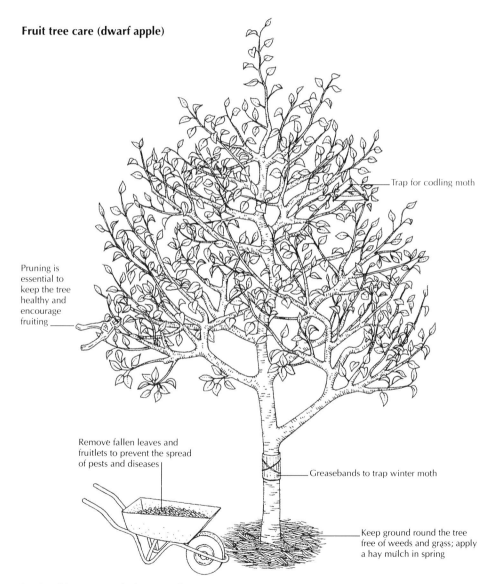

Trap for codling moth

Pruning is essential to keep the tree healthy and encourage fruiting

Remove fallen leaves and fruitlets to prevent the spread of pests and diseases

Greasebands to trap winter moth

Keep ground round the tree free of weeds and grass; apply a hay mulch in spring

For healthy mature fruit trees, there are certain tasks to be done throughout the year.

Watering is necessary in dry spells, especially before the tree has become established.

Soft fruit

Soft fruit can be grown around the garden, mixed with ornamental plants; for example, standard gooseberries and redcurrants on a long leg (a bushy top on a long length of clear stem) look particularly attractive. However, netting against birds can be a problem – fruit grown together in a fruit cage is much easier to protect see (page 106). Many types of soft fruit can also be trained on walls and fences or a system of posts and wires. This method of growth has many advantages: it takes up little space and it is easy to net, pick and inspect for pests and diseases.

Growing conditions
Most types of soft fruit do best in a fairly sunny, sheltered spot. Some fruit will tolerate partial shade but not overhanging trees. Avoid frost pockets, as bush fruit generally flowers early and its blossom is easily damaged; cane fruit is less susceptible. Wind causes direct damage and deters pollinating insects. Good drainage is essential.

Soil
A deep, moisture-retentive soil with a pH of 6.5 is ideal. Nutrient deficiencies can occur on very alkaline soils, particularly with raspberries (see pages 32–5). Leafmould and/or compost are essential in preparing heavy or very light soils (see pages 50–9). Correct any mineral deficiencies before planting (see page 102–3). Do not to overfeed with nitrogen-rich manures or fertilizers as these can encourage leafy growth at the expense of fruit.

Requirements of individual crops
• **Blackberries and hybrid berries z 7** Hybrid berries like loganberries need an application of well-rotted manure before planting, with extra compost or leafmould added to light and heavy soils. Blackberries are more tolerant of a range of soils and will fruit in partial shade.
• **Blackcurrants z 5** These benefit from a slightly richer soil than most soft fruit and a position in full sun. Fork in manure before planting, and add extra compost or leafmould on heavy or light soils.
• **Red and whitecurrants z 6, gooseberries z 6** Fork in compost before planting or, on light soil, well-rotted manure. They will tolerate partial shade.

•**Raspberries z 3** Fork in well-rotted manure before planting, and add extra compost or leafmould to light and heavy soils. Raspberries prefer full sun.
• **Strawberries z 5** Fork in compost before planting; subsequent feeding is not usually necessary. Replace the crop every 3–4 years (as their yield falls) and replant in another spot. Strawberries do best in full sun.

Clearing the ground
Clear the ground of deep-rooted persistent weeds such as bindweed before planting any soft fruit. Otherwise, fruit bushes can be planted into fairly weedy ground provided you fork out the weeds from the immediate area round the roots and put down a light-excluding mulch (see pages 146–9). Clear the ground thoroughly when growing cane fruit and strawberries.

Choice of varieties
You can choose varieties to give you soft fruit over a long period, from gooseberries picked in late spring to autumn-fruiting raspberries. It is worth looking for varieties that have resistance to specific diseases (see page 92) and for late-flowering varieties for frost-prone areas. Virus diseases (see page 99) are a particular problem in many types of soft fruit; if possible, buy plants that are certified as coming from virus-free stock. Be wary of propagating from your own or neighbours' plants if they are not healthy, as virus diseases are carried over in cuttings and strawberry runners. Specialist garden nurseries are likely to have a range of varieties and virus-free stock, and may have ready-trained cordons, fans and standards.

Maintenance
Mulching (see pages 36–7)
Hay is a good mulch for cane and bush fruit. As well as keeping weeds down and retaining moisture, it often provides sufficient nutrients to feed the plants. Do not apply it until late spring or early summer, as its light colour can increase the risk of frost damages. Rake off any remains of the previous year's mulch in late autumn or early spring. If extra feeding is required – for blackcurrants or raspberries on light soils, for example – mulch with compost every two or three years during spring.

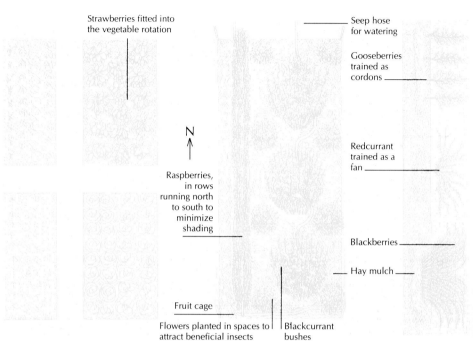

Strawberries fitted into the vegetable rotation

Seep hose for watering

Gooseberries trained as cordons

N

Raspberries, in rows running north to south to minimize shading

Redcurrant trained as a fan

Blackberries

Hay mulch

Fruit cage

Flowers planted in spaces to attract beneficial insects

Blackcurrant bushes

This layout for soft fruit includes both a fruit cage and fruit trained on fences. The fruit is netted in summer, but the nets are removed in winter so that birds can deal with pests.

Strawberries can be planted through a light-excluding sheet mulch so that no weeding is necessary. Otherwise, mulch them with straw when the fruit begins to swell so as to keep them clean.

Pruning and tidying (see pages 168–9)
Prune redcurrants, whitecurrants and goose-berries any time from late autumn to late winter to shape bushes and train cordons and fans. Prune again in mid-summer to remove excess new growth; this makes it easier to pick the fruit as well as helping the fruit to ripen and improving air circulation; it also directly removes any aphids and mildew at the tips of the shoots.

Blackcurrants fruit best on one-year-old wood. Prune every year any time from early autumn to late winter, removing about a quarter to a third of the oldest wood from the base

Cut out old canes of raspberries and black-berries as soon as they have finished fruiting (or in late winter for autumn-fruiting raspberries). Tie the new canes to supporting wires.

Cut off the old leaves of strawberries approximately 7.5cm (3in) above the crown immediately after cropping; removing old growth promptly helps to prevent the carry-over of pests and disease.

Watering
Water regularly in dry spells when the fruit is swelling. It is particularly important not to get water on the foliage or fruit because this encourages fungal diseases. Water by hand or use a seep hose (see page 167).

Pests and diseases
Correct pruning and training is one of the best measures for preventing problems in soft fruit. If you have a large fruit cage, find room within it for some attractant plants to encourage beneficial insects (see pages 24–7).

Keep a close eye on fruit so that you spot problems, such as gooseberry sawfly, as early as possible. Details of the most troublesome pests and diseases affecting soft fruit are given on pages 130–2.

Ornamental borders

A border that contains a mixture of different types of plant – shrubs, herbaceous plants, bulbs and annuals – is usually the most practical type of border for a small garden. It is easy to create year-round interest and, at the same time, encourage wildlife.

Shrubs form the backbone of the border and provide winter interest: plant evergreens and deciduous shrubs in roughly equal proportions, including some that have fruit or berries (see page 27). Climbers like clematis (z 3–9), climbing roses (*Rosa* spp. z 2–7) and honeysuckle (*Lonicera* spp. z 2–10) are also useful for height and shelter for wildlife (see page 15). Train them on stout posts or fences.

Herbaceous perennials provide summer colour and are the best sources of nectar and seeds for wildlife in autumn (see pages 18–23). Bulbs are most important for spring flowers, bringing a welcome splash of colour: use dwarf bulbs such as snowdrops (*Galanthus*

spp. z 4–6), crocuses (z 4–8) and scilla (z 5–9) under deciduous shrubs or through ground cover; plant larger narcissi (z 4–9) at the back of the border where other plants will cover up the dying foliage.

Use annuals to fill in any spaces in the border, particularly in the early years while the shrubs mature. You can even plant pots of half-hardy bedding to fill a temporary gap.

Growing conditions

There are ornamental plants to suit almost any garden situation – dry, wet, sunny or shady – therefore, sites that would not be suitable for fruit or vegetables can be put to good use. However, the widest range of plants will grow in sunny, sheltered places, and beneficial insects will favour flowers in such spots.

An over-rich soil can encourage leaf growth at the expense of flowers. Use compost to improve the soil before planting, or leafmould

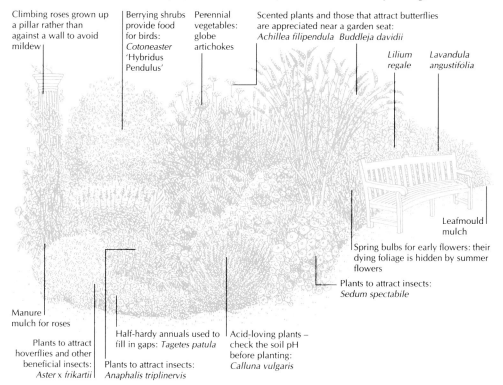

Climbing roses grown up a pillar rather than against a wall to avoid mildew

Berrying shrubs provide food for birds: *Cotoneaster* 'Hybridus Pendulus'

Perennial vegetables: globe artichokes

Scented plants and those that attract butterflies are appreciated near a garden seat: *Achillea filipendula* *Buddleja davidii*

Lilium regale

Lavandula angustifolia

Leafmould mulch

Spring bulbs for early flowers: their dying foliage is hidden by summer flowers

Plants to attract insects: *Sedum spectabile*

Manure mulch for roses

Plants to attract hoverflies and other beneficial insects: *Aster* x *frikartii*

Half-hardy annuals used to fill in gaps: *Tagetes patula*

Plants to attract insects: *Anaphalis triplinervis*

Acid-loving plants – check the soil pH before planting: *Calluna vulgaris*

This small ornamental border contains a mixture of shrubs, herbaceous plants, bulbs and annuals. There are some plants in flower or with berries nearly all the year round.

on heavy soils. Manure is only essential on very poor soils and for a few plants such as modern bush or climbing roses which are pruned hard and need to make a lot of vigorous growth each year.

Clear the ground thoroughly before planting (see pages 146–7) – once weed roots get among herbaceous plants they are almost impossible to eradicate.

Obtaining plants

Grow hardy annuals from seed, sowing them directly outside in their growing positions. They will often self-seed in future years. Half-hardy bedding plants need to be raised in trays or modules in a greenhouse and planted out each year. Some herbaceous plants can also be grown from seed, although you will generally have to buy plants of named varieties (see pages 154–9).

Be wary of accepting clumps of plants from friends and neighbours, as soil diseases and persistent weeds are easily transmitted in this way. Cuttings from shrubs are generally healthy, although even these can sometimes carry virus diseases. Specialist nurseries are more likely than garden centres to have a range of herbaceous plants and shrubs suited to particular conditions, and they should also carry varieties that are resistant to pests and diseases (see page 92).

Revitalize clumps of herbaceous plants every three to four years by lifting and dividing them; dig a fresh supply of compost into the soil and plant young pieces from the outside of the clump. Similarly clumps of spring bulbs benefit from being lifted and the best replanted before they become overcrowded. Most shrubs last for many years. If you replace old roses, do not plant new ones in the same place.

Maintenance

Mulching (see pages 36–7) Disturb the soil in an established border as little as possible. Mulch in spring to protect the soil surface and help control weeds. Leafmould (see page 56) is an ideal material among herbaceous and annual plants where the mulch is likely to become incorporated into the soil when you divide and plant. Fine-grade bark looks attractive in areas where there are groups of small

shrubs, and coarse bark or shredded prunings can be used round large shrubs. The mulch should be sufficient to feed the plants, but top-dress with compost or bonemeal on poor soils if necessary.

Weeding Hand-weed or hoe weeds that grow through the mulch (see pages 152–3). Do not give any perennial weeds the chance to become established.

Watering In dry spells, water new plants individually using a watering can until they become established (see page 167). Otherwise, try to avoid watering: overhead sprinklers can flatten the stems and spoil the blooms of flowers. In dry areas, choose drought-resistant varieties of plants.

Pruning and tidying (see pages 168–9)

It is important to remove diseased foliage or debris regularly – the fallen leaves of roses with blackspot, for example. However, do not be too neat and tidy as this will deter wildlife.

Deadheading some annual and herbaceous plants during the summer can encourage more blooms, but as autumn approaches leave some flower heads on the stems to form seedheads. Remove these only when the birds have had a chance to eat the seeds.

Leave the foliage of spring and summer bulbs to die back naturally. If you cut it off while it is still green then you prevent plant foods going back into the bulb to build up next year's flowers. In late autumn or early spring pull up dead annual flowers and cut back the stems of herbaceous plants.

Remove any dead, diseased or damaged wood from shrubs as soon as you spot it. In addition, prune the shrubs annually if necessary so as to keep them in shape and encourage flowering.

Pests and diseases

Barriers that are used against pests on organic vegetables are rarely useful on an ornamental border, which you want to be as attractive as possible. Generally speaking, if the plants are growing strongly, most pests and diseases will not cause enough damage to look unsightly so there is no need for action. Sometimes ornamentals can even act as useful nursery plants. Details of the most troublesome pests and diseases are given on pages 137–9.

Trees and hedges

Trees and hedges help to screen the garden and filter wind and noise. They can also be attractive features in their own right, and are excellent for wildlife (see pages 12–13). Try to find room for a hedge on at least one boundary, and plant a tree if you can, as part of a mixed border, on its own in a lawn or meadow or in a hedge.

In a small or medium-sized garden, choose the tree and site with care. Many species will be too tall and will cause shading and other problems in years to come. They can also cause damage to foundations and drains if they are planted too close to the house. Look for species whose ultimate height is around 4.5–6.0m (15–20ft). The choice of hedging plants will depend on the function of the hedge. Is it to be a formal backdrop, an impenetrable barrier or an informal but attractive ornamental screen?

Growing conditions

Most trees and hedging plants are hardy and will thrive in all reasonable garden soils, provided they are well drained. However, some types will not withstand cold winds and frost, so choose plants carefully if you live in cold, exposed areas. If you are planting on uncultivated ground, the soil can be improved as you plant (see pages 50–7).

Obtaining plants

Although you can grow some trees and hedging plants from seed, this is a slow process and some ornamental trees can only be propagated by grafting. Specialist tree and shrub nurseries are most likely to have a range of ornamental and native species. These are usually sold bare-rooted or, in the case of conifers, with the rootball wrapped in sacking or nylon netting. Look for small, vigorous plants which usually establish much better than older ones; they are also less expensive and more often than not do not need staking.

Maintenance

Until trees and hedges are established, keep the immediate area around them free from weeds and grass (see page 150), and water in dry spells; mulch plants that lack vigour with compost in spring. It is not usually necessary to weed, water or feed them once they are established. Trim hedges regularly. Established trees do not generally need pruning except to remove diseased or damaged branches (see pages 168–9). Remove suckers which appear from the bark of the tree. Carefully check that stakes or ties are not damaging the stem of the tree as it grows.

For information on pests and diseases see pages 137–41.

Hedges

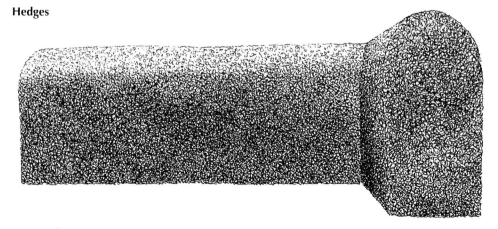

Formal or semi-formal hedges should be clipped regularly – that is to say, at least once a year – but never in the nesting season.

Taper the hedge slightly so that the base is wider than the top to help avoid damage from wind and snow.

Tree care

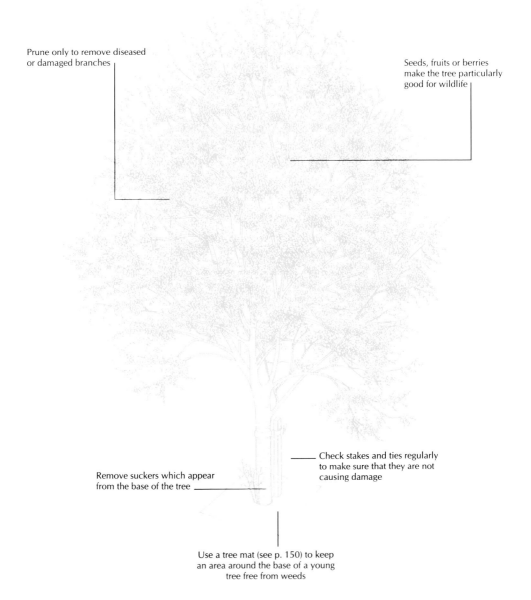

Prune only to remove diseased
or damaged branches

Seeds, fruits or berries
make the tree particularly
good for wildlife

Check stakes and ties regularly
to make sure that they are not
causing damage

Remove suckers which appear
from the base of the tree

Use a tree mat (see p. 150) to keep
an area around the base of a young
tree free from weeds

Lawns

Lawns are often overlooked, but the correct growing conditions, a balanced environment and nutrients supplied by recycled organic matter are as important to an organic lawn as to the rest of the garden.

The ideal site for a lawn is one that is sunny, level and well drained. Improve the drainage of wet areas and choose suitable grass mixtures for partially shaded sites if necessary. However, do not even attempt to grow a lawn in deep shade, on a waterlogged soil or on steep banks. As an alternative in such situations, think about using ornamental mulches (see page 37), ground cover plants (see page 24) or perhaps a planting of wild flowers (see pages 16 and 157).

If you are sowing a new lawn, choose a suitable grass mixture: a lawn used as a play area, for example, needs more of a hard-wearing mixture than a lawn which is primarily decorative. Whatever type of lawn you have, however, the following general principles apply to maintaining it.

pH
Check the pH regularly with a testing kit (see page 35). On a soil that is too acid, grass debris will not decompose and a layer of dead material (known as the "thatch") will build up on the surface. Nutrients are not recycled and moisture may not be able to penetrate. If necessary add ground limestone to bring the pH above the level of 5.5.

Mowing
The key to a successful lawn is not to mow too closely or too often.

A minimum cutting height of approximately 3cm (1¼in) is adequate for most lawns. This will encourage a thick sward which is more resistant to wear and swamps weeds. Mow when necessary – frequently when the grass is growing quickly, but less often at other times. As a rough guide, mow the grass as soon as it is approximately 1.2cm (½in) taller than the cutting height. Do not allow the grass to get long and then cut it severely because this will weaken it.

Leave the mowings on the lawn whenever possible because if you always remove them you will be taking away fertility which has to be put back in some other way. However, it is advisable to collect the mowings when the weather is cold and wet, otherwise they will sit in clumps on the surface and starts killing the grass beneath the clumps. The mowings should also be removed if the grass has been left to grow too long before it is cut, or if weeds that you are trying to eliminate are in the process of seeding.

It does no harm to take away mowings every few cuts if you want to use them on the compost heap or in the garden.

Feeding
Make sure the lawn is well fed. For an initial treatment of a lawn in poor condition, a dressing of blood, fish and bone at approximately 70g/sq m (2oz/sq yd) applied in mid-spring is a good tonic. Otherwise, most of the nutrients a lawn required are supplied by returning the mowings.

An adequate supply of nitrogen is essential, and this is usually available if clover is present (see page 103).

If clover does not occur naturally as a "weed" in your lawn, scatter seed into the grass in spring just after you have mown. Use wild white clover from a supplier of wildflower seeds or a dwarf pasture white cultivar from an agricultural seed merchant at a rate of 5g/sq m (⅕oz/sq yd).

The only additional nutrient that may then be required on some soils is phosphorus, which can be supplied to phosphorus-deficient lawns with a dressing of bonemeal at approximately 70g/sq m (2oz/sq yd) applied in spring. Never apply a fertilizer or other nitrogen-rich materials to the lawn during the autumn months.

Weeding
As long as the grass is growing strongly, most weeds will be kept under control. A few weeds are not only tolerable but desirable; remove problem weeds such as dandelions and plantain by hand (see pages 152–3).

General maintenance
Little other maintenance is required on a healthy lawn because the earthworms will do most of the work for you. They draw almost all the debris down into the soil so thatch should not build up and therefore routine

scarifying of the lawn to remove it should not be necessary. The earthworm burrows will also aerate the lawn, so no regular spiking needs to be done either. At the same time, the casts which the worms deposit on the surface act as a top-dressing into which new grass shoots can root. Spread the casts with a brush if necessary.

Encourage earthworms by making sure the pH level is over 5.5 because they dislike very acid soil conditions. Leaving some mowings on the lawn also helps by supplying the worms with a constant supply of succulent food and so increases their activity.

The most troublesome pests and diseases of lawns are described on page 141.

Renovating a neglected lawn
If a thick layer of thatch has built up on a neglected lawn, this can be removed by vigorous raking or scarifying in autumn. Press the rake down on the surface of the lawn and pull it vigorously along to bring out as much dead material as possible. Once the pH has been corrected and the lawn is being regularly fed by returning the mowings, routine scarifying should not be necessary.

If small areas of a lawn have been particularly compacted through overuse, spike them with a garden fork. Drive the fork in vertically to a depth of about 10cm (4in), rock it gently back and forth and then remove it.

Top-dressing in autumn can even out bumps and hollows in a lawn. It can also improve the surface structure of a lawn on poor or heavy soils. Make up a mixture of approximately 4 parts loam, 2 parts sand and 1 part leafmould. You can modify the mixture to suit your soil by, for example, using more leafmould and less sand on a sandy soil. The loam should ideally come from a turf stack (see pages 162–3), but good garden soil and used potting compost are suitable alternatives. Spread the mixture over the surface with a shovel at a rate of about 1.6kg/sq m (3lb/sq yd). Spread it as evenly as possible, using the back of a rake.

If bare patches appear after top dressing because large hollows have been filled in, sow these with grass seed before weeds establish themselves.

Lawn care

1 **Scarify small areas of lawn** with a garden rake: press down and pull it along vigorously to remove some of the thatch. 2 Aerate the area by spiking it with a garden fork.

3 Top-dress the lawn in autumn to even out bumps: broadcast a mixture of loam, sand and leafmould, 4 spreading it as evenly as possible with the back of a wooden rake.

Greenhouses

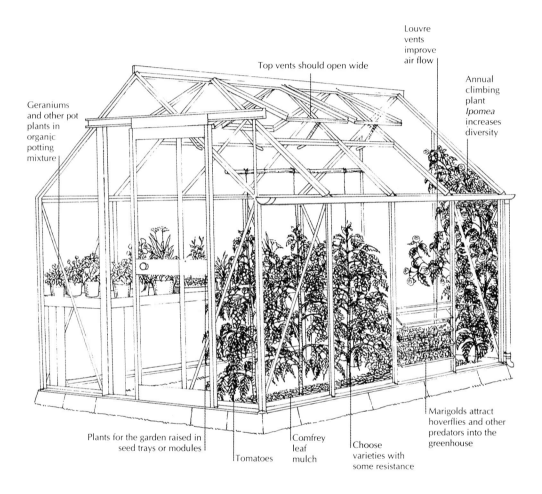

Louvre vents improve air flow

Top vents should open wide

Annual climbing plant *Ipomea* increases diversity

Geraniums and other pot plants in organic potting mixture

Plants for the garden raised in seed trays or modules

Tomatoes

Comfrey leaf mulch

Choose varieties with some resistance

Marigolds attract hoverflies and other predators into the greenhouse

A small aluminium greenhouse 2.4m x 3m (8ft x 10ft) allows you to raise your own plants for the garden, grow half-hardy summer crops and provides winter protection

A greenhouse is valuable in an organic garden not only for extending the range of plants you are able to grow, but also for giving a good start to vegetables and flowers that will be transplanted outdoors later. As in the garden, plants in the greenhouse will thrive if they have a balanced environment and the right growing conditions.

for tender plants. Site the greenhouse in a sunny sheltered spot, orientated so that the ridge runs from east to west if possible, as this will allow in maximum light.

Creating a balance
Growing a varied range of plants from different families and with different habits will help to establish a balanced environment where pests and diseases are less likely to get out of hand. Many greenhouse pests have natural predators that will find their way in from the garden. You can encourage them by, for example, planting

a few flowers in the greenhouse border that will attract hoverflies and other beneficial insects (see pages 18–23).

The right conditions
• **Light** To get the best light, site a greenhouse away from buildings and trees. Good light is essential, especially for raising plants early in the year and for autumn, winter and spring crops. Some shading may be necessary in summer to reduce temperatures and prevent scorching. Exterior blinds are ideal for this, but shading paints are cheaper and easy to apply.

• **Water** Correct watering of plants in pots is critical (see page 167); overwatering is as damaging as underwatering. The amount of water required depends on the weather, how vigorously the plants are growing and the type of potting mixture you have used.

In cold, cloudy weather, plants may not need much water – check the look and feel of the mixture in the pot first. Water carefully if necessary: avoid splashing water onto plant leaves and round the greenhouse as this will encourage fungal diseases and increase humidity. In sunny summer weather, more watering will be needed. Conserve moisture and increase humidity in sunny, hot weather by standing pots on trays of moist sand or on capillary matting. Grow cropping plants in the greenhouse border whenever possible as watering is less critical here.

• **Air** Ventilation in the greenhouse is essential, not only to keep temperatures down but also to increase the flow of air and hence aid in the prevention of fungal diseases.

Open the vents for a few hours whenever the weather permits, even if there is no danger of overheating.

• **Heat** You can help a greenhouse maintain heat by making sure that there are no gaps in the glass or structure. Put up a windbreak for greenhouses in exposed positions. In winter, line the greenhouse with bubble polythene or other insulating material.

A little extra heat can be useful, especially during extreme winter conditions. However, factors such as light and day length also play a part in plant growth, so beware of upsetting the balance. Paraffin and gas heaters increase the humidity and make ventilation all the more important. For raising plants in spring, an electric propagator which provides heat beneath the seed trays and pots is invaluable.

Feeding plants
The plants' basic diet should come from the organic matter in the greenhouse soil or potting mixture (see pages 162–5). Treat a greenhouse border as you would an intensively cultivated plot outdoors. Fork in compost, well-rotted manure or other organic matter as appropriate to the crop (see pages 50–7). Mulch plants where possible (see pages 36–7): this conserves moisture, provides extra nutrients and protects the soil surface from the damage done by continual watering.

When plants are fruiting, you may need to top up this supply with an organic liquid feed (see pages 86–7). If you are not growing winter crops, sow a green manure (see pages 80–5). Even green manures such as phacelia and fenugreek that are slightly tender outside will often overwinter in an unheated greenhouse.

For plants in pots, use a good organic potting mixture. When extra feeding is required, top-dress with organic fertilizers or a 1.5cm (⅝in) layer of worm compost or use an organic liquid feed.

Pest and disease control (see pages 110–41)
Good hygiene is very important. Remove dead leaves and debris from the greenhouse regularly. Throw away plants that are badly affected by pests or diseases. At least once a year, have a thorough clean-up of the structure – glass, pots, seed trays and water butts – using hot soapy water.

Be particularly careful not to bring problems into the greenhouse with new plants. This is almost the only way several common greenhouse pests and diseases can arrive.

Plan a rotation of crops for the greenhouse border if possible (see pages 46–9). Where you wish to keep growing the same crop, change the soil every two to three years, replacing it with good topsoil from the garden.

Common pest and disease problems you are likely to encounter in a greenhouse include damping off, grey mould, powdery mildew, sooty mould, aphids, vine weevil, red spider mite and whitefly. One of the most important ways of controlling the outbreak of many pests is by biological control (see pages 104–5).

Seasonal checklist

MID-WINTER
- Plan vegetable plot
- Order seeds
- Make cabbage root fly mats, bottle cloches, lacewing refuges and bird and bat boxes
- Wash pots and trays ready for sowing
- Remove any damaged or diseased branches from trees and shrubs
- Cut down herbaceous plants after birds have taken seeds
- Fork over soil where soil pests have been a problem
- Winter-prune canes of autumn raspberries
- Cover wall-trained peach trees to prevent peach leaf curl

LATE WINTER
- Make up sowing and potting mixtures
- Sow early vegetable crops if you have a heated propagator
- Put potatoes out to sprout in cool, light, frost-free place
- Add organic matter to vegetable beds for early spring planting and put out cloches and polythene to warm soil
- Dig up over-wintering brassicas as soon as you have finished harvesting as they can harbour pests and diseases
- Check ties on trees

EARLY SPRING
- Last opportunity to plant bare-rooted trees, fruit bushes and shrubs
- Best time to plant evergreens
Last chance to prune apples, pears and soft fruit
- Sow early vegetable crops in greenhouse and under cloches; only sow outside if the soil is warm enough
- Sow early peas to miss pea moth
- Sow half-hardy annuals if you have a heated propagator
- Plant early potatoes if you can protect tops from late frosts
- Mulch over-wintering vegetables such as Japanese onions with nutrient-rich mulch or top-dress with fish, blood and bone
- Prepare vegetable beds for summer crops
- Sow quick-growing green manures on ground that will not be used until mid-summer
- Protect fruit blossom from frost if possible
- Prune roses

- Prune shrubs, such as *Buddleja davidii*, that flower on new shoots
- Cut back shrubby herbs such as lavender, sage and thyme
- Give lawn an initial cut if weather is mild, but not too closely; do not cut if the weather is wet but wait until the grass is dry

MID-SPRING
- Sow and plant hardy vegetables outside
- Protect newly sown vegetables with barriers where necessary; for example, put cabbage root fly mats on brassicas and fleece on early carrots
- Sow hardy annuals like pot marigolds outside (a good choice of plant because they attract hoverflies)
- Sow tender vegetables such as tomatoes in greenhouse
- Plant main crop potatoes and onion sets
Mulch ornamental borders with materials such as leafmould, bark and shreddings when soil is moist
- Top-dress established plants in pots with worm compost or begin liquid feeding
- Feed neglected lawns
- Start cutting lawn in mid-spring and continue regularly until early autumn
- Check regularly from mid-spring onwards for fruit pests, diseases and other problems, in particular, canker, aphids, winter moths and tortrix moths
- Inspect gooseberries and currants for sawfly and eggs from mid-spring

LATE SPRING
- Continue sowing vegetables outdoors and plant out early crops sown inside
- Keep early-sown crops well weeded
- Mulch top and soft fruit with hay or straw
- Watch for aphids but do not spray unless damage is severe; predator numbers should be building up by now
- Look for first signs of greenhouse whitefly and order biological control
- Hang codling moth traps in apple and pear trees from late spring onwards until the end of late summer
- Remove covers from wall-trained peaches
- Remove tied-on grease bands
- Apply shade paint to greenhouse roof and/or walls or fix blinds

EARLY SUMMER
• Continue sowing and planting vegetables
• Sow main crop carrots in early summer to miss first generation of carrot fly
• Sow peas late to miss pea moth
• Plant out tender crops after the last frost
• Prune plums and cherries now until end of late summer to avoid silver leaf disease
• Net fruit bushes, raspberries and main crop strawberries; thin plums, pears and apples
• Look out for cabbage caterpillars or eggs until early autumn
• Water plants as needed until early autumn, especially those that are newly planted

MID-SUMMER
• Cut spring wild-flower meadows; move hay
• Cover flowering peas with mesh to protect against pea moth
• Summer-prune red and white currants and gooseberries to keep bush open and help control disease
• Collect immature fallen fruitlets from apples and pears

LATE SUMMER
• Start sowing overwintering green manures
• Sow winter salad crops such as endive and overwintering vegetables like spring cabbage
• Lift onions and dry thoroughly before storing to avoid storage diseases
• Prune out old raspberry canes after fruiting
• Cut off strawberry leaves after harvest
• Plant new strawberries if needed
• Cut hedges after birds have finished nesting
• Remove and compost early-fallen apples or pears in case they contain pests
• Summer-prune cordons, espaliers, fans and other restricted forms of apples and pears

EARLY AUTUMN
• Sow overwintering green manures
• Sow new wild-flower meadows
• Sow hardy annual attractants to overwinter and flower early
• Harvest potatoes early on heavy soils to avoid slug damage
• Prune out old canes of hybrid berries
• Take nets off fruit after harvesting to allow birds to get at overwintering pests
• Cover ponds with netting to keep leaves out
• Remove greenhouse shading

MID-AUTUMN
• Last chance to sow grazing rye
• Cover root crops with straw to protect from frost damage and lift and store those that are not frost hardy
• Dig a compost trench on next year's runner bean bed
• Insulate worm bins
• Cut summer wild-flower meadows and then remove hay
• Clean out greenhouse thoroughly
• Top-dress neglected lawns
• Trim back flowerheads of shrubby herbs and herbaceous plants after birds have eaten seeds
• Prune blackcurrant bushes any time from mid- to late autumn
• Prune out old canes of blackberries
• Apply greasebands to apple, pear and plum trees and to the stakes
• Lift, divide and replant herbaceous plants any time from now until early spring if soil conditions permit
• Collect up fallen leaves from apple and pear trees to help control scab
• Collect leaves from lawns and paths to make leafmould; this will also prevent them from rotting on the ground

LATE AUTUMN
• Fork-over seed beds on clay soils and leave to weather over winter
• Mulch roses after leaf fall to help prevent reinfection with blackspot
• Prune red and white currant bushes and gooseberries any time from leaf-fall until early spring
• Harvest remaining apples and pears before severe frosts occur

EARLY WINTER
• Check for hibernating hedgehogs before having bonfires
• Best time to plant any new trees, fruit bushes, shrubs and hedges
• Remove any mummified fruit from tree to help prevent spread of disease
• Prune apple and pear trees, gooseberry bushes and red and white currants anytime from now until early spring
• Check greasebands remain sticky through winter until mid-spring
• Feed wild birds from now until spring

Index 1

Index 2/Acknowledgements

Acknowledgements

Editor: Emily Wright
Executive Art Editor: Mark Richardson
Designer: Michael Whitehead
Artists: Chris Forsey, William Giles, Andrew McDonald, Coral Mula, Sandra Pond

The Royal Horticultural Society and publishers have made every effort to ensure that all instructions given in this book are accurate and safe, but they cannot accept liability for any resulting injury, damage or loss to either person or property whether direct or consequential and howsoever arising. The author and publishers will be grateful for any information which will assist them in keeping future editions up to date. We specifically draw our readers' attention to the necessity of carefully reading and accurately following the manufacturer's instruction on any product.

THE R.H.S ENCYCLOPEDIA OF PRACTICAL GARDENING

EDITOR-IN-CHIEF: CHRISTOPHER BRICKELL

A complete range of titles in this series is available from all good bookshops or by mail order direct from the publisher. Payment can be made by credit card or cheque/postal order in the following ways:

BY PHONE Phone through your order on our special credit card hotline on 01903 828503; speak to our customer services team during office hours (9am to 5pm) or leave a message on the answer machine, quoting your full credit card number plus expiry date and your full name, address and contact telephone number.

BY POST Simply fill out the order form below (it can be photocopied) and send together with your payment to LITTLEHAMPTON BOOK SERVICES, FARADAY CLOSE, DURRINGTON, WORTHING, WEST SUSSEX BN13 3RB

ISBN	TITLE	PRICE	QUANTITY	TOTAL
1 84000 160 7	Garden Planning	£8.99		
1 84000 159 3	Water Gardening	£8.99		
1 84000 157 7	Garden Structures	£8.99		
1 84000 151 8	Pruning	£8.99		
1 84000 156 9	Plant Propagation	£8.99		
1 84000 153 4	Growing Fruit	£8.99		
1 84000 152 6	Growing Vegetables	£8.99		
1 84000 154 2	Growing Under Glass	£8.99		
1 84000 158 5	Organic Gardening	£8.99		
1 84000 155 0	Garden Pests and Diseases	£8.99		
			Postage & Packing	£2.50
			Grand Total	

Name..(BLOCK CAPITALS)

Address..

....Postcode........................

I enclose a cheque/postal order for £...................... made payable to Octopus Publishing Group Ltd. or:

please debit my: Access ❑   Visa ❑   AmEx ❑   Diners ❑   account

by £...........................   Expiry date...................

Account number ❑❑❑❑❑❑❑❑❑❑❑❑❑❑❑❑

Signature................................